GOD AND HIS PEOPLE

Covenant and Theology in the
Old Testament

ERNEST W. NICHOLSON

CLARENDON PRESS · OXFORD

1986

Oxford University Press, Walton Street, Oxford OX2 6DP
Oxford New York Toronto
Delhi Bombay Calcutta Madras Karachi
Petaling Jaya Singapore Hong Kong Tokyo
Nairobi Dar es Salaam Cape Town
Melbourne Auckland

and associated companies in
Berlin Ibadan

Oxford is a trade mark of Oxford University Press

Published in the United States
by Oxford University Press, New York

© Ernest W. Nicholson 1986

Reissued in paperback 1988

British Library Cataloguing in Publication Data

Nicholson, Ernest W.
God and his people: covenant and theology in the Old Testament.
1. Bible. O.T.—Criticism, interpretation, etc.
2. Covenants (Theology)—Biblical teaching
I. Title
231.7 ´6 BS1199.C6
ISBN 0-19-826684-7
ISBN 0-19-826727-4 (Pbk.)

Library of Congress Cataloging in Publication Data

Nicholson, Ernest W. (Ernest Wilson)
God and his people.
Bibliography: p.
Includes indexes.
1. Covenants (Theology)—Biblical teaching. 2. Bible.
O.T.—Criticism, interpretation, etc. I. Title.
BS1199.C6N53 1986 231.7 ´6 85-21559
ISBN 0-19-826684-7
ISBN 0-19-826727-4 (Pbk.)

Set by Joshua Associates Limited, Oxford
Printed in Great Britain
at the University Press, Oxford
by David Stanford,
Printer to the University

TO HAZEL

Preface

GOD's covenant with Israel has been a central theme in understanding the Old Testament from ancient times, but in the last hundred years it has been a particularly prominent issue in critical biblical study. In some ways, however, the study of the covenant may be thought to have come full circle in scholarly criticism, and it may be wondered whether the whole debate has run itself into the ground, leaving 'covenant' as a played-out concept for the student of the Old Testament.

This book is an endeavour to show that, while in some important respects we are indeed in much the same position today with regard to the covenant as were some leading scholars a century ago, in other ways the intervening debate has made it possible to see far more clearly than they did just how crucial the covenant idea was in the development of what is distinctive in the faith of ancient Israel. So far from being merely one among a wide range of terms and ideas that emerged, flourished, and had their day, 'covenant' is a central theme that served to focus an entirely idiosyncratic way of looking at the relationship between God and his chosen people, and indeed, between God and the world. As such it deserves to be put back squarely on the agenda for students of the Old Testament.

Four chapters (Part One) survey the discussion of 'covenant' in the century since Julius Wellhausen. In chapter 1 we shall see how, in the generation or so of debate that followed the publication of his *Prolegomena to the History of Israel* in 1878, there was little agreement about the antiquity and meaning of the covenant idea; but it becomes clear that by 'covenant' scholars understood primarily a certain theological *theme* or *vision* of God's relationship to Israel. Unanimity was reached, as chapter 2 explains, only when the growing influence of sociological insights on Old Testament study—as a result, most notably, of Max Weber's work on ancient Judaism—led scholars to see the covenant far less as an 'idea' and much more as a social *institution*, the principle of unity among the tribes of Israel, made concrete in centralized social organization. With the triumph of Martin Noth's theory of an ancient Israelite 'amphictyony' a point of stability was reached for this approach. Chapter 3 charts a development that built on the sociological understanding of the covenant, but tried to relate it more specifically to one particular institution in the ancient Near East that was felt to offer a model for understanding how and why Israel placed so much emphasis on 'covenant': the vassal treaty. It is argued, however, that this development was primarily a negative one, running the study of covenant into a blind alley, though perhaps at the same time serving to highlight some basic flaws in the whole quest for a theory of 'covenant' as a social institution rather than as an ideal or theological theory. The demise of the 'treaty' theory leaves the debate in some ways back where it was in the pre-Weberian times, before sociological theories made their mark on the subject. Chapter 4, which completes the first part of the book, shows the direction which covenant-research has taken in more recent years. It reviews linguistic arguments about the word *bᵉrīt* 'covenant', controversy about which has come into prominence again recently largely through the work of E. Kutsch, and looks also at the recent and influential work of L. Perlitt, which has had the effect of bringing the origins of the covenant idea down to a much later period than was allowed for in the consensus-view from the 1920s to the 1960s, and in the process shifts the emphasis from the 'institutional' to the theological.

In chapters 5–9 (Part Two) key texts bearing on the antiquity of the covenant are discussed in some detail. Perlitt's general thesis that the covenant as a full-blown theory was a late arrival in Israel is seen to be substantially vindicated, but he is shown to have been on shaky ground in insisting that it is so late as to have been completely unknown to the eighth-century prophets. Rather, the idea emerged at some point during the late monarchical period; Hosea shows it to have been already forming in his day, and there is some other pre-Deuteronomic evidence of it. On the whole, however, it is fair to regard 'covenant' as a theological theory about God's relationship with Israel which, though first formulated in earlier times, came into its own at the hands of the Deuteronomic circles in the years leading up to the Exile.

This might seem to leave the issue almost where Perlitt himself leaves it, and indeed to represent a 'back to Wellhausen' position. Old Testament scholarship in general is indeed moving in some such direction, and there are good reasons for this; many of Wellhausen's lines of thought were abandoned all too hastily, and some of them—perhaps especially his ideas on questions of 'introduction' such as the dates of sources and the period in which particular theological themes, 'covenant' included, belonged—do deserve reconsideration.

Nevertheless, as chapter 10 (Part Three) goes on to argue, there is much more to be said about the covenant, even if on the mere question of its date Perlitt has already drawn approximately the correct conclusions. For 'covenant' theology proves, on closer examination, to hold the key to a question that has long occupied the attention of Old Testament scholars: the question of the distinctiveness of Israel's religious faith. And here the sociological dimension, which seemed in earlier chapters to have been an attractive but ultimately misleading line of enquiry, since it diverted scholarship into a wild goose chase for a very early, socially operative covenant, still has some useful insights to offer. Sociology since Weber has been interested not only in the social institutions which religion may generate and in which it may play a part, but also in the social function of religion itself. Such writers as Peter Berger have argued that religion and religious concepts have as one of their most important roles the legitimation of particular sorts of social order.

Now if such an analysis is applied to ancient Israel (as it has been, at least implicitly, by H. H. Schmid) one can trace a highly distinctive development, in which a phase where religion legitimates society is succeeded by one in which a new style of religious thought emerges that challenges and *de*-legitimates the apparently stable and divinely ordained social structures. The crucial figures in bringing about this transformation were (as Wellhausen correctly saw) the classical prophets, beginning in the eighth century BC. But if, as preceding chapters have argued, covenant-theology was also a creation of this same period, then the conclusion that the covenant idea itself is intimately bound up with the vast religious change which these prophets initiated lies close to hand.

Thus the conclusion to which this book moves is that covenant-language served as the focal point for that desacralization of a religious society of which the prophets were the chief agents. The concept of a covenant between Yahweh and Israel is, in terms of 'cash value', the concept that religion is based, not on a natural or ontological equivalence between the divine realm and the human, but on *choice*: God's choice of his people and their 'choice' of him, that is, their free decision to be obedient and faithful to him. Thus understood, 'covenant' is the central expression of the distinctive faith of Israel as 'the people of Yahweh', children of God by adoption and free decision rather than by nature or necessity.

E.W.N.

Oriel College, Oxford
January 1985

Acknowledgements

I GLADLY record my gratitude to several colleagues and friends. John Barton has been a constant source of stimulus and help in the writing of this book, from the earliest to the final stages of its preparation. I owe him much more than this brief acknowledgement can possibly convey. At all stages I have also had the invaluable advice and help of James Barr who has been ever ready to give me generously of his time and learning. John Emerton has likewise placed me deeply in his debt for much help in the course of my reading and research and for many suggestions for the improvement of the final typescript.

Others too have come to my aid on various aspects of the subject, and I record my gratitude to them also: Stephanie Dalley, Christopher Begg, John Day, and Graham Davies.

In the midst of a busy family life my wife Hazel has listened untiringly to the drafting and redrafting of many parts of this book. To her I dedicate it with deepest gratitude and love.

Contents

Abbreviations

ANET	J. B. Pritchard, *Ancient Near Eastern Texts Relating to Old Testament*, third edition with Supplement, Princeton 1969.
AOT	H. Gressmann, *Altorientalische Texte zum alten Testament*, second edition, Berlin and Leipzig 1926.
ATANT	Abhandlungen zur Theologie des Alten und Neuen Testaments
ATD	Das Alte Testament Deutsch
BA	*The Biblical Archaeologist*
BASOR	*Bulletin of the American Schools of Oriental Research*
BBB	Bonner Biblische Beiträge
BDB	*A Hebrew and English Lexicon of the Old Testament* (edited by F. Brown, S. R. Driver, and C. A. Briggs), Oxford 1907.
BFChrTh	*Beiträge zur Förderung Christlicher Theologie*
BKAT	Biblischer Kommentar: Altes Testament
BWANT	Beiträge zur Wissenschaft vom Alten und Neuen Testament
BWAT	Beiträge zur Wissenschaft vom Alten Testament
BZAW	Beihefte zur Zeitschrift für die alttestamentliche Wissenschaft
CBQ	*The Catholic Biblical Quarterly*
FRLANT	Forschungen zur Religion und Literatur des Alten und Neuen Testaments
HDB	*Hastings Dictionary of the Bible*
JBL	*Journal of Biblical Literature*
JNES	*Journal of Near Eastern Studies*
JSOT	*Journal for the Study of the Old Testament*
JSS	*Journal of Semitic Studies*
JTS	*Journal of Theological Studies*
KAT	Kommentar zum Alten Testament
KS	A. Alt, *Kleine Schriften*
LXX	The Septuagint
NKZ	*Neue Kirchliche Zeitschrift*
OTS	*Oudtestamentische Studiën*

RGG[1]	*Die Religion in Geschichte und Gegenwart*, first edition, Tübingen 1909–13.
RGG[2]	*Die Religion in Geschichte und Gegenwart*, second edition, Tübingen 1927–32.
SBL	Society of Biblical Literature
SJT	*Scottish Journal of Theology*
S*VT*	Supplements to *Vetus Testamentum*
TLZ	*Theologische Literaturzeitung*
ThStK	*Theologische Studien und Kritiken*
TZ	*Theologische Zeitschrift*
VT	*Vetus Testamentum*
WMANT	Wissenschaftliche Monographien zum Alten und Neuen Testament
ZA	*Zeitschrift für Assyriologie*
ZAW	*Zeitschrift für die alttestamentliche Wissenschaft*
ZTK	*Zeitschrift für Theologie und Kirche*

PART ONE

COVENANT IN A CENTURY OF STUDY SINCE WELLHAUSEN

I

A Time of Controversy
(1878-1918)

JULIUS WELLHAUSEN'S *Prolegomena zur Geschichte Israels*[1] marked the high point of nineteenth-century Old Testament study. It brought to fruition the main critical advances of preceding research. But it no less marked the beginning of a period of fresh research and debate for which it provided not only the stimulus but also in large measure the agenda. Of no aspect of his work is this more true than of his conclusions concerning the origin and nature of the Sinaitic covenant which found their first expression in the *Prolegomena* and remained unaltered in his subsequent shorter writings.[2] The origin and significance of the Old Testament covenant traditions as a whole in Israelite religion and theology now became a subject of renewed interest. In addition to discussions of it in numerous more general works on Israelite history and religion, a number of detailed studies were devoted to it and yielded insights which, though they commanded no consensus at the time, were to be of lasting importance and, as we shall see in chapter two below, were later to gain widespread acceptance.

Wellhausen's reconstruction of the history of Israelite religion led him to the conclusion that the presentation of Israel's relation with Yahweh in terms of a covenant was a late development and came about as a result of the preaching of the great prophets. In the period before their time and

---

[1] It was first published as *Geschichte Israels*, vol. I, Berlin 1878, and was renamed *Prolegomena zur Geschichte Israels* for the second and subsequent editions. The English translation was made from the second edition (1883) and published as *Prolegomena to the History of Israel*, Edinburgh 1885.

[2] Especially his article 'Israel' first published in the ninth edition of *Encyclopaedia Britannica*, vol. XIII, 1881 (republished as an Appendix to the English translation of the *Prolegomena* in 1885; references to it below are to this Appendix), and his *Israelitisch-jüdische Religion*, first published in *Die Kultur der Gegenwart*, ed. P. Hinneberg, I. 4, Berlin and Leipzig 1905, pp. 1–38, and reprinted in J. Wellhausen, *Grundrisse zum Alten Testament*, ed. R. Smend, Munich 1965, pp. 65–109 (references below are to the latter edition).

beginning with Moses, the relation between Yahweh and Israel is best understood as a 'natural bond', like that of a son to his father:

As for the substance of the national faith, it was summed up principally in the proposition that Jehovah is the god of Israel. But 'God' was equivalent to 'helper'; that was the meaning of the word. 'Help', assistance in all occasions of life—that was what Israel looked for from Jehovah, not 'salvation' in the theological sense. The forgiveness of sins was a matter of subordinate importance; it was involved in the 'help', and was a matter not of faith but of experience. The relation between the people and God was a natural one as that of son to father; it did not rest upon observance of the conditions of a pact.[3]

In recovering the earliest stage in the history of Israelite religion, the role of the historical Moses must be sharply distinguished from that of the quite unhistorical Moses of the extensive Sinaitic legislation of the present Pentateuchal narrative. Historically Moses was 'the people's leader, judge, and centre of unity';[4] he it was who led them forth from Egypt, and through him the faith in Yahweh who had delivered them from bondage became ever thereafter the basis and sustaining power of the nation's life.[5] Moses the law-giver at Sinai, through whom God gave to Israel the extensive and minute legislation of the theocratic community, is but the fictitious creation of much later periods, beginning in the writings of J and E, developing through the work of the redactor who combined these two documents (the Jehovist) and the book of Deuteronomy, and finding its culmination in the Priestly presentation of the Sinai events.[6]

According to Wellhausen it is still possible to discern behind the narrative of JE a tradition which knew nothing of the journey of Israel to Sinai and the events which took place there. Instead, the Israelites, after their escape from Egypt, journeyed to Kadesh, and it was there that they spent the forty years of their residence in the wilderness.[7] The story of their journey to Sinai and the giving of the law there, beginning at Exodus 19 and continuing to Numbers 10, was only secondarily imposed upon this earlier and historical tradition, as is evidenced, for example, by the fact that the narratives which are related immediately before the arrival at Sinai are repeated after the departure from it (cf. Exod. 16 with Num. 11, and Exod. 17 with Num. 20).[8]

---

[3] 'Israel', p. 469.   [4] 'Israel', p. 439.
[5] 'Israel', pp. 432 ff.   [6] *Prolegomena*, pp. 362 ff.; E. trs. 342 ff.
[7] *Prolegomena*, pp. 363 f.; E. trs. 342 f.   [8] *Prolegomena*, p. 363; E. trs. 343.

Kadesh was the original scene of the legislation (Exod. 15: 25). But this legislation was of a different nature from that now described as having been given at Sinai. The legislation at Kadesh represented not 'a single act in which Moses promulgates to the Israelites once for all a complete and comprehensive body of laws'; rather it was a process which went on for the duration of Israel's sojourn at Kadesh and was the 'professional activity of Moses' to whom the people turned for guidance when occasion arose.[9] *Torah* in this sense had its place in the historical events which followed the exodus, and in this sense it was to continue to be administered down through the centuries.

Thus Moses was not regarded as the promulgator once for all of a national constitution, but rather as the first to call into activity the actual sense for law and justice, and to begin the series of oral decisions which were continued after him by the priests. He was the founder of the nation out of which the Torah and prophecy came as later growths.[10]

Thus 'law' in this period was conceived of as Yahweh's help, his guidance, for his people.

The story of the giving of the law at Sinai arose at a much later time when the necessity was felt to describe the legislation governing the life of the nation as having been given in one dramatic moment in the past: 'For the sake of producing a solemn and vivid impression, that is represented as having taken place in a single thrilling moment which in reality occurred slowly and almost unobserved.'[11] Since Sinai historically was 'the seat of the deity', Yahweh's ancient mountain abode, it was naturally chosen as the scene of this momentous event. In this way the Sinai legislation made its way into the narrative, and once admitted continued to expand.[12]

This emphasis upon the law in the present Pentateuchal narrative is in large measure due to the influence of the preaching of the great prophets. As understood by Wellhausen, it was these prophets who brought to an end the old religion of Israel. That old religion rested on the conviction of an indestructible bond between Yahweh and his people; in Israel Yahweh was worshipped, and not among the surrounding nations; in Israel were his altars and his dwelling. 'His cultus was the bond between Him and the

---

[9] *Prolegomena*, p. 364; E. trs. 343.   [10] 'Israel', p. 438.
[11] 'Israel', p. 439.   [12] *Prolegomena*, pp. 383 f.; E. trs. 361 f.

nation; when therefore it was desired to draw the bond still closer, the solemn services of religion were redoubled.'[13] But first Elijah, who was 'like a bird whose song heralds the coming of morning',[14] and then especially the great series of prophets beginning with Amos, raised Yahweh high above the people. To these prophets Yahweh

was the God of righteousness in the first place, and the God of Israel in the second place, and even that only in so far as Israel came up to the righteous demands which in His grace He had revealed to him . . . Thus the nature of the conditions which Jehovah required of His people came to the very front in considering His relations with them: the Torah of Jehovah, which originally, like all His dealings, fell under the category of divine aid, especially in the doing of justice, of divine guidance in the solution of difficult questions, was now conceived of as incorporating the demands on the fulfilment of which His attitude towards Israel entirely depended.[15]

Thus the 'natural bond between the two was severed, and the relation was henceforth viewed as conditional . . . The ethical element destroyed the national character of the old religion'.[16] As a result of this there arose, according to Wellhausen, 'from ideas which easily suggested it, but yet as an entirely new thing, the substance of the notion of covenant or treaty'.[17]

The word *bᵉrīt* itself does not occur in the eighth-century prophets as a designation of the relationship between God and Israel—not even in Hosea, even though this prophet's 'marriage metaphor' 'presents us as clearly as possible with the thing'.[18] According to Wellhausen, the word *bᵉrīt* derived from a quite different source. 'The ancient Hebrews had no other conception of law nor any other designation for it than that of a treaty. A law only obtained force by the fact of those to whom it was given binding themselves to keep it.'[19] Accordingly, he concluded that the use of the term *bᵉrīt* 'treaty' for law

fitted very well with the great idea of the prophets, and received from it in turn an interpretation, according to which the relation of Jehovah to Israel was conditioned by the demands of His righteousness, as set forth in His word and instruction. In this view of the matter Jehovah and Israel came to be regarded as

---

[13] 'Israel', p. 471.
[14] *Israelitisch-jüdische Religion*, p. 90: 'Elias glich einem Vogel, der vor dem Morgen singt'; cf. 'Israel', pp. 461 ff.   [15] *Prolegomena*, pp. 442 f.; E. trs. pp. 417 f.
[16] 'Israel', pp. 473 f.   [17] *Prolegomena*, p. 443; E. trs. 418.
[18] *Prolegomena*, p. 443; E. trs. 418.   [19] *Prolegomena*, p. 443; E. trs. 418.

the contracting parties of the covenant by which the various representatives of the people had originally pledged each other to keep, say, the Deuteronomic law. After the solemn and far-reaching act by which Josiah introduced this law, the notion of covenant-making between Jehovah and Israel appears to have occupied the central position in religious thought: it prevails in Deuteronomy, in Jeremiah, Ezekiel, in Isaiah xl.–lxvi., Lev. xvii–xxvi., and most of all the Book of the Four Covenants. The Babylonian exile no doubt helped, as the Assyrian exile had previously done, to familiarise the Jewish mind with the idea that the covenant depended on conditions, and might possibly be dissolved.[20]

As this brief survey has shown, Wellhausen's work directed attention to four main issues which arise in the study of the origin and nature of the covenant between Yahweh and Israel. These are: the historicity of the tradition of a journey to Sinai by the Israelites after the exodus; the meaning of the term *bᵉrīt* when applied to the relationship between God and his people; the nature of early Israelite religion; and the silence of the eighth-century prophets about the covenant. Controversy on all four of these issues came quickly and was to last for a generation, as we shall now see. These issues are of course to a greater or lesser extent interrelated, but as far as possible I shall deal with them separately in the ensuing sections of this chapter which review the debate set in motion by Wellhausen's work.

I

On the first of these four issues, the pattern of divided opinion which characterized this period of discussion was established in the two major histories of Israel which were published within a decade of the appearance of the *Prolegomena*, the one by B. Stade in 1887, the other by R. Kittel in 1888.[21]

Stade arrived at even more radical conclusions than Wellhausen, arguing that the oldest Pentateuchal source (J) originally contained no description of a wilderness sojourn and itinerary by the Israelites. The

---

[20] *Prolegomena*, p. 444; E. trs. 418 f. (The 'Book of the Four Covenants' was Wellhausen's description of the Priestly document, the four covenants being that with Adam, that with Noah, the covenant with Abraham in Genesis 17, and the Sinai covenant.)

[21] B. Stade, *Geschichte des Volkes Israel* vol. I, Berlin 1887; R. Kittel *Geschichte der Hebräer*, vol. I, Gotha 1888; E. trs. *A History of the Hebrews*, vol. I, London and Edinburgh 1895.

narratives concerning this were composed only subsequently, using locations regarded by the surrounding peoples as holy places, including Kadesh itself, as the 'camping sites' of the tribes on their journey from Egypt to Canaan (p. 132). Stade subsequently considerably modified such a negative assessment of the wilderness traditions, now finding historical evidence of the significance of Kadesh and of Moses' role there in the post-exodus period.[22] But he still adhered to Wellhausen's view that the narratives of a journey to Sinai and the making of a covenant there have no historical basis.[23] The notion of a covenant between Yahweh and Israel played no part in the older period of Israelite religion, but emerged only at a late stage and is not adequately attested before the seventh century BC.[24]

Kittel, on the other hand, sought to defend the historicity of the journey to Sinai and of the covenant ceremony there. He agreed with Wellhausen that Israel had a long sojourn at Kadesh; he found that the Pentateuchal sources were unanimous on this. But he argued also that a journey to the holy mountain took place immediately after the events at the Red Sea whence the people turned southwards into the Sinai peninsula where, he believed, Sinai lay.[25] It was only subsequently that they made their way northwards to Kadesh. But it was at Sinai and under the leadership of Moses that the new religion came into being; its 'programme' was contained in the sentence which introduces the decalogue ('I am Yahweh your God'), and its moral content was the ten commandments in an original, shorter formulation.[26] Kittel rejected the sharp dichotomy drawn by Wellhausen between early Israelite religion and that which arose from the preaching of the eighth-century prophets. These prophets never aimed at founding a new faith: 'their constant purpose was simply to uphold and renew the old faith which in their time had been forgotten and left aside',[27] though this does not mean that important developments did not take place as a result of their preaching. With regard to the covenant at Sinai, originally it was conceived of as an arrangement decreed by one of the parties, Yahweh, which subsequently

---

[22] 'Die Entstehung des Volkes Israel', in *Ausgewählte akademische Reden und Abhandlungen*, Giessen 1899, pp. 99–121.

[23] Ibid., p. 101. Cf. his *Biblische Theologie des Alten Testaments*, vol. I, Tübingen 1905, p. 34.   [24] *Geschichte*, p. 507; *Biblische Theologie*, p. 36.

[25] *Geschichte*, vol. I, pp. 201–16; E. trs. 222–38.

[26] *Geschichte*, vol. I, pp. 221 f.; E. trs. 244 f.

[27] *Geschichte*, vol. I, p. 220; E. trs. p. 243.

advanced to the 'idea of a reciprocal obligation which is involved in the word itself'.[28]

The division of opinion which now emerged on this matter remained not only during this period under survey, but, with the new dimensions which form-criticism and tradition-criticism added to the problem, continued into subsequent periods of research when, as we shall see, agreement was reached on other major aspects of the origin and nature of the Old Testament covenant traditions.[29] The immediate effect of form-criticism on the discussion of this problem in the years following the turn of the century was to sharpen the historical question, for, in the light of H. Gunkel's pioneering work on Genesis,[30] the nature of the narratives in Exodus as *Sagen* ('folk-tales') was now more definitively emphasized. The question now was whether any historical information could be derived from such material, which was now more than ever seen to be far removed from historiographical writing; it was a question not merely about the historicity of a journey to Sinai but about the bondage-exodus-wilderness complex of stories as a whole.

That a kernel of such information can be derived from them was generally agreed, but with much variation in the results achieved and no lessening in the controversy about the historicity of the making of a covenant at Sinai. Thus E. Meyer concluded that the figure of Moses was originally and exclusively limited to priestly traditions at Kadesh and that his association with other traditions in the Pentateuch, including the exodus, was wholly secondary.[31] The stories of a journey to Sinai and of the making of a covenant there are without historical foundation. Instead, Meyer argued for the view, subsequently supported by some others, that Israel's covenant with Yahweh had its roots in the cult at Shechem, as attested in the original core of Joshua 24, and that the tradition of the making of a covenant and of the giving of the law at Sinai is a secondary development based upon the Shechemite covenant tradition (pp. 550 ff.)

O. Procksch, on the other hand, whilst accepting that Kadesh was the home of the Israelites after the exodus, argued that their sojourn there

---

[28] *Geschichte*, vol. I, p. 224; E. trs. p. 248.   [29] See below, Ch. 2, section V. 3.

[30] *Genesis, übersetzt und erklärt*, Göttingen 1901. See also his article 'Sagen und Legenden Israels', *RGG*[1], vol. V, 1913, cols. 179–98, and 'Sagen und Legenden: II. Zu Israel', *RGG*[2], vol. V, 1931, cols. 49–60.

[31] B. Luther and E. Meyer, *Die Israeliten und ihre Nachbarstämme. Alttestamentliche Untersuchungen*, Halle 1906, pp. 47, 72 ff.

enabled them to make a pilgrimage to Sinai, the sacred abode of Yahweh.[32] Such a pilgrimage may have involved only Moses and leading representatives of the people, and the occasion for it may have been a solemn festival held by the Midianites at Sinai. It was at Sinai that Israel formally became the people of Yahweh on the basis of a covenant, the covenant law being the ten commandments in an original, shorter form. Procksch argued that there is nothing in this series of commandments which necessitates assigning its formulation to a later period than that of Moses; on the contrary, once one concedes the historicity of the making of a covenant at Sinai, commandments such as these are entirely apt as the basis of such a covenant; they are easily remembered and are striking in their simplicity. As for their purpose: 'Essentially they base the relationship between God and people upon a more spiritual religion and morality.' (p. 371).

With Gunkel himself the opposing view was again represented.[33] He granted a historical basis for the tradition of Israel's experience of a theophany of Yahweh at Sinai, which he took to have been a volcano in Midianite territory, but not for that of the making of a covenant between Israel and Yahweh. This reflects developments of a much later time which have transformed an original tradition of a covenant at Sinai between the Israelites, led by Moses, and the Midianites—a view which had already been advanced by several scholars earlier (col. 521. See section IV below). Significantly, however, in a later edition of the same article, published in 1930, he abandoned this suggestion and now wrote of a covenant between Yahweh and Israel at Sinai[34]—an indication of the considerable shift in opinion concerning the antiquity of the covenant between Yahweh and Israel which had taken place among scholars at large in the intervening years, as we shall see.

H. Gressmann, however, Gunkel's close colleague, favoured the contrary view, though not in precisely the same form as argued earlier by, for example, Kittel or Procksch. In his study of the narratives in Exodus, the most thorough to be attempted during the period with which we are here concerned,[35] Gressmann drew a relatively full picture both of the

---

[32] *Das nordhebräische Sagenbuch. Die Elohimquelle*, Leipzig 1906.
[33] In his article on Moses in *RGG* [1], 1913, vol. IV, cols. 516-24.
[34] See below, introduction to Ch. 2.
[35] *Mose und seine Zeit*, FRLANT, NF I, Göttingen 1913.

events of the bondage-exodus period and of the founding and nature of early Israelite religion. He concluded that Kadesh was the historical centre of the Israelite community after the exodus; it was there under Moses and with the help of the Midianites that the political and religious organization of Israel was founded. This included the making of a covenant between Israel and Yahweh; by such means alone Yahweh and Israel, hitherto unknown to each other, became related as God and people. It is true that the stories specifically concerning Kadesh do not mention the making of a *bᵉrīt*. But the ancient material in Deuteronomy 33: 2-5 preserves the memory of the enthronement of Yahweh as Israel's divine king, and the effect of this was the same as the making of a covenant; by such means the God of Sinai became the God of Israel at Kadesh (pp. 439 f.)

The specifically Sinaitic stories of the making of a *bᵉrīt* were subsequent developments. But although they have no basis in historical events, Gressmann pointed to one of them which he believed to be a tradition of great antiquity, that is, Exodus 24: 1-2, 9-11 (pp. 182 ff.). The antiquity of what is here recorded is indicated by, for example, the fact that as yet the leaders of Israel referred to are on an equal footing with each other; all alike ascend the holy mountain and no special significance is attached to Moses over the others who are with him. The implied 'mythical' notion of Mount Sinai's peak touching the heavens and the description of what was under God's 'feet' also point to ancient beliefs. That the scene described concerns the making of a covenant is indicated by its closing words 'they ate and drank', the eating of a common meal being attested elsewhere as a means of making a covenant. Gressmann also argued that such a covenant between Yahweh and Israel would originally have been bilateral, with obligations not only placed upon the Israelites but also assumed by Yahweh himself. It was only in later traditions, such as that in Exodus 24: 3-8, that the covenant came to be understood as having imposed obligations upon Israel alone (pp. 184 f.).

This evidence that the Sinai narratives contain such a nucleus of ancient tradition also led Gressmann to reject as an oversimplification Wellhausen's purely literary explanation of the relationship between the Sinai narratives and the exodus-Kadesh narrative. The way in which the Sinai tradition had imposed itself upon the Kadesh traditions was the result of a more complex process in the history of the traditions. The

Kadesh traditions, Gressmann argued, which reflect historical events, were initially dominant, but subsequently receded when the Sinai tradition developed, asserted itself more and more and finally came to occupy the centre of the stage (pp. 388 ff.). This suggestion that the relationship between the exodus and Sinai traditions could not be solved by purely literary-critical means, but involves also the study of the history of traditions, was an indication of the new approach to such problems, which form-critical and traditio-historical research now opened up and which was to be further developed in ensuing decades.[36]

As we have seen, Gressmann pointed to Exodus 24: 1-2, 9-11 as a tradition of great antiquity concerning the making of a covenant at Sinai. By contrast, other descriptions of such a covenant, such as Exodus 24: 3-8 which has been editorially linked with this ancient tradition, are later formulations reflecting a development in the concept of the covenant from an original reciprocal arrangement to one in which Yahweh's law was unilaterally imposed upon Israel. His argument for the antiquity of Exodus 24: 1-2, 9-11 subsequently found widespread acceptance. That Exodus 24: 3-8 is likewise a tradition of great antiquity had, however, been earlier and forcefully argued by C. Steuernagel, and though Gressmann himself did not refer to this contribution, it was Steuernagel's view that eventually became, and has remained, influential.[37] It may be appropriately noted at this point.

The predominant view hitherto among critical scholars concerning this passage had been that it is a late composition. This is evident, it was maintained, by the fact that in the ritual described Yahweh, though one of the covenant partners, is not portrayed as participating directly in this ritual in the same way as in the older narrative of the making of a covenant with Abraham in Genesis 15.[38] Against this view, Steuernagel argued that in describing 'the young men' of Israel (v. 5) as having offered the sacrifices here, this passage is based upon an ancient record and pre-dates the rise of the Levites as the accepted priesthood of Israel. Since already by the end of the period of the Judges this status of the Levites

[36] For a detailed survey of these developments see D. A. Knight, *Rediscovering the Traditions of Israel*, SBL Dissertation Series 9, Missoula 1975.

[37] 'Der jehovistische Bericht über den Bundesschluss am Sinai', *ThStK* 72, 1899, pp. 319–50.

[38] See, for example, R. Kraetzschmar, *Die Bundesvorstellung im Alten Testament in ihrer geschichtlichen Entwickelung*, Marburg 1896, p. 84.

appears to have been established—the narratives about Shiloh in 1 Samuel 1 ff. indicate this—and since even earlier, as the narrative in Judges 17 indicates, Levites were already preferred as priests, the tradition in Exodus 24: 3–8 must have originated at a still earlier period when the Levites either were unknown as priests or at least were not yet favoured as such (p. 350). Thus the possibility presents itself, Steuernagel suggested, that Exodus 24: 3–8, though not in all its details, narrates the actual event of the making of a covenant at Sinai, though he refrained from pressing this beyond a possibility.

As for the nature of the covenant, according to Steuernagel it was understood in J and in the earliest E material[39] as Israel's solemn and binding commitment to Yahweh; in neither source, as originally formulated, was there any suggestion that it was conceived of as a reciprocal arrangement, a contract (pp. 346 f.)

II

This already brings us to another important aspect of the debate generated by Wellhausen's work, namely, the meaning of the term *bᵉrīt* when applied to the relationship between Yahweh and Israel. The foregoing pages have given some indication of the disagreement which emerged on this issue. Thus Wellhausen himself, as we have seen, understood the word in terms of a reciprocal arrangement between Yahweh and Israel, a contract or treaty; in this way its innovation at a late time in the history of Israelite religion marked the transition from early Israelite religion to Judaism as a religion of law. Kittel on the other hand thought in terms of a development from an original unilateral declaration of Yahweh's will for Israel to the idea of a reciprocal arrangement. Steuernagel, as noted above, rejected any suggestion that the covenant was originally conceived of as a contract or the like, whilst Gressmann argued that originally it would have been just such a reciprocal arrangement and that it was only later that it came to be understood as imposing obligations upon Israel alone. To these may be added, for example, the view of R. Smend who argued that the idea of a contractual arrangement

---

[39] He ascribes Exodus 24: 3–8 to J, and Exodus 24: 9–11 to the earliest stage of the composition of E (E¹).

came in only with the book of Deuteronomy.[40] In the earlier narrative of Yahweh's *berīt* with Abraham in Genesis 15 the word designates Yahweh's solemn oath to give the land of Canaan to the patriarch's descendants without any reference to obligations being laid upon Abraham. Nor in the case of the covenant referred to in Exodus 24: 3–8, 34: 10–28 is such a contractual and conditional concept of *berīt* present. The word in these latter texts designates the ordinances given by Yahweh and accepted by the people when he became Lord of his people. Just as a king gives his laws to his people in the arrangement whereby he becomes their king, so Yahweh gave his people his law when he became their Lord (p. 296).

The questions raised by such different proposals as these were (*a*) whether and to what extent the word underwent change when adopted from the secular sphere into the theological, or (*b*) whether in its secular usage it already displayed a semantic range which enabled it to be used for various notions in the theological sphere, such as God's gracious promise or oath to his people, or the imposition of his law upon Israel, or the mutual acceptance of obligations by both God and people and thus an 'agreement' or 'contract'. A more systematic discussion of this came in three notable studies at this time which merit special attention at this point.

In 1892 and 1893 J. J. P. Valeton published three detailed articles in which he surveyed and discussed the occurrences of the word both in its secular and in its religious usage.[41] He argued that the specifically religious usage of it occurs only rarely in the literature before the period of Deuteronomy and Jeremiah. In the earlier strata of the Pentateuch only J refers to a covenant between Yahweh and Israel at Sinai (Exod. 24: 3–8; 34: 10–28a; possibly Exod. 19: 3–8). The narrative of the covenant with Abraham in Genesis 15 also belongs to the old JE material. 1 Kings 19: 10–14 also contains a pre-Deuteronomic reference to the covenant, though it is not clear whether the Sinai covenant is intended. Of the prophets before Jeremiah, only Hosea employed the word in its religious usage

---

[40]*Lehrbuch der alttestamentlichen Religionsgeschichte*, Freiburg im Breisgau and Leipzig 1893, p. 298.

[41] 'Bedeutung und Stellung des Wortes *berīt* im Priestercodex', *ZAW* 12, 1892, pp. 1–22; 'Das Wort *berīt* in den jehovistischen und deuteronomischen Stücken des Hexateuchs, sowie in den verwandten historischen Büchern', *ZAW* 12, 1892, pp. 224–60; 'Das Wort *berīt* bei den Propheten und in den Ketubim. Resultat', *ZAW* 13, 1893, pp. 245–79.

(Hos. 8: 1).[42] It was only from the period of Deuteronomy and Jeremiah onwards that *bᵉrīt* became a term of emphasized and central importance in Israelite religion.[43] At this time also originated the belief in a covenant between Yahweh and the house of Levi (Deut. 33: 8–11; Jer. 33: 20 f.; Mal. 2: 4–9; Num. 25: 12 f.; Neh. 13: 29), and of a covenant between Yahweh and the dynasty of David (2 Sam. 23: 5; Jer. 33: 20 f.; Ps. 89; 2 Chron. 7: 18; 13: 5; 21: 7). In the Priestly material in the Pentateuch *bᵉrīt* is nowhere used in a secular sense but has become a theological, technical term, though P does not use it of the law-giving at Sinai.[44]

From his review of the secular usages of the word, Valeton concluded that it designated an agreement established by oath between two parties. Such an agreement could have the character of a mutual commitment to a common goal on the part of both parties, or of a solemn declaration of the will of a superior accepted by an inferior party. In the case of the latter, the *bᵉrīt* could be the self-imposition of obligations by a superior in favour of an inferior party, that is, a binding promise, or the imposition of obligations upon the inferior party.[45]

In its religious usage *bᵉrīt* could designate a promise made on oath by God to men as a guarantee of his gracious relationship with them. It is used in this sense of the *bᵉrīt* with Abraham, with David, and with the Levites. Alternatively, it could connote the obligations imposed by God upon people in return for his benevolence to them. It is in this latter sense that Deuteronomy uses the term for the relationship between God and Israel. In this way the Deuteronomic understanding of the term is the opposite of that of the Priestly authors for whom it meant consistently God's solemn promise; in Deuteronomy God's promise to Israel recedes markedly, whilst the obligations he imposes upon the people are sharply emphasized.[46] Yahweh's promise to his people is also what is meant by the word in the narrative in Exodus 34: 10–28. The laws set out here are not to be understood as conditions upon which the *bᵉrīt* would be granted; rather, the observance of these commands was to be the means whereby Israel would enter fully into the benefits of Yahweh's *bᵉrīt*, that is, Yahweh's promise.

In his important monograph *Die Bundesvorstellung im Alten Testament*

---

[42] *ZAW* 13, 1893, pp. 246 ff.
[43] *ZAW* 12, 1892, pp. 249 ff.
[44] *ZAW* 13, 1893, p. 279.
[45] *ZAW* 12, 1892, pp. 233 f.
[46] *ZAW* 12, 1892, p. 252.

(Marburg 1896) R. Kraetzschmar reopened the question of the original meaning of the word and its subsequent development. Up to this time two main understandings of the word had been held. The first and more widely accepted view was that it originally designated an agreement entered into by two parties involving reciprocal obligations. Such an agreement could be between equals or between a stronger and a weaker party. The meaning 'law' was a secondary development and arose from the nature of such agreements as involving mutually accepted and binding obligations. The other understanding was that the word originally meant 'law' from which was derived secondarily the meaning 'agreement', 'treaty', 'contract' to designate a relationship established between two parties by mutually accepted stipulations.

Kraetzschmar argued that *bᵉrīt* originally referred to the solemn cultic ceremony by which a relationship between two parties was established, and that its meaning was secondarily extended to designate the relationship itself and the obligations or stipulations involved (p. 29). As employed in this derived sense in the Old Testament, *bᵉrīt* connotes different kinds of relationships and commitments. It can mean an agreement (*Bund*) between two parties to achieve a mutually desired goal; a treaty or contract (*Vertrag*) between two states or individuals; a solemn assurance (*Zusicherung*) pledged by a superior to an inferior party, or, by contrast, the imposition of obligations upon an inferior party; it can also refer to a vow (*Gelübde*) taken by a group who pledge themselves to perform certain duties or tasks, or a vow taken at the instigation of a third party, a mediator, the vows in both cases being made to God.

Thus, according to Kraetzschmar, *bᵉrīt* was a cultic act whereby obligations or agreements of whatever kind were in solemn manner made absolutely binding and unbreakable. Its content and meaning were determined by the nature of the obligations it involved, according as it had the sense of agreement, treaty or contract, solemn assurance or promise, an obligation imposed by one party upon another, or a vow (pp. 40 f.).

On the basis of this consideration of the range of meanings of the word, Kraetzschmar discussed briefly God's *bᵉrīt* with Abraham, with David, and with Levi (pp. 57 ff.). In the case of the first of these, he found its earliest attestation in the most ancient stratum of the J narrative (J¹) in Genesis 15: 1–12a, 17–18aα (pp. 58 ff.). Elsewhere in J¹ he found it only in

Genesis 12: 7 and 24: 7. In these texts the *b͑rīt* consisted solely of Yahweh's promise to Abraham that his descendants would inherit the land of Canaan. This record of the divine assurance to the patriarch presupposed and gave expression to Israel's claim to the land in which it dwelt as having its basis in just such a divine promise to its great ancestor.

The *b͑rīt* with David, the earliest testimony to which is 2 Samuel 23: 1–7 ('The Last Words of David'), likewise consisted of Yahweh's solemn promise to David that his dynasty would endure forever (pp. 63 ff.). The concept of such a *berīt* originated soon after David's death when legend began to surround him and he was more and more seen to have been one who had been the special object of Yahweh's grace. The belief in a *b͑rīt* between Yahweh and the house of Levi, the oldest testimony to which is Deuteronomy 33: 9, originated in the second half of the eighth century BC (pp. 66 ff.). Here again the term designates Yahweh's promise, in this case that Levi and his descendants would be priests of Yahweh forever.

Thus, according to Kraetzschmar, during the monarchical period the unalterable, enduring entitlement of Israel to the land of Canaan, of the descendants to David to the throne of Israel, and of the Levites to the priesthood of Yahweh's people, were believed to be founded upon three divine covenants granted to the respective ancestors, Abraham, David, and Levi; and thus the three pillars of the Israelite state—possession of the land, the monarchy and dynasty, and the priesthood—were believed to be based upon God's eternal pledges to his people (p. 69).

It may here be interposed that there was little support for Kraetzschmar's view that the covenant with Levi is of such early origin. It is doubtful whether Deuteronomy 33: 9 refers to it, whilst other texts which concern it are no earlier than the exilic period (Num. 25: 12 f. (P); Jer. 33: 21; Mal. 2: 4–9; Neh. 13: 29). Whether or not the tradition of a *b͑rīt* with Abraham was of early origin was also disputed during the period here under survey. The relatively early dating proposed by Kraetzschmar was not accepted by, for example, Gunkel who argued that with its emphasis upon the land as divinely given to Israel it presupposes a time when future possession of the land was under threat, that is, the period after the fall of the Northern Kingdom in 721 BC.[47] On the other hand, though many argued that the tradition of a *b͑rīt* between Yahweh and David arose only at a very late time, perhaps as late as the exile, Kraetzschmar's view that

[47] *Genesis*, p. 167.

'The Last Words of David' in 2 Samuel 23: 1–7 was of much earlier origin found fresh support from Procksch and Gressmann.[48] As we shall see, that the tradition in Genesis 15 as well as the tradition of a covenant with David are both of early origin became widely accepted by Old Testament scholars of a subsequent generation.

According to Kraetzschmar, in the oldest stratum of the J and E narratives concerning Sinai the covenant consisted of Yahweh's giving the sacred ark as the sign of his presence with his people (p. 94 f.). That is, like the covenants with Abraham, David, and Levi, *bᵉrīt* here was also conceived of as Yahweh's promise to Israel. It was only later, under the influence of the preaching of the eighth-century prophets, that this earlier notion was replaced. This arose from the inclusion of a decalogue in both the J narrative (Exod. 34: 10–28) and E (Exod. 20: 1–17); the *bᵉrīt* now came to designate an agreement (*Bund*) with reciprocal obligations. The presence of law rendered the content of the *bᵉrīt* an arrangement based upon conditions to be observed by both parties (pp. 94, 98 f.). Yahweh's obligation was to take Israel under his divine protection; Israel's obligation was to obey the will of Yahweh set out in his law. This new concept of the covenant between Yahweh and Israel arose about the end of the eighth century BC and received full expression in Deuteronomy and other literature of the seventh and sixth centuries BC (pp. 99, 123 ff., 145 ff.). That P also knew of such a covenant is reflected in Exodus 6: 2 ff. (p. 187). For P, however, the most important covenant was that between God and Abraham (Gen. 17). Against Valeton, Kraetzschmar argued that this was also conceived of as an agreement involving mutual obligations. The same was true of the P narrative of a covenant with Noah (Gen. 9) (pp. 188 ff., 192 ff).

We return to the question of the meaning of the word *bᵉrīt* which was the subject of yet another significant work during the period here under survey, that of J. Pedersen in his notable study *Der Eid bei den Semiten* (Strasburg 1914). As its title indicates, Pedersen now brought into the discussion comparative material, specifically from pre-Islamic Arabic literature. He also sought, however, to deepen our understanding of the role and significance of covenant-making among ancient Semitic peoples in the light of what we can discern about their mentality and psychology. On this basis he rejected previous understandings of the word *bᵉrīt* in

[48] See below, ch. 2, section IV, first para.

terms of such concepts as agreement, treaty, contract, and the like; such views had been governed by modern European ideas and institutions rather than properly founded upon a knowledge and understanding of ancient Semitic society and mentality. Contrary therefore to the view that the making of a covenant meant the establishment of an agreement, contract, treaty, or the like, whence one could claim the forming of a relationship between the parties involved, Pedersen argued that the word, like the Arabic *'ahd*, signified the creation by word and rite of a *relationship* between two parties; the making of a covenant effected a 'union of spheres' which had hitherto been separate, and so had the effect of creating the same solidarity between them as in the case of natural blood-relationship. The new community of interests or 'union of spheres' thus created brought with it specific rights and duties which the relationship in itself made binding and inviolable. Pedersen's definition was therefore that *bᵉrīt* designated a 'mutual relationship of solidarity with all the rights and obligations which this relationship entailed for the parties involved' (pp. 33 f.). Whether both parties had prescribed rights, whether they both undertook specific obligations, or whether one party could command something which the other had to honour and fulfil could vary; the chief emphasis lay in the mutuality of the relationship and the obligation(s) this entailed whatever the precise nature or extent of these might be.

What was peculiar to Pedersen's conclusion was simply his strong emphasis upon *bᵉrīt* as a relationship, a so-called 'union of spheres'. This apart, however, his definition cited above was clearly in line with what most others at this time held—however much the etymology or the 'original meaning' of *bᵉrīt* or the particular ceremonies involved in the making of a *bᵉrīt* remained disputed—namely, that the making of a covenant created a bond between two parties which involved an obligation of some sort, whether taken on by one of the parties in favour of the other, or imposed by one upon the other, or accepted mutually by both parties. Thus, the effect of Pedersen's definition covered most if not all of the terms with which Kraetzschmar translated the word. For example, Pedersen too argued that the covenant with Abraham in Genesis 15 or with David in 2 Samuel 23: 5 was Yahweh's promise to these individuals (pp. 41 f.). Similarly, Pedersen, like Kraetzschmar, understood Yahweh's *bᵉrīt* with Israel to involve the imposition of obligations by Yahweh upon Israel (pp. 35 f.). The difference between them was that by emphasizing

that the word means primarily a 'relationship' Pedersen understood the
making of a covenant between Yahweh and Israel to have been an original
element in Israelite religion—references to Yahweh as Israel's 'owner' or
'husband' or 'king' are at the same time references to his *bᵉrīt* with Israel
(p. 63)—whereas Kraetzschmar, arguing that one must not confuse 'relationship with Yahweh' with 'covenant relationship'[49] concluded that the
latter arose only at a late stage in the history of Israelite religion.

Without therefore necessarily accepting all the grounds on which
Pedersen argued his view, subsequent scholars were able to accept his
definition itself, that is, that the word designates a bond between parties
with prescribed obligations. As we shall see, however, such an understanding of the meaning of *bᵉrīt* has since been challenged.[50]

One further feature of Pedersen's work must be noted here. He
restricted the comparative evidence he employed to pre-Islamic Arabic
literature, and specifically rejected the use of ancient Mesopotamian
sources. These latter, he argued, derive from a centralized state and city
culture in which 'covenant' acquired a different role and significance
(already in the modern sense of 'treaty' or 'arrangement') than in the
different cultural setting of the Arabic and Old Testament texts (p. 51).
Again as we shall see, it was to such Mesopotamian and also Hittite
political texts that attention was later to be forcefully directed for an
elucidation of the nature and significance of covenant-making in Israel,[51]
though in fairness to Pedersen it must be borne in mind that the main
texts which were to make this possible had either not yet been discovered
or had not yet been published at the time he was writing his book.

III

Like Wellhausen, Kraetzschmar argued that the notion of a covenant
would have been foreign to early Israelite religion which centred upon a
'natural bond' between Yahweh and Israel (p. 98). But he did allow for the
conclusion of a covenant of a different nature at Sinai. He suggested that
at an early time a number of Hebrew tribes, perhaps the Rachel tribes,

---

[49] *Bundesvorstellung*, p. 100. Cf. Pedersen's comment on this, op. cit., pp. 39 f.
[50] For a discussion see chapter 4 below.
[51] See below, chapter 3.

living in the vicinity of Sinai, entered into a *bᵉrīt* with each other for mutual protection and help in war. As witness to this pact they placed sacred stones in a box, that is, the ark, which was brought out in times of war to spur the tribes to full commitment to their obligations. At a later time Moses adopted this ark in introducing the religion of Yahweh to those who had escaped from Egypt. At his hands it was reinterpreted as a means of representing the presence of Yahweh of Sinai among his people, though at the same time it retained its function as a means of uniting the disparate tribes of Israel (pp. 209 ff., 215).

That originally the covenant functioned as a means of uniting diverse groups with each other was argued by others at this time. According to F. Schwally, at Sinai some Israelite tribes entered into a covenant with the Midianites, and Yahweh was invoked as guarantor of the oath sworn by both parties.[52] In later times, however, 'the actual course of things faded from memory, and the notion could establish itself that at Sinai what was concluded was not a covenant between Israel and Midian under the protection of Yahweh, but simply a covenant of Yahweh with his chosen people' (p. 3.) B. D. Eerdmans suggested that the covenant at Sinai originally consisted of the union of a number of nomadic tribes into a tribal confederation, accompanied by the invoking of Yahweh as the God to whom some of these tribes believed they owed their deliverance from bondage in Egypt.[53]

A somewhat similar view had been argued by K. Budde.[54] Referring to Exodus 18, he argued:

What the prophets and historians of Israel later called 'Israel's covenant with Yahweh and Yahweh's with Israel' is here described in a sober, historical narrative, in a form which offers nothing at all wonderful when read in the light of ethnology and the history of religions. Expressed in the language of sober historical narration, this covenant is nothing else than an alliance of Israel with the nomad tribe of the Kenites at Sinai, which had as its self-evident condition the adoption of their religion, Yahweh-worship.[55]

---

[52] *Semitische Kriegsaltertümer*, I, *Der heilige Krieg im alten Israel*, Leipzig 1901, p. 2.

[53] 'Oorsprong en beteekenis van de "Tien Woorden"', *Theologisch Tijdschrift* 37, 1903, pp. 19–35.

[54] K. Budde, *the Religion of Israel to the Exile*, New York and London 1899; *Die Religion des Volkes Israel bis zur Verbannung*, Giessen 1900.

[55] *The Religion of Israel*, p. 24; *Die Religion*, p. 19.

But, he went on to suggest,

> this alliance is rightly called in the Old Testament tradition a covenant of Israel, not with the Kenites, but with Yahweh. For Israel had made the acquaintance of this God earlier than that of the desert tribe which served Him. It had been won to Him by the preaching of Moses in Egypt, and had vowed to dedicate itself to His service before it met the Kenites. We must recognise therefore as a fact historically well attested and supported by many later witnesses, that Israel, simultaneously with its exodus from Egypt and the beginning of its history as a distinct nation, turned to a new religion, the worship of Yahweh, the mountain-god of the Kenites, at Sinai.[56]

Neither Schwally nor Eerdmans was able adequately to explain why such an originally secular arrangement should subsequently have been understood as a covenant between Yahweh and Israel, whilst Budde's view left some confusion about whether or not Yahweh was a party to the covenant made between the Kenites and the Israelites. The question was whether a covenant between different groups could also have been one between such groups and Yahweh. To this W. Robertson Smith had in fact earlier given a much more direct answer.[57] He drew a distinction between religions and societies based upon kinship on the one hand, and, on the other, Israelite society and religion, which was not so based. In the former the idea of a covenant, whether between the worshippers mutually or between them and their god, is not applicable, for a covenant means 'artificial brotherhood'; it would have had no place in a society where the natural brotherhood of which it is an imitation already existed: '. . . in purely natural religions, where the god and his community are looked upon as forming a physical unity, the idea that religion rests on a compact is out of place, and acts of religious communion can only be directed to quicken and confirm the life-bond that already subsists between the parties' (p. 319). By contrast, he argued, from the time of Moses Yahweh's relation to Israel was not natural but ethical, and though the great prophets were later to give this fresh and powerful application, they did not regard the concept as an innovation. 'In fact, a nation like Israel is not a natural unity like a clan, and Jehovah as the national God was, from the time of Moses downward, no mere natural clan God, but

---

[56] *The Religion of Israel*, p. 24; *Die Religion*, p. 19.
[57] *The Religion of the Semites*, London 1889, 1894², third edition by S. A. Cook, 1927. (References here are to the second edition.)

the god of a confederation, so that here the idea of a covenant religion is entirely justified.' (p. 319 note 2.)

In short, here already Robertson Smith set out briefly an understanding of the covenant between Yahweh and Israel as something which was not a *theological idea* born of a late period in Israelite religion, as Wellhausen and others maintained, but that which lay at the foundation of Israel as a society of tribes and of their worship of Yahweh. That is, the covenant performed a *religio-sociological function* of uniting diverse groups with each other and with their common God Yahweh. As we shall see, such an understanding of the covenant between Yahweh and Israel was later to become widely accepted.

Independently of Robertson Smith's work, others also argued strongly against Wellhausen's understanding of pre-prophetic religion as centring on a 'natural bond' between Israel and Yahweh. Most notable among these was F. Giesebrecht in his influential monograph *Die Geschichtlichkeit des Sinaibundes* (Königsberg 1900). He argued that Wellhausen's description of early Israelite religion as centring on such a bond was misconceived and indeed, on Wellhausen's own understanding of how Israel came to worship Yahweh, anomalous (pp. 25 ff.). Wellhausen had rightly attached great significance to Moses as the founder of the Israelite nation, and, closely bound up with this, of Israel's religion. After the deliverance from Egypt and through the agency of Moses Yahweh became the God of Israel and Israel the people of Yahweh, and this relationship, Wellhausen had also rightly maintained, remained the guiding principle of Israel's life and history thereafter. But this means, Giesebrecht argued, that Israel's relationship with Yahweh was *historically* founded and did not emerge, as in the case of the so-called 'natural' religions, from the people's own religious consciousness. Israel came to know Yahweh as the result of specific historical events and through the teaching of a historical individual who pointed to those events as the manifestation of Yahweh's actions on his people's behalf. In short, it was not a 'natural' religion but one based upon *election*, and as such it was from the outset distinctively different from the 'natural' religion of, say, the Moabites with their native god Chemosh. Further, it was this belief in divine election that shaped the peculiar history and development of Israelite religion subsequently, for it brought with it from the beginning an aggressive exclusivism of Yahwism, a belief in the incomparability of Yahweh, which led inevitably to monotheism, a monotheism which had in essence already developed before the preaching of the great prophets and which in effect began with the achievements of Moses (pp. 28 ff.). If such was the essential nature of early Israelite religion and of its concept of God and of his relationship with his people, then, argued Giesebrecht, the main argument of Wellhausen and others against the possibility that this religion was founded upon a covenant is removed.

A number of scholars subsequently argued the same view, amongst them, for example, E. Kautzsch, P. Karge, G. Beer, and Gressmann.[58] For these scholars the making of a covenant between Yahweh and Israel was a *sine qua non* of the nature of Israelite religion as a 'religion of election'; by the singularly appropriate means of a covenant Israel became united with this God, whom they believed to have revealed himself to them in the stirring event of the exodus. Thus Israel's belief in its divine election became formalized in the covenant, and these together, election and covenant, were what gave Israelite religion its distinctiveness from the outset over against the religions of its ancient Near Eastern environment.

IV

But for those who held such a view there remained a major problem on which Wellhausen's work had sharply focused attention. This is the striking sparsity if not total absence of references to this covenant in the literature of the eighth-century prophets. Among those who rejected Wellhausen's view of the post-prophetic origin of the notion of a covenant between Yahweh and Israel various attempts were made to explain this. The following are just a few of them.

Giesebrecht, for example, argued that as Israel down through the centuries continued to experience Yahweh's grace in the ever-changing circumstances and fortunes of its history, so the memory of the formal act of the more and more distant past by which its relationship with Yahweh had been sealed became less and less important; the people '*lived* the

---

[58] E. Kautzsch's article on the 'Religion of Israel' in *HDB*, extra volume, Edinburgh 1904, esp. pp. 629 ff.; cf. his *Biblische Theologie des Alten Testaments*, Tübingen 1911, pp. 60 ff.; P. Karge, *Geschichte des Bundesgedankens im Alten Testament*, Münster 1910; G. Beer, *Mose und sein Werk. Ein Vortrag*, Giessen 1912, pp. 32 f.; H. Gressmann, *Mose und seine Zeit*, pp. 469 ff.

relationship with its God in faith and in his grace' without forever reflecting afresh on its inauguration in the remote past (p. 63). It was only in the wake of the frightening doubt cast upon the continuation of the relationship between Yahweh and Israel by the eighth-century prophets that the memory of how it had begun came powerfully to the forefront of national life again. As Amos saw the mounting power of Assyria, he called to mind that the relationship between Yahweh and Israel had been founded upon a historical event and that therefore God and the people were not necessarily bound together irrevocably. Hosea developed this idea further, employing the metaphor of a marriage which demands loyalty and can experience divorce although still allowing for subsequent reconciliation. Then later came the further intensification of the covenant demands, non-observance of which must involve the end of the relationship between Yahweh and Israel (pp. 64 f.).

A different suggestion had been made earlier by the conservative scholar C. J. Bredencamp.[59] He argued that the existence of a covenant between Yahweh and Israel based upon a law stipulating mutual obligations and rights was the very reason the prophets so often depict Yahweh disputing with his people (p. 23). That apart from Hosea 6: 7 and 8: 1 they did not employ the word *bᵉrīt* is no argument that they did not know of the covenant and all that it entailed, for the different images they used—the image of Yahweh as king, or as father, or as owner of a vineyard,—are simply paraphrases of the covenant relationship: 'It is not the word that was the source of the idea, as Wellhausen imagines, but on the contrary the idea expresses itself in the various though similar popular similes and images' (p. 25). In a review of Bredencamp's book, Stade responded to this that Bredencamp had confused 'relationship with God' with 'covenant with God'.[60]

Different again was the suggestion made by A. B. Davidson.[61] He offered the explanation that the reason the earlier prophets do not refer to the covenant was not that it had come into existence later than their time; after all, later prophets such as Zephaniah, Nahum, Habakkuk, Haggai, Jonah, Joel, Zecharia 1–8 do not use the term either, though it was certainly current in their time. The reason was, he suggested, that for

---

[59] *Gesetz und Propheten. Ein Beitrag zur alttestamentlichen Kritik*, Erlangen 1881.
[60] *TLZ* 7, 1882, Cols. 241–8.
[61] Article on 'Covenant' in *HDB*, Edinburgh 1898, vol. I, pp. 509–15.

these pre-exilic prophets the relation between Yahweh and Israel was brought about and sustained by Yahweh's love for his people in his redeeming acts on their behalf. The nature of this relationship was perfectly well understood; it was given in the conception of Yahweh and was purely ethical.

> What is required of the people is to seek 'good'—civil and moral righteousness and the service of Jehovah alone. In demanding this from the people the prophets do not found on a book or on laws, they speak off their own minds. To themselves their principles are axiomatic, and wherever these principles were learned they coincide with the Moral Law (Hos 4: 1–3) ... Thus the prophetic idea differs from the idea of a covenant as real differs from formal; the assurance of redemption reposes, not on the divine promise, but on the divine nature, on God Himself as men have historically found Him in His acts of redemption already done, as He is known in the heart of man. (p. 512)

Different yet again was the view of, for example, W. Lotz.[62] He regarded the references to the covenant in Hosea 6: 7 and 8: 1 as authentic, and also attributed to this period Zechariah 9: 11. But the paucity of references in the eighth-century prophets was because at that time the concept of the covenant had not been sufficiently developed to embrace the relationship between Yahweh and Israel in the comprehensive way in which it was later to be used in such writings as Deuteronomy, Jeremiah and Ezekiel.[63] In these latter writings the relationship between God and Israel could be summed up by the term *berīt*. Earlier, however, it was used only of a specific agreement between God and his people, after the analogy of a covenant between two human partners, and involving mutual obligations. The term did not at this earlier time designate the relationship *in toto*; it would have been inconceivable, for example, that had there been no covenant there would have been no relationship between Yahweh and Israel. Lotz drew an analogy between this early understanding of the covenant between Yahweh and Israel and that between David and Jonathan (1 Sam. 18: 3; 20: 8). The latter involved mutual obligations, but the relationship between David and his great friend was wider and deeper than their covenant together.

---

[62] W. Lotz in a series of articles under the title 'Der Bund vom Sinai' in *NKZ* 12, 1901, pp. 561–80, 631–55, 859–75; *NKZ* 13, 1902, pp. 181–204; *NKZ* 14, 1903, pp. 128–53; *NKZ* 15, 1904, pp. 281–304, 532–59.

[63] *NKZ* 15, 1904, pp. 281 ff.

These few examples show that amongst those who opposed Wellhausen's view no agreed solution for the sparsity of references to the covenant by the eighth-century prophets was arrived at. And no one who did not already believe that the covenant was an ancient aspect of Israelite religion was persuaded by any of them. On this question of the prophets and the covenant, no less than on the other issues raised by Wellhausen's work, opinions remained sharply polarized. But a dramatic change was soon to come from this generation of controversy to a long period of virtual unanimity of opinion against Wellhausen that the covenant was indeed an ancient and fundamental feature of Israelite religion. It is to this remarkable change in the history of covenant study that I now turn.

2

The Controversy Ended

In his article on Moses in the first edition of *Die Religion in Geschichte und Gegenwart*, published in 1913, Gunkel wrote: 'Um Sinai hat M(ose) dann die Stämme gesammelt und einen Bund mit den Midianitern geschlossen.' ('Moses then assembled the tribes at Sinai and made a covenant with the Midianites.' vol. IV, col. 521.)[1] In his revision of this article for the second edition of the same work in 1930, however, this sentence reads: 'Um Sinai hat M(ose) dann die Stämme gesammelt und durch einen "Bund" Jahves mit ihnen sie innerlich geeinigt.' ('Moses then assembled the tribes at Sinai and by means of a "covenant" of Yahweh with them gave them an inner unity." vol. IV, col. 234.)

These quotations from Gunkel's two editions of his essay are a striking pointer to the way in which the marked division of opinion during the period described in the foregoing chapter rapidly gave way afterwards to widespread agreement on the antiquity and significance of the covenant between Yahweh and Israel. Indeed, within little more than a decade after the end of the First World War such agreement, even if with much variation in detail, had established itself. Further, this agreement extended also to the origin and significance of other covenantal traditions in the Old Testament, notably those concerning Abraham and David. Nor was this agreement a passing, brief episode; on the contrary, in all essentials the conclusions arrived at and so widely accepted at this time were to continue to command the support of the great majority of scholars for more than a generation to come, the only difference being, as we shall see in the next chapter, that fresh evidence was introduced which, it was believed, further strengthened these conclusions.

How did this new-found, widespread agreement among scholars on these hitherto so controversial issues come about? What arguments were now adduced, in these years following the First World War, and why did they command such support where others before had failed to do so?

[1] See also the views of F. Schwally, B. D. Eerdmans, and K. Budde, in ch. 1, section III.

I

With regard to the covenant between Yahweh and Israel, three main arguments now prevailed. Briefly stated they were as follows:

(1) First, the view expressed at an earlier time that the covenant was from the outset a necessary feature of Israelite religion as a religion founded upon historical events, that is, a religion of 'election' and not a 'natural' religion, now found fresh and widespread emphasis. The significance of the covenant in this respect was now stressed by, for example, J. Hempel in his influential work *Gott und Mensch im Alten Testament* (Stuttgart 1926). Hempel saw the significance of the notion of the covenant to be that it removed the relationship between God and the people from the sphere of the natural and transferred it to the realm of history in which Yahweh's power, the declaration of his will, and his holiness were made manifest (p. 126). A. Weiser, who was later to become one of the chief exponents of the significance of the covenant in Israel's cult (see under (2) below), likewise argued at this time that the covenant mediated by Moses at Sinai was the outward expression of Israel's belief in divine election,[2] whilst K. Galling, in his well-known monograph on Israel's election traditions published in 1928, argued that the covenant was an important element in these traditions and arose from, and gave expression to, the belief in Yahweh as the God of history, a belief which rendered Israelite religion unique among the religions of the ancient Near East.[3] Most influential of all, however, was W. Eichrodt's *Theologie des Alten Testaments*, the first volume of which appeared in 1933, in which the covenant and its theology is employed in a large-scale, programmatic manner.[4] The fundamental importance of the covenant was summed up by Eichrodt as follows:

---

[2] *Die Bedeutung des Alten Testaments für den Religionsunterricht*, Giessen 1925, reprinted in his *Glaube und Geschichte im Alten Testament und andere ausgewählte Schriften*, Göttingen 1961, pp. 19–50.

[3] *Die Erwählungstraditionen Israels*, BZAW 48, Giessen 1928, pp. 26 ff., 92 ff.

[4] Vol. I, Leipzig 1933. The second volume was published in 1935, and the third in 1939. E. trs. *Theology of the Old Testament*, vol. I, London 1961 (from the sixth German edition of *Theologie des Alten Testaments*, I, Stuttgart 1959); vol. II, London 1967 (from the fifth German edition, II and III, Stuttgart 1964). In citing the original German work below I refer to the first edition.

any understanding of God's involvement with his people in terms of popular Nature religion was rejected. The covenant agreement excluded the idea, which prevailed widely and was disseminated among Israel's neighbours as well, that between the national God and his worshippers there existed a bond inherent in the order of Nature, whether this were a kind of blood relationship, or a link between the God and the country which created an indissoluble association between himself and the inhabitants. This type of popular religion, in which the divinity displays only the higher aspect of the national self-consciousness, the national 'genius', or the *mysterium* of the forces of Nature peculiar to a particular country, was overcome principally by the concept of the covenant. Israel's religion is thus stamped as a 'religion of election', using this phrase to mean that it is the divine election which makes it the exact opposite of the nature religions.[5]

Eichrodt also sought to explain the virtual absence of references to the Sinai covenant in the preaching of the eighth-century prophets.[6] He suggested that although as originally founded and properly understood the covenant was inaugurated as a free and gracious act of Yahweh, there was inherent in it a weakness which made it a potential danger to religious life, namely, its legal aspect because of which it was liable to become the basis of a *do ut des* religion. Eventually, he argued, this is what in fact happened so that the prophets faced a dead externalism in religious practice and a mechanical routine in religious thought, a formal pre-occupation with the performance of duties and a corresponding reckoning on God's automatic performance of his obligations towards Israel in return. The prophets thus strove to eradicate all thought of an *opus operatum* in the people's concept of its relation with God.

When, therefore, the prophets come to speak of the founding of Israel's privileged standing, it is not hard to see why they make no reference to the Sinai covenant, but instead call to mind the deliverance from Egypt. In no other way could they have illuminated more clearly the gracious favour of Yahweh, or guarded against the false perversion of his activity into an obligatory performance by the covenant deity.[7]

Thus they presented God's acts as the working out of a fully personal love and loyalty, the proper response to which, on the part of the people, was

[5] *Theologie*, I, p. 10, E. trs., I, pp. 42 f.
[6] *Theologie*, I, pp. 15 f., E. trs., I, pp. 51 f.
[7] *Theologie*, I, p. 16, E. trs., I, p. 52.

not the performance of a mere external rite or duty but a spontaneous reaction coming from the heart.

(2) A further area of research which came to prominence during the 1920s contributed significantly to the emerging agreement among scholars on the antiquity and importance of the covenant. This was the new interest in, and investigation of, the role of the cult in Israelite religion. The ground for this trend had already been prepared, especially by Gunkel and Gressmann, but it was most notably S. Mowinckel in his epoch-making *Psalmenstudien I-VI* (Kristiana 1921-4) who now developed and presented it in compelling manner. Influenced not only by Gunkel and Gressmann, but even more strongly by Pedersen and the Danish philologist and historian Vilhelm Grønbech,[8] Mowinckel, in the second volume of these Studies, argued in detail his well-known view that the autumn feast of Tabernacles in Israel centred upon a celebration, a cultic 'actualization' of Yahweh's kingship as creator and sustainer of the world. For our present purposes two aspects of what Mowinckel here argued are particularly important. First, he contended that integral to this festival was a cultic renewal of the covenant between Yahweh and Israel. The historic foundation of the covenant at Sinai was annually re-experienced in this cultic 'drama'. He pointed to such Psalms as 81 and 95 as evidence of this element in the festival as a whole.[9] Secondly, Mowinckel, here particularly reflecting ideas suggested by Pedersen and Grønbech, understood the covenant to have been of the essence of Israelite society, that which was constitutive of it and which governed the relationships between the individual Israelites and between Israel as a whole and Yahweh. 'Blessing' belonged to an individual in so far as he was a member of the covenant community, and 'blessing' and 'divine power' belonged to the community from Yahweh as 'Lord of the covenant' (pp. 150 f).

A few years later Mowinckel returned to this subject in his influential work *Le Décalogue* (Paris 1927), now arguing that the narratives in Exodus 19-24 concerning the making of the covenant at Sinai are nothing other

[8] The major, though not the only source of influence from Grønbech was his *Vor Folkeaet in Oldtiden*, 1909-12, E. trs. *The Culture of the Teutons*, London and Copenhagen 1931. Mowinckel dedicated the second volume of his *Psalmenstudien* to V. Grønbech, J. Pedersen, H. Gunkel, and H. Gressmann.

[9] *Psalmenstudien II. Das Thronbesteigungsfest Jahwäs und der Ursprung der Eschatologie*, Kristiania 1922, pp. 152 ff.

than a description, in the language of 'historical myth', of a cultic celebration in Israel during the monarchical period, that is, of a covenant-renewal celebration which, as his earlier work on the Psalms had already argued, included amongst other things a proclamation of Yahweh's divine law (pp. 114 ff.).

It was to this view that G. von Rad was later directly indebted in his well-known study *Das formgeschichtliche Problem des Hexateuch*.[10] Weiser reviewed Mowinckel's *Le Décalogue* favourably,[11] and later, especially in his commentary on the Psalms, developed Mowinckel's insights further, arguing that the festival in question should properly be understood as a festival of covenant-renewal; that is, he gave more prominence, indeed a central position, to this feature of the 'New Year Festival'.[12] Mowinckel himself in his later work *The Psalms in Israel's Worship*[13] also gave greater emphasis to the covenant-renewal aspect of this festival. A. Alt too, in his influential monograph on the origins of Israelite law,[14] accepted the theory of a recurring covenant festival, differing from Mowinckel and other scholars only in regarding it as having been celebrated not annually but every seventh year, as Deuteronomy 31: 10–13 suggests.[15]

This view that the covenant was the subject of a recurring cultic festival which included a proclamation of the divine law was subsequently seen as a key to understanding the basis of the ethical teaching of the great prophets, who in this as in other respects, it was now argued, were the spokesmen of the covenant. Thus, even if they did not use the word *bᵉrīt* itself, in a number of important ways they nevertheless presupposed the covenant tradition which had been transmitted through the centuries in Israel's cult and so was familiar to them and their contem-

---

[10] BWANT IV: 26, Stuttgart 1938, reprinted in his *Gesammelte Studien zum Alten Testament*, Munich 1958, pp. 9–86, E. trs. 'The Form-Critical Problem of the Hexateuch', in *The Problem of the Hexateuch and Other Essays*, Edinburgh and London 1966, pp. 1–78.

[11] *TLZ* 53, 1928, cols. 553–7.

[12] *Die Psalmen*, fifth revised edition, Göttingen 1959, E. trs. *The Psalms*, London 1962 (from the fifth German edition). Earlier editions of the German have not been available to me.

[13] E. trs. in 2 volumes, Oxford 1962, from *Offersang og Sangoffer*, Oslo 1951.

[14] *Die Ursprünge des israelitischen Rechts*, Leipzig 1934, reprinted in *KS* I, Munich 1953, pp. 278–332, E. trs. 'The Origins of Israelite Law', in *Essays on Old Testament History and Religion*, Oxford 1966, pp. 79–132.

[15] Ibid., p. 326; E. trs., p. 127.

poraries.[16] Scholarship on this matter had indeed come a long way from Wellhausen.

(3) Most important of all, however, was M. Noth's famous monograph *Das System der zwölf Stämme Israels*[17] which took up and brilliantly argued the view, already suggested by a number of scholars at earlier times, that the tribes of Israel in the pre-monarchical period constituted a sacral confederation which is best understood on the analogy of the Greek 'amphictyonies' of a later period. Noth maintained that Joshua 24 preserves the memory of the foundation of this twelve-tribe 'amphictyony' at Shechem, an event in which Joshua as the leader of the 'house of Joseph' took the initiative. He assembled the representatives of the other tribes and by means of a covenant bound the tribes to each other and to Yahweh whom they now adopted as their common God. Further, the covenant whereby the Israelite 'amphictyony' came into being became the subject of an annual cultic festival at the central sanctuary of the tribal league (pp. 74 ff.)[18] Thus Noth's work illuminated the religio-sociological context in which the covenant between Yahweh and Israel functioned. It established the view that the covenant is not to be understood as a theological *idea*, as Wellhausen and others had earlier maintained, but was an *institution* with a definable function in ancient Israelite society and religion.

Noth rejected the view that the Sinai covenant was developed on the basis of the Shechemite traditions represented by Joshua 24. Following E. Sellin,[19] he argued that two separate historical situations are presupposed by these two covenant traditions: on the one hand the making of a covenant between a group of Israelites and Yahweh at Sinai, and, on the other, the assembly at Shechem at a later time in which this group took part with other Israelites who had already been settled in the land. The Old Testament errs only in regarding all twelve tribes as having been at Sinai.[20]

---

[16] For a survey with extensive bibliography see R. E. Clements, *Prophecy and Covenant*, London 1965, chs. 4 and 5.   [17] BWANT IV: 1, Stuttgart 1930.
[18] Cf. his *Geschichte Israels*, Göttingen 1950, pp. 80 f., E. trs. *The History of Israel* (revised by P. R. Ackroyd) London 1960, pp. 91 f.
[19] 'Seit welcher Zeit verehrten die nordisraelitischen Stämme Jahwe?', *Oriental Studies dedicated to Paul Haupt*, Baltimore and Leipzig 1926, pp. 124–34; *Geschichte des israelitisch-jüdischen Volkes*, I, Leipzig 1924, pp. 98 ff.
[20] *Das System der zwölf Stämme Israels*, pp. 88 f.

II

Why was it that these arguments concerning the antiquity and importance of the covenant now gained such widespread acceptance? After all, they were by no means wholly new. For example, the view that the covenant was a necessary and distinctive feature of Israel's religion as a religion of 'election' had been strongly advocated by a number of scholars during the period surveyed in the foregoing chapter. Or again, the view that the covenant would have performed an essential religio-sociological function in early Israel as a tribal society had also been suggested much earlier, notably by Robertson Smith.

One must not of course underestimate the vigour and cogency with which such arguments were now freshly presented in the years immediately following the First World War, or the new insights which lent them added support. Thus, whilst earlier scholars had suggested that pre-monarchic Israel took the form of an 'amphictyony', it was not until Noth's epoch-making work that it was presented in such detail and so compellingly. Nor does one find Mowinckel's influential insights into the nature and role of the cult in Israelite religion represented at an earlier stage of scholarship in this matter, even though the ground for his work was in part prepared by such scholars as Gunkel and Gressmann. But when allowance has been made for all this, it remains the case that other important trends contributed significantly both to the formulation and to the widespread acceptance of the arguments briefly outlined in the foregoing section of this chapter.

I mention first two such trends in Old Testament study at this time which favoured the fresh emphasis upon, and general acceptance of, the view that the covenant between Yahweh and Israel was a *distinctive* feature of Israelite religion, that indeed it contributed significantly to the distinctiveness of that religion over against those of Israel's neighbours.

(1) First, as is well known, the 1920s saw the rebirth of interest in Old Testament theology. There were several impulses for this. During the nineteenth and early twentieth centuries attention had become increasingly focused upon an investigation of the history and development of Israelite religion to the virtual exclusion of any interest in a theological treatment or assessment of the Old Testament. In the 1920s, however, a

reaction set in against this. It was now felt that if scholarship hitherto had succeeded in wresting the Old Testament from the chains of dogmatic theology, it has also replaced that erstwhile bondage with a new one, in this instance bondage to a purely historical or 'history-of-religions' approach. This was the judgement of C. Steuernagel in his well-known article in the K. Marti *Festschrift* in 1925, an article which is often cited as marking the beginning of the renewed concern with Old Testament theology at this time.[21]

A second impulse derived from the new theological climate which came about after the First World War. K. Barth's 'bomb' had 'exploded in the playground of the theologians', and although, as the foregoing remarks indicate, Old Testament scholars in general had long since forsaken that particular playground, they were not unaware of the distant bang, and from now onwards became increasingly influenced by the new theological movement and spirit of these years. Neo-orthodoxy's emphasis upon revelation *von oben nach unten* (revelation 'from above to below') and its corresponding assault upon 'natural theology' and 'religion' created a climate conducive to an emphasis upon Israel's history as the arena of God's self-revelation, and with this to a new impetus towards discerning the uniqueness of Israel's faith which from now onwards became more and more regarded as having been radically discontinuous with the religious thought-world of its environment. All this led to increased attention to the 'particularist' elements of Israelite faith such as 'saving history', 'election' and 'covenant'. The notion that Israelite religion began as something of a 'natural bond' between God and people was now increasingly being abandoned.

Thirdly, these post-First World War years saw the beginnings in Germany of an upsurge of anti-Semitic feeling, one manifestation of which was a renewed challenge to the relevance of the Old Testament as part of the church's scriptures. Though A. von Harnack's well-known call at the turn of the century for the abandonment of the Old Testament had met with a general lack of concern among Old Testament scholars, this new and perniciously motivated challenge compelled a response, and this response gave added urgency to a renewed concern with a theological

---

[21] 'Alttestamentliche Theologie und alttestamentliche Religionsgeschichte', *Vom Alten Testament. Festschrift für K. Marti*, ed. K. Budde, BZAW 41, Giessen 1925, pp. 266–73.

evaluation of the Old Testament and, with this, of those elements in Israelite faith and piety which are of abiding value.

In their different ways works such as those referred to above which made their appearance during these years witness to these various impulses. Significantly, from the point of view of our purpose here, they each, in their different ways, saw in the covenant that which was normative in, and creative of, Israelite faith and piety, that which gave definitive and distinctive expression to the relation between God and Israel, to the nature of God and to his will as well as to what response this required of Israel.

(2) Such emphasis upon the covenant between Yahweh and Israel as a distinctive feature of Israelite religion also came as a legacy of the 'history-of-religions movement', one of the main aims of which was an evaluation of the distinctiveness of Israelite religion among the religions of its environment. Behind this movement can be discerned the influence of a revival of Romanticism which took place around the turn of the century. Amongst other things, this renewed Romanticism, reacting against what was believed to be renewed rationalism or 'new enlightenment' trends in late nineteenth-century thought, revived Herder's emphasis, made against the 'universalism' or 'uniformitarianism' of the eighteenth-century Enlightenment, upon the 'individuality' (*Eigentümlichkeit*) of nations, upon individual national *Volksgeist*.

In Old Testament studies this renewed emphasis upon the 'individuality' of nations, upon what was distinctive of a people over against other peoples, can be seen in, for example, H. Gunkel's early work *Schöpfung und Chaos in Urzeit und Endzeit* (Göttingen 1895) which endeavoured to demonstrate the distinctiveness of Israel's development of ancient Near Eastern creation mythology. Reaction to the so-called 'pan-Babylonian' school in the early years of the century which threatened to dissolve Israelite religion into its ancient Near Eastern environment gave added impetus to the quest for that which was peculiar to Israel's religion. It was a quest which was to receive increasing attention among scholars. Significant for our purposes was the renewed emphasis placed upon it in the years following the First World War. Thus H. Gressmann, who was a leading member of the 'history-of-religions movement', in a programmatic essay in 1924 on the future tasks of Old Testament research, specifically called for such an awareness of the individuality and distinctiveness of Israel including its religion, language, politics, its literature and culture over against those of its ancient Near Eastern neighbours about whom archaeological discoveries had in the meantime been yielding so much new information. And he did so in terms very characteristic of the 'new-romantic' spirit to which I have referred: 'jedes Volk had seine individuelle Seele, mit ihren spezifischen Fähigkeiten und Gaben, seine persönliche Note, die es von allen anderen unterscheidet' ('each people has its own individual soul, with its specific capabilities and gifts, its own personal character, which distinguishes it from all others.')[22] Here too, therefore, the view that the covenant between Yahweh and Israel was a distinctive feature of Israelite religion, that it was of the *Eigenart* of that religion over against the religions of its ancient environment, found a congenial background in Old Testament studies for the renewed emphasis now placed upon it at this time.

III

But more important than the influence of all these trends upon the understanding of the role and significance of the covenant during these years was that which now came from the study of the sociology of religion. This had recently entered a new phase, its modern era, largely through the work of Emil Durkheim and, of direct relevance for Old Testament research, Max Weber.

One might say, in broad terms, that whereas hitherto a society's religion had come to be regarded as one feature among others in its life, one social phenomenon among other such phenomena—late nineteenth-century positivism indeed had tended to regard it as of less significance than other activities, such as economics, in the shaping and development of a society's life—it was now seen to be a normative and formative force, creative in forms of social life and organization. Religious beliefs and practices with their related institutions such as the cult were now viewed as belonging to the very 'nuts and bolts', so to speak, of a society, creating solidarity among its members and powerfully influencing many aspects and activities of its life, including its economic activity. As a result, attention was

---

[22] 'Die Aufgaben der alttestamentlichen Forschung', *ZAW* 42, 1924, p. 10.

now increasingly focused upon the *function* of religious beliefs and commitments in the making and development of a society.

A direct and important influence of this new trend in the study of the sociology of religion upon Old Testament research was made by Max Weber's study of ancient Israel which first appeared as a series of articles in the 1917–19 issues of the *Archiv für Sozialwissenschaft und Sozialforschung* and was subsequently published in 1921 (posthumously) as the third volume of his *Gesammelte Aufsätze zur Religionssoziologie* under the title *Das antike Judentum (Ancient Judaism)*.[23] Weber's research here was not of course carried out simply in the interests of Old Testament studies, though his knowledge of this field at that time was impressive.[24] His main interest and the motivation for his work lay elsewhere, specifically in investigating the role of religion in the development of a society's economic activity and structures.[25] The stimulus for this derived from earlier studies, especially from his famous *Die protestantische Ethik und der Geist des Kapitalismus (The Protestant Ethic and the Spirit of Capitalism)*, originally published in two parts in 1904–5.[26] Against Marxist historians, who had argued that the economic factor was the most dominant in the development of a society, Weber contended that religion was itself one of the dominant forces in economic motivation and development. It was this interest in how a society's religious beliefs were a motivation in its economic activity (or lack of it) which subsequently led Weber to a study, first of ancient Chinese religion, then of Indian religions, and finally of ancient Israel.

For our purposes what is important here is the predominant role Weber assigned to the covenant between Yahweh and Israel in the foundation of Israelite religion and society and in their subsequent history.

---

[23] Tübingen 1921, E. trs. *Ancient Judaism*, London 1952.

[24] A brief discussion is provided by C. S. Rodd, 'Max Weber and Ancient Judaism', *SJT* 32, 1979, pp. 457–69. On the influence of the sociology of religion on Old Testament study see H. F. Hahn, *The Old Testament in Modern Research*, London 1956, ch. 5; H.-J. Kraus, *Geschichte der historisch-kritischen Erforschung des Alten Testaments*, second edition, Neukirchen 1969, pp. 324–7; W. Schluchter (ed.), *Max Webers Studie über das antike Judentum. Interpretation und Kritik*, Frankfurt am Main 1981; C. Schäfer-Lichtenberger, *Stadt und Eidgenossenschaft im Alten Testament. Eine Auseinandersetzung mit Max Webers Studie 'Das antike Judentum'*, BZAW 156, Berlin and New York 1983.

[25] For an introduction to Weber's thought see, for example, R. Bendix, *Max Weber: An Intellectual Portrait*, University Paperbacks, London 1966.

[26] E. trs. London 1930.

According to Weber 'Israel as a political community was conceived as an oathbound confederation.'[27] Whilst, however, in other ancient confederations the god guaranteed the oath sworn by the members to each other, in Israel the *bᵉrīt* was not merely between the tribes but also between them and Yahweh who was thus a party to the *bᵉrīt*. By this means Yahweh became 'the contractual partner to the ritualistic and social order of the confederacy'.[28] Herein lay the uniqueness of Israelite religion:

In its special relation to God, Israel stood in contrast to all other nations, because of this very unique historical event and the unique conclusion of a covenant. Israel's special relationship to God was not merely guaranteed by God, but had been concluded with God as a party to it. The entire Israelite tradition unanimously traced its origins back to the concrete event assumed to have set the process in motion.[29]

This covenant was no mere 'theoretical construction'; rather it was the basis of the cohesion which existed between the otherwise diverse groups which became known as Israel:

The 'covenant' concept was important for Israel because the ancient social structure of Israel in part rested essentially upon a contractually regulated, permanent relationship of landed warrior sibs with guest tribes as legally protected metics: itinerant herdsmen and guest artisans, merchants and priests.[30]

On the question why Israel's covenant was not one made simply between such groups themselves but with Yahweh as a party to it, Weber wrote:

all political organizations among Bedouins and stock-breeders were quite unstable due to their life conditions. All these tribal organizations tended now to split into sibs, again to coalesce ... With this instability contrasts strikingly the extraordinary stability of a definite type of organization to be found precisely among these unsettled strata: namely, the religious order or 'cult' organization of similar pattern. Apparently only such a religious organization provided solid basis for permanent political and military structures. Such an organization was that of the Rechabites: for centuries, from Jehu's time to Jeremiah we see their continued existence and religious-political activities ... Also, the strictly Yahwistic Kenite tribe, to which the Rechabites belonged, seems to have based its cohesion on religion.[31]

---

[27] *Das antike Judentum*, p. 82; E. trs. p. 75.
[28] p. 128; E. trs. 120.
[29] pp. 126 f.; E. trs. p. 118.
[30] p. 87; E. trs. p. 79.
[31] pp. 87 f.; E. trs. p. 79.

These Rechabites, who were also stock-breeders, achieved their enduring cohesion by means of divine commandments laid down by their founding father Jonadab ben Rechab. In like manner, such cohesion as early Israel achieved was dependent upon the $b^e r\bar{\imath}t$ with Yahweh.

Weber insisted that it was not a case of the particular life conditions of, say, the Rechabites 'producing' an order 'whose establishment could be considered as something like the "ideological exponent" of its economic conditions'.[32] Rather, the emergence of such an order 'was determined by quite concrete religious-historical and often highly personal circumstances and vicissitudes'.[33] That is to say, the particular religious beliefs should not be understood as the deposit of an already realized social organization. Rather, such beliefs originated quite fortuitously, in a historical context in which, in the case of the Rechabites, the founding father narrated his own personal religious experiences and intentions. On the other hand, once

the religious fraternization had proven its efficiency as a political and economic instrument of power and was recognized as such it contributed, of course, tremendously to the diffusion of the pattern. Mohammed's as well as Jonadab ben Rechab's religious promises are not to be 'explained' as products of population phenomena or economic conditions, though their content was co-determined thereby. They were, rather, the expression of personal experiences and intentions. However, the intellectual and social means which they utilized and further the great success of creations of this very type are indeed to be understood in terms of such life conditions. The same goes for ancient Israel.[34]

For Israel the deliverance from bondage in Egypt was seen as a token of God's power and the absolute dependability of his promises and of Israel's lasting debt of gratitude. 'The uniqueness of the event was constituted by the fact that this miracle was effected by a god till then unknown by Israel and who thereupon was accepted through solemn *berith* by Moses' establishment of Yahwe worship. This reception was based on mutual pledges bilaterally mediated through the prophet Moses.'[35]

The confederacy which came into existence was characterized as a war confederacy, with Yahweh as its war god and also god of Israel's social organization:

[32] p. 88; E. trs. pp. 79 f.   [33] p. 88; E. trs. p. 80.
[34] pp. 88 f.; E. trs. p. 80.   [35] p. 127; E. trs. p. 118.

We must assume that, since Moses, he was the god of the covenant of the Israelite confederacy, and corresponding to the purpose of the confederacy, he was primarily its war god. He played this role in a very special manner. He became war god by virtue of a treaty of confederation. This contract had to be concluded, not only among the confederates, but also with him, for he was no god residing in the midst of the people, a familiar god, but rather a god hitherto strange. He continued to be a 'god from afar.' This was the decisive element in the relationship. Yahwe was an elective God. The confederate people had chosen him through *berith* with him . . . Yahwe, in turn, had chosen this people before all others by .free resolve . . . He has given them promises as to no other people and in compensation accepted their pledges.[36]

Since Yahweh was a party to the *berīt*, 'All violations of the holy enactments were not merely violations of orders guaranteed by him as other gods guarantee their orders, but violations of the most solemn contractual obligations toward him personally.'[37] Thus observance of confederacy law 'was jealously watched by Yahwe'.[38]

In this manner Yahwe became not only the war god of the confederacy but also the contractual partner of its law established by *berith*, above all of the socio-legal orders. Since the confederacy was at first a stateless association of tribes, new statutes, whether cultic or legal in nature, could in principle originate only by way of agreement (*berith*) based on oracle like the original covenant. Therewith all statutes were based on the same ground as the old contract relation which existed between the god and the people.[39]

Weber also argued that already in the pre-monarchical period, that is, the period of the confederacy, the Levites became exponents and teachers of the divine law; a 'Levitical Torah' thus began to develop at their hands and continued through the centuries.[40] The pre-classical prophetic circles were also guardians of the old confederacy law. Their antecedents were the ecstatic prophets who played a role as charismatically inspired crusaders in the holy wars of the confederacy, these wars having been fought by peasant militias led by a charismatic leader and hero. With the coming of kingship and the creation of a standing, professional army the old confederacy peasant militia with its tradition of charismatic leadership as well as the role of these prophetic circles gradually died out,

---

[36] p. 140; E. trs. p. 130.
[38] p. 142; E. trs. p. 132.
[40] pp. 181 ff.; E. trs. pp. 169 ff.

[37] p. 140; E. trs. p. 130.
[39] p. 141; E. trs. p. 131.

though not without bitterness.[41] When at a later time the pre-classical prophets, most notably Elijah—the real forerunner of the classical prophets—attacked the social abuses of the monarchy, the basis of their condemnation was nothing other than 'the time-honoured "law" of the ancient Israelite confederacy'.[42]

With regard to the classical prophets, Weber rejected any suggestion that their invective against king and people was motivated by political or socio-political considerations. They are not to be understood as champions of 'democratic' ideals'; nor were they motivated by any commitment to 'natural laws', even less 'to revolution or self-help of the masses suppressed by the mighty'.[43] 'The socio-ethical demands which they rather presuppose than raise, suggest the Levite exhortation, the existence and knowledge of which all prophets treat as self-evident.'[44] '. . . the Torah is always the completely self-evident presupposition of all prophecy. It is seldom explicitly referred to because it went without saying'.[45]

In a field of study such as that of the Old Testament, where many scholars had long since emphasized the creative role of religion in the making of the Israelite nation, the new trend in the sociology of religion had a responsive audience. Further, form-criticism with its quest for the *Sitz im Leben* of Israelite beliefs and traditions had already given Old Testament studies a sociological orientation which facilitated the reception of such a new trend which now gave added impetus to the investigation of the concrete, social manifestations of religion in the life of Israel as a society. Not surprisingly, therefore, the new insights in the study of the sociology of religion made an increasingly important impact upon Old Testament studies during the 1920s and beyond,[46] not least upon the understanding of the significance of the covenant in Israelite religion and society. Against such a background the view that the

---

[41] pp. 110, 119 f.; E. trs. pp. 101, 110 f.

[42] pp. 120; cf. pp. 86 f., 291; E. trs. p. 111; cf. pp. 78, 277.

[43] p. 292; E. trs. p. 278.

[44] p. 292; E. trs. p. 278.   [45] p. 310; E. trs. p. 295.

[46] In addition to the works cited in note 24 above, see also S. T. Kimbrough, *Israelite Religion in Sociological Perspective: The Work of Antonin Causse*, Studies in Oriental Religions, vol. IV, Wiesbaden 1978. Causse worked largely under the influence of the French school of sociology, notably Lévy-Bruhl and Emil Durkheim (cf. Kimbrough, pp. 98 ff.), rather than Weber.

covenant *functioned* as a means of uniting the disparate elements of early Israel with each other and with Yahweh, though it had earlier been suggested, now found widespread emphasis and acceptance. That is, the covenant was now understood to have been not a 'theological idea', a 'theoretical model' coined as an apt way for describing the particular relationship of Israel with Yahweh as his elected people, but an institution which was formative in the creation of Israel and normative in its development, and in its ethos.

Beyond any doubt, it was from Weber's *Ancient Judaism* that the main and direct influence derived for fresh research by Old Testament scholars in this area. Gressmann, in his programmatic essay already referred to, drew particular attention to the need for scholars to concern themselves with the new ideas in the sociology of religion, and referred specifically to Weber's work.[47] Just a few years earlier Kittel, in a similar essay, had done likewise, again mentioning specifically Weber's work.[48] They were not banging upon closed doors; the scholarly literature on the Old Testament at this time contains numerous references to that work. Thus, for example, Weiser, Hempel, Galling, and Eichrodt, in their works referred to above, appealed to it for support for their views on the importance and antiquity of the covenant in Israelite religion.[49] Its influence can also be seen in Noth's well-known monograph on early Israel which also makes explicit mention of it. Indeed, though there are important differences in detail between Noth's work and that of Weber, in their broad outlines Noth's conclusions with regard to early Israel approximate to Weber's views. This is manifestly so of Weber's understanding of early Israel as a confederation or 'amphictyony' (he also employs this latter term)[50] of tribes bound to each other and to Yahweh by means of a covenant, and of his understanding of the role of the covenant law in the life of the confederation, as also of his description of the wars of the league as 'holy

---

[47] *ZAW* 42, 1924, p. 17.

[48] 'Die Zukunft der alttestamentlichen Wissenschaft', *ZAW* 39, 1921, p. 99.

[49] Amongst Old Testament scholars at that time, as far as I am aware, critical opposition to Weber's work came only from W. Caspari, especially in his *Die Gottesgemeinde am Sinai und das nachmalige Volk Israel*, BFChrTh 27, Gütersloh 1922, in which he argued, for example, that the view, crucial for Weber's work, that the covenant was a central feature of Israelite religion from the beginning was merely an assumption (pp. 137 ff. For comments on Caspari's work see Schäfer-Lichtenberger, pp. 13 ff.)

[50] *Das antike Judentum*, p. 98; E. trs. p. 90.

wars'[51] fought by tribal militias under the leadership of charismatic heroes. Add to all this Weber's view that the basis of the ethical teaching of the prophets, including the classical prophets, was the old confederacy covenant law tradition, and we have an overall understanding of the antiquity, role and influence of the covenant tradition which, again in its broad outlines, has been the dominant view with regard to this issue among Old Testament scholars since that time.[52]

IV

With this new-found agreement among scholars concerning the antiquity and significance of the covenant between Yahweh and Israel came also widespread agreement on the origin and nature of the other two main covenantal traditions in the Old Testament, the Abrahamic and Davidic covenants. With regard to the former in Genesis 15, whilst earlier scholars had in general argued that this was a late or relatively late formulation—such was the view of Wellhausen and Gunkel; Kraetzsch-mar dated it no earlier than the monarchical period—the 1920s brought a reversal of this view, and, as in the case of the Sinai covenant, this covenant too now came to be widely regarded as being of much more ancient origin. At the same time the view that the Davidic covenant was likewise of early origin, that indeed it arose in the time of David himself, now also began to command widespread support. The view of Kraetzsch-mar, who traced it to the period immediately following the death of David, was improved upon, so to speak, by H. Gressmann who argued in 1910 that the 'Last Words of David' in 2 Samuel 23: 1–7 with its specific reference to this covenant was contemporaneous with David himself.[53] He further argued that the divine promise concerning the Davidic dynasty mediated to David by Nathan (2 Sam. 7) belongs to an equally ancient layer of material in this chapter (pp. 141 ff). Subsequently, O. Procksch, in 1913, argued likewise for the antiquity of 2 Samuel 23: 1–7,

---

[51] Cf. Noth, *Das System der zwölf Stämme Israels*, pp. 100 ff. Weber referred especially to the work of F. Schwally, *Semitische Kriegsaltertümer*, vol. I: *Der heilige Krieg im alten Israel*, Leipzig 1901. From a later time is G. von Rad's well-known *Der heilige Krieg im alten Israel*, Göttingen 1958.

[52] For a comprehensive survey see Clements, *Prophecy and Covenant*.

[53] *Die älteste Geschichtsschreibung und Prophetie Israels (von Samuel bis Amos und Hosea)*, Göttingen 1910, pp. 186 f.

suggesting indeed that there are no good reasons for questioning that David himself composed it, as the text itself claims.[54] Both of these scholars were supported by L. Rost in his influential study of the 'Succession Narrative' in 1926.[55] Most influential of all, however, was A. Alt's understanding of the origin and purpose of this covenant, advanced in his essay on the formation of the Israelite state published in 1930. Alt too accepted the antiquity of 2 Samuel 23: 1–7 and of the promise to David in 2 Samuel 7, and argued that the covenant in question had a specific religio-political function, that of legitimizing the dynastic principle in the face of the charismatic principle of leadership which had characterized tribal life in pre-monarchical Israel.[56] That is, the ideal of kingship which arose in Israel under David found expression in this eternal covenant between Yahweh and David, the purpose of which was to guarantee the undisturbed continuance of the Davidic dynasty as the divinely appointed rulers of Israel. Thus, as in the case of the Sinai covenant, in arguing for the antiquity of the Davidic covenant, emphasis was now also placed upon the particular *function* it had in Israelite society; it was no longer to be regarded simply as a 'theological idea' but as having pertained to a specific institution. This understanding of the antiquity and significance of the Davidic covenant was henceforth widely accepted.

There was an equally influential shift in the matter of the antiquity and significance of the Abrahamic covenant in Genesis 15 with Alt's epoch-making monograph *Der Gott der Väter*, published in 1929.[57] Wellhausen had argued that this narrative was a late composition, whilst of the patriarchal narratives in general he had written that 'we attain to no historical knowledge of the patriarchs, but only of the time when the stories about them arose in the Israelite people; this later age is here unconsciously projected, in its inner and outward features, into hoar antiquity,

---

[54] 'Die letzten Worte Davids. 2 Sam. 23: 1–7', *Alttestamentliche Studien Rudolph Kittel zum 60. Geburtstag dargebracht*, BWAT 13, Leipzig 1913, pp. 112–25.

[55] *Die Überlieferung von der Thronnachfolge Davids*, BWANT III: 6, Stuttgart 1926, reprinted in his *Das kleine Credo und andere Studien zum Alten Testament*, Heidelberg 1965, pp. 119–253; E. trs. *The Succession to the Throne of David*, Sheffield 1982.

[56] *Die Staatenbildung der Israeliten in Palästina*, Reformationsprogramm der Universität Leipzig, 1930. Reprinted in *KS* II, Munich 1953, pp. 1–65 (see esp. p. 63); E. trs. 'The Formation of the Israelite State in Palestine', *Essays on Old Testament History and Religion*, pp. 171–237 (see esp. p. 235).

[57] BWANT III: 12, Stuttgart 1929, reprinted in *KS* I, pp. 1–79; E. trs. 'The God of the Fathers', *Essays on Old Testament History and Religion*, pp. 1–77.

and is reflected there like a glorified mirage'.[58] By contrast, Alt believed it possible to uncover the nature and content of patriarchal religion from the material in Genesis. In between Wellhausen and Alt's study lay the pioneering work of Gunkel who, notably in his commentary on Genesis, as we saw earlier, argued that many of the stories in Genesis concerning the patriarchs are *Sagen* or cycles of *Sagen* (*Sagenkränze*) very much more ancient than the literary narratives in which they are now embodied, and in many instances even of pre-Israelite origin.

Alt discerned in the patriarchal stories evidence of the pre-Yahwistic religion of Israel's ancestors which the introduction of the worship of Yahweh among the tribes did not entirely obliterate. Two types of deity are evidenced in these narratives. On the one hand there are the *ʾēlīm*, recognizable in the titles *ʾēl bētēl* of Bethel (Gen. 31: 13; 35: 7), *ʾēl ʿōlām* of Beersheba (Gen. 21: 33), *ʾēl rᵒʾī* at a sanctuary further south (Gen. 16: 13), and, without indication of their location, *ʾēl ʿelyōn* (Gen. 14: 18–24) and *ʾēl šaddai* (Gen. 17: 1; etc.). The book of Judges adds *ʾēl bᵉrīt* or *baʿal bᵉrīt* of Shechem (Jud. 9: 4, 46). As a rule, Alt suggested, the original purpose of the stories in which these deities are mentioned was the legitimation of the sanctuaries where they were worshipped. These *ʾēlīm* were local Canaanite deities whom the Israelites worshipped during and after their settlement in the areas where they were acknowledged.[59] This means that these deities cannot have been worshipped by the Israelites before their settlement in Canaan.

At this point Alt drew attention to a distinctive element in these stories hitherto unexplored by scholars, that is, the frequent references to 'the god of my (your, etc.) father', and he argued that it is in these references that we come upon the ancestral cults of the diverse Israelite clans before their settlement in the land. He adduced evidence of this type of cult from Nabataean and Palmyrene inscriptions from a much later time (*c.* 100 BC to the fourth century AD). The gods in question were not related to a specific sanctuary, as in the case of the *ʾēlīm* referred to above, but originated in personal revelations to the semi-nomadic patriarchal figures by whom they were first worshipped. Thus, when texts refer to the 'god of my father', for example, 'the god of Abraham' or 'the god of Isaac', what was originally meant was the god first worshipped by these individuals.

[58] *Prolegomena*, p. 336; E. trs. pp. 318 f.
[59] *KS* I, p. 8; E. trs. p. 9.

Hence 'the Mighty One of Jacob' (*ᵃbīr yaʿakōb*) designated the god originally worshipped by Jacob and his clan; 'the Fear of Isaac' (*paḥad yiṣḥāq*) was the god originally worshipped by Isaac and his clan, whilst on the basis of Genesis 15: 1, the name of Abraham's clan deity may have been 'the Shield of Abraham' (*māgēn ʾabrāhām*).[60] The relationship between these gods and their worshippers embodied two promises directed to the deepest needs of such clans, first the promise of descendants, and, second, the promise of land. The first expressed the concern of such clans for their continued maintenance and increase in their semi-nomadic wanderings; the second represented the claim of settlers to their land.[61] The first originated before the entry into the land, the second in Palestine itself after they had settled there permanently.

When, after their permanent settlement in the land, these various clans adopted the worship of the *ʾelīm* at the local sanctuaries, the ancestral gods were identified with them. Thus it has come about that the patriarchal figures, originally recipients of divine revelations in the pre-settlement period, are now described in the narratives as recipients of the revelations of these local Canaanite deities. At a later stage when the worship of Yahweh was introduced it gradually penetrated the older sanctuaries and imposed itself as the newest stratum upon the cults hitherto practised at them. In this way the patriarchal traditions advanced to the Yahwistic stage in which we now find them in the JE material in Genesis. The identification of the ancestral gods of the fathers with Yahweh was facilitated, according to Alt, by the similarity in character between them: 'What the gods of the Fathers were to the smaller communities, he was to the whole confederation of the tribes';[62] 'the gods of the Fathers were the παιδαγωγοί leading to the greater God, who later replaced them completely'.[63]

In the light of these considerations Alt turned to the narrative in Genesis 15 concerning the covenant between Yahweh and Abraham. Gunkel, as we noted earlier, did not include this story among the ancient materials he isolated in Genesis; most likely it was composed, he argued, at a much later time when Israel's continued possession of the land was under threat.[64] By contrast, Alt now argued that the original layer of

[60] pp. 24 ff., 67 note 4; E. trs. pp. 25 ff., 66 note 179.
[61] p. 66; E. trs. p. 65.　　[62] p. 62; E. trs. p. 60.
[63] p. 63; E. trs. p. 62.　　[64] *Genesis*, Göttingen 1901, p. 167.

material in this chapter (vv. 1a, bα, 3-4, 8-11, 17-18a which he ascribed to J)[65] is based upon an ancient aetiological story concerning the God of Abraham:

The Yahwist's account in this chapter of a covenant made by God with Abraham contains cultic and mythological elements which give the impression of great antiquity, and it is very unlike the theophanies composed entirely by this author. A distinct and independent story almost undoubtedly lies behind this passage. In accordance with his basic theme, the Yahwist has associated it with Yahweh; but this of course does not show with which God Abraham was originally supposed to have made this covenant. It can hardly be a local Palestinian numen, for in that case we would presumably be told the place where the scene was enacted. This makes it highly probable that it was the God of Abraham, especially since its earliest Yahwist form concludes with the simple promise of a son to Abraham. It would seem to be a genuinely ancient passage, standing first in the series of revelations by the God of the Fathers, which the Yahwist continues through Isaac and Jacob, composing each account himself.[66]

V

The ancient setting which Alt thus found for the covenant between Yahweh and Abraham as well as his argument concerning the origin and significance of the Davidic covenant proved as compelling among scholars as the view concurrently being advanced concerning the nature and antiquity of the Sinai covenant tradition. The result was that widespread agreement rapidly emerged during these years concerning the origin and significance of all three major Old Testament covenant traditions (the Sinaitic, Abrahamic, and Davidic) where previously there had been marked division of opinion. Further, though there remained variation in detail, this agreement proved lasting. Thus, to give but the briefest indication of this:

(1) Alt's view of the antiquity of the covenant tradition in Genesis 15: 7-21 gained general support among scholars, including, for example, von Rad—he regarded the passage in question as 'one of the oldest narratives in

---

[65] *KS* I, p. 66 note 2; E. trs. p. 65 note 175.
[66] pp. 66 f.; E. trs. 65 f.

the traditions about the patriarchs'[67]—and Noth;[68] likewise O. Kaiser, who otherwise pointed to late elements in this chapter as a whole, nonetheless accepted the antiquity of the covenant element in it.[69] Later still, N. Lohfink, for example, freshly argued the antiquity of the tradition here,[70] as also did R. E. Clements who, though questioning some aspects of Alt's arguments, maintained that this Abrahamic tradition directly influenced the development of the Davidic covenant, and further suggested that the Yahwist author saw in the ancient Abraham covenant an expression of the divine providence which pointed forward to the rise of the great Davidic empire.[71] Until recently the only notable challenge to Alt's view came from J. Hoftijzer who, in a monograph in 1956,[72] argued that Genesis 15 and a number of related passages are late additions. But his views made virtually no impact at that time, and it was not until more recent years that an increasing number of scholars have again questioned the antiquity of Genesis 15.[73]

(2) Matters have been no different in the case of the Davidic covenant. Here too the view which gained ground in the 1920s and which Alt's essay in 1930 particularly enhanced continued to command majority support. Alt himself reaffirmed it in a later essay.[74] It found additional support from a different quarter among scholars who concerned themselves with the sacral nature of Israelite kingship, and who saw in the Davidic

---

[67] *Das erste Buch Mose, Genesis*, fifth edition, Götingen 1958, p. 159; E. trs. *Genesis*, London 1961, p. 184.

[68] *Überlieferungsgeschichte des Pentateuch*, Stuttgart 1948, p. 252 note 610; E. trs. *A History of Pentateuchal Traditions*, Englewood Cliffs 1972, p. 232 note 610: 'the portrayal of the promise of the land in the solemn and archaic covenant-making scene (Gen. 15: 7 ff.), which is now set off from the epiphany scene and was thought of as a prelude to the Sinai covenant, certainly belongs to a preliterary stage of the narrative development antedating J'.

[69] 'Traditionsgeschichtliche Untersuchung von Genesis 15', *ZAW* 70, 1958, pp. 107–26.

[70] *Die Landverheissung als Eid*, Stuttgarter Bibel Studien 28, Stuttgart 1967.

[71] *Abraham and David: Genesis 15 and its Meaning for Israelite Tradition*, London 1967.

[72] *Die Verheissung an die drei Erzväter*, Leiden 1956.

[73] For a survey and extensive bibliography see C. Westermann, *Genesis* (12–36), BKAT I, Neukirchen 1981, pp. 247–75.

[74] 'Das Königtum in den Reichen Israel und Juda', *VT* 1, 1951, pp. 2–22, reprinted in *KS* II, pp. 116–34 (see esp. p. 132); E. trs. 'The Monarchy in Israel and Judah', *Essays on Old Testament History and Religion*, pp. 239–59 (see esp. p. 257).

covenant one of the foundation elements of Judah's royal ideology.[75] Notwithstanding variation in detail and emphasis, there was also general agreement that the covenantal promises to the Davidic dynasty were the subject of annual cultic reaffirmation, specifically within the context of the autumn festival at the temple in Jerusalem. For most, the only remaining matter of serious dispute concerned the relationship, if any, between the Davidic covenant and the more ancient Sinai covenant, some arguing that the latter was transmitted solely in northern Israel whilst the Davidic tradition displaced it in Jerusalem until late in the monarchical period when, with the Deuteronomic reformation, it regained a footing in Judah.[76] Others contended that both traditions remained together throughout the monarchical period in Jerusalem.[77]

As in the case of the Abrahamic covenant in Genesis 15, dissent from this view concerning the antiquity of the Davidic covenant tradition was a minority position. As far as I am aware it came in this instance especially from Noth who argued that the notion of a covenant between Yahweh and David was a late innovation.[78] Once again, however, it was not until recently that this view has received fresh support.[79]

(3) In the case of the covenant between Yahweh and Israel, the general agreement concerning its antiquity and significance which emerged soon after the First World War proved lasting. Scant support now remained for the view that the notion of such a covenant was a late innovation in Israelite religion.[80] A few scholars continued to advocate the view that the

---

[75] For example, A. R. Johnson, 'The Rôle of the King in the Jerusalem Cultus', *The Labyrinth*, ed. S. H. Hooke, London 1935, pp. 71–111, and his later *Sacral Kingship in Ancient Israel*, Cardiff 1955, second edition 1967.

[76] For example, L. Rost, 'Sinaibund und Davidsbund', *TLZ* 72, 1947, cols. 129–34.

[77] For example, H.-J. Kraus, *Gottesdienst in Israel*, Munich 1962, pp. 222 ff.; E. trs. *Worship in Israel*, Oxford 1966, pp. 189 ff.

[78] *Die Gesetze im Pentateuch*, Halle 1940, reprinted in his *Gesammelte Studien zum Alten Testament*, second edition, Munich 1960, pp. 9–141 (see esp. 122 f.); E. trs. 'The Laws in the Pentateuch', in *The Laws in the Pentateuch and Other Essays*, Edinburgh and London 1966, pp. 1–107 (see esp. p. 93.).

[79] For example, L. Perlitt, *Bundestheologie im Alten Testament*, WMANT 36, Neukirchen-Vluyn 1969, pp. 47 ff. For a recent discussion see T. N. D. Mettinger, *King and Messiah: The Civil and Sacral Legitimation of the Israelite Kings*, Coniectanea Biblica, Old Testament Series 8, Lund 1976, pp. 275 ff.

[80] R. H. Pfeiffer was one of a very few who continued to argue this view. See his *Religion in the Old Testament*, London 1961, p. 55: 'Every mention of the covenant of Jehovah

Sinai covenant tradition was a secondary creation on the basis of the historical Shechemite covenant tradition.[81] But most now accepted at least a nucleus of historicity behind the Sinai tradition, and what debate there was concerned the original relationship, if any, between this tradition and the exodus-settlement tradition, the events behind them, and how, if they were originally unrelated, they came to be associated with each other in the development of the Pentateuchal narrative as a whole.

Von Rad's well-known monograph published in 1938 gave fresh impetus to the discussion of this latter issue. He argued that the two sets of tradition, the so-called *Landnahme* tradition and the Sinai tradition, were originally transmitted separately, the former within the context of the feast of Weeks in early summer, the latter being the subject of the autumn festival of Tabernacles in pre-monarchical Israel.[82] It was the Yahwist, whose work he dated to the tenth century BC, who first combined them.[83] Noth accepted von Rad's basic thesis concerning the original independence of the Sinai tradition, but argued that it had already been combined with the other traditions in the pre-monarchical period to form a Pentateuchal *Grundlage* which later became the basis of the work of both the Yahwist and the Elohist.[84] Weiser, on the other hand, maintained that both sets of traditions belonged together from the outset as separate parts of the autumn festival of the tribes from the pre-monarchical period onwards.[85] Different again, for example, was the solution proposed by H. H. Rowley who argued that separate events involving separate groups of Israelites can be discerned behind the exodus-Kadesh narratives and the Sinai narratives, the one group having journeyed to Sinai, the other having sojourned at Kadesh. After the settlement both traditions were

with Israel in the Bible is later than 621 BC'; 'Facts and Faith in Biblical History', *JBL* 70, 1951, pp. 1–14.

[81] For example, T. J. Meek, *Hebrew Origins*, New York 1936, pp. 26 f.; C. A. Simpson, *The Early Traditions of Israel*, Oxford 1948, p. 648. Cf. E. Nielsen, *Shechem: A Traditio-Historical Investigation*, second revised edition, Copenhagen 1959, pp. 117 f. For a recent discussion see R. E. Clements, 'Baal-Berith of Shechem', *JSS* 13 1968, pp. 21–32.
[82] 'Das formgeschichtliche Problem des Hexateuch', *Gesammelte Studien*, pp. 41 ff., 48 ff.; E. trs. pp. 33 ff., 41 ff. [83] pp. 58 ff.; E. trs. pp. 50 ff.
[84] *Überlieferungsgeschichte des Pentateuch*, pp. 40–67; E. trs. pp. 38–62.
[85] *Einleitung in das Alte Testament*, Göttingen 1948, second edition 1949, pp. 70 ff.; E. trs. from the fourth edition, *Introduction to the Old Testament*, London 1961, pp. 81–99.

combined, but though the conflation as such yields an unhistorical picture 'the separate traditions may be accepted as genuinely historical'.[86] The debate on this issue was to continue, and entered a new phase when what was claimed to be fresh and decisive evidence for a resolution of it was introduced in the 1950s.[87]

But this issue apart, the consensus which emerged during the 1920s concerning the role of the covenant in Israelite history and religion was sustained in the period which ensued. To give but a brief sketch of this, I take in turn each of the three main arguments outlined in section I above.

First, the renewed emphasis upon Israelite religion as a historically oriented religion, a religion of 'election' as against the 'natural' religions of other ancient Near Eastern nations, gathered momentum from that time onwards, largely as a result of the rebirth of interest in Old Testament theology which had now also emerged. Weiser, for example, returned to it in an influential essay in 1931, stressing again the role of the covenant as one of the ways in which Israel's conviction of having been divinely chosen acquired concrete expression.[88] Eichrodt's renowned *Theologie des Alten Testaments* in which, as we noted, the same ideas were extensively presented, appeared in the 1930s and made a lasting impact, whilst Galling's monograph likewise remained widely influential. The understanding of Israelite religion as historically oriented was given fresh impetus by von Rad, again in his monograph of 1938 in which it was argued that Israel's earliest confession of faith took the form of a 'creed' centring upon Yahweh's saving actions in history on his people's behalf.

The role of the covenant in Israel's historically founded religion also gained increasing support from this time onwards among British and American scholars. Among the former, N. W. Porteous, for example, argued it in 1936.[89] He was followed later by such scholars as H. Wheeler Robinson in his *Inspiration and Revelation in the Old Testament* (Oxford

[86] *From Joseph to Joshua: Biblical Traditions in the Light of Archaeology*, London 1950, p. 107.

[87] For a survey see E. W. Nicholson, *Exodus and Sinai in History and Tradition*, Oxford 1973.

[88] *Glaube und Geschichte im Alten Testament*, BWANT IV: 4, Stuttgart 1931, reprinted in his *Glaube und Geschichte im Alten Testament und andere ausgewählte Schriften*, Göttingen 1961, pp. 99–182.

[89] 'Volk und Gottesvolk im Alten Testament', *Theologische Aufsätze: Karl Barth zum 50. Geburtstag*, ed. E. Wolf, Munich 1936, pp. 146–63.

1946, pp. 153–5) and most notably H. H. Rowley in a number of popular works and especially his influential monograph *The Biblical Doctrine of Election* (London, 1950, *passim*).[90]

Most prominent of all, however, was the reception and further working out of such a view among scholars of the so-called 'Biblical Theology Movement' which began and gathered momentum in the United States from the 1940s onwards.[91] Here the contrast between Israelite faith, understood as history-centred, and the myth-oriented and 'cyclic' religions of Israel's neighbours was more sharply drawn than ever, with corresponding emphasis upon election and covenant as the fundamental elements in that faith from its inception. Amongst the considerable literature in which this view found expression, particular mention may be made of several influential contributions by G. E. Wright, one of the leading figures of that movement.[92]

The cultic 'actualization' or 'renewal' of the covenant, including a proclamation of the covenant law, in Israel's life from ancient times was the subject of the second of the three main arguments outlined in Section I above. Von Rad compellingly developed Mowinckel's pioneering thesis of a recurring renewal of the covenant at the autumn festival of Tabernacles, and traced its origins to the pre-monarchical period. Through von Rad's work and no less through Alt's influential study of the origins of Israelite law, as well as several notable contributions by Weiser, it gradually became common currency among scholars in both Europe and the United States. Evidence was also found of an office of 'covenant mediator' whose function was the proclamation of the divine law within

[90] N. H. Snaith's view was a somewhat curious mixture of Wellhausen's conclusions and the more widely accepted view (*The Distinctive Ideas of the Old Testament*, London 1944, pp. 107–10): Israel was from the outset 'the covenant people of Yahweh', but in the pre-prophetic period this signified a relationship materially no different from that of other nations of the time with their gods; the distinctive Israelite development of the notion came only as a result of the preaching of the eighth-century prophets. A reading of Snaith's argument reveals that he was able to hold this unusual view only because he understood 'covenant' to mean simply 'relationship'.

[91] The rise and decline of this movement is described in B. S. Childs, *Biblical Theology in Crisis*, Philadelphia 1970.

[92] *The Challenge of Israel's Faith*, Chicago 1944 (published in England 1946); 'How did Early Israel differ from her Neighbours?', *BA* 6, 1943, pp. 1–20; *The Old Testament Against Its Environment*, London 1950; *God Who Acts*, London 1952; 'The Faith of Israel', *The Interpreter's Bible*, vol. I, New York and Nashville 1952, pp. 352–89.

the context of this covenant-renewal festival.[93] In this way Yahweh's law for his people was continuously made known as the fundamental standard of conduct required of them. The view, already known at an earlier period, that an original form of the decalogue (a so-called *Urdekalog*) can be isolated from Exodus 20: 1–17 and Deuteronomy 5: 6–21 now became much more widely accepted, but with the added dimension that its original *Sitz im Leben* was this covenant-renewal festival.[94] In arguing therefore that the covenant law was the basis of the ethical teaching of the prophets, scholars were thus able to point to its annual proclamation in Israel's cult as the concrete background and source of that ethical teaching.

This view of a recurring cultic 'actualization' of Israel's covenant tradition, and especially the proclamation of the covenant law which it included, carried with it an understanding of the covenant not as a theological idea but as having a particular religio-sociological function: the ordering of Israelite society as the people of Yahweh. According to the third of the main arguments outlined in section I above, this functioning of the covenant in the continuing life of Israel followed and sustained the function it initially performed as the means whereby disparate groups were constituted into the ancient tribal confederation of Israel, the Israelite 'amphictyony', an understanding of the structure of early Israel which Weber and especially Noth so illumined. Thus Noth found in the narrative of the 'diet at Shechem' in Joshua 24 a historical nucleus recording the foundation of the Israelite confederation. At the same time, he understood this chapter to reflect not merely a once-for-all event, but a recurring renewal of the covenant whereby this confederation had been constituted and its life ordered.

The claim is justified that nothing contributed more to the continued and increasing acceptance by scholars of the antiquity and significance of the covenant in Israelite life and religion than Noth's detailed and compelling study. So long as such an understanding of the origin of Israel

[93] Cf. for example, A. Alt, 'Die Ursprünge des israelitischen Rechts', *KS* I, pp. 300 f.; E. trs. p. 102; M. Noth, 'Das Amt des Richters Israels', *Festschrift für A. Bertholet*, Tübingen 1950, pp. 404–17; H.-J. Kraus, *Die prophetische Verkündigung des Rechts in Israel*, Theologische Studien 51, Zollikon 1957.

[94] For a survey see J. J. Stamm and M. E. Andrew, *Der Dekalog im Lichte der neueren Forschung*, second edition, revised and enlarged, Bern and Stuttgart 1962; E. trs. *The Ten Commandments in Recent Research*, London 1967.

was maintained, a plausible context for the institutional role of a covenant in the formation and life and religion of Israel was provided. All the more serious, therefore, for this widely accepted theory of the origin of the covenant, has been the increasing rejection of Noth's understanding of early Israel as an 'amphictyony',[95] as we shall see.

Before this more recent development emerged, however, a new phase in the study of covenant in the Old Testament began in the mid-1950s which seemed, at least initially, to offer striking new support for the consensus which had arisen in the preceding decades. For many, indeed, the new evidence (which was now thought to have been uncovered) was seen as the crowning climax to the investigation of the origin and significance of the covenant. What this new evidence is, and how justified the claims based upon it are, is the subject of our next chapter.

[95] See, for example, J. Hoftijzer, 'Enige Opmerkingen rond het israëlitischen 12-Stammensysteem', *Nederlands Theologisch Tijdschrift*, 14, 1959-60, pp. 241-63; G. W. Anderson, 'Israel: Amphictyony: ʿAM; ḴĀHĀL; ʿĒDĀH', *Translating and Understanding the Old Testament, Essays in Honor of H. G. May*, ed. H. T. Frank and W. L. Reed, Nashville and New York 1970, pp. 135-51; R. de Vaux, *Histoire ancienne d'Israël: la periode des Juges*, Paris 1973, pp. 19-36; E. trs. *The Early History of Israel: From the Entry into Canaan to the Period of the Judges*, London 1978, pp. 695-715; A. D. H. Mayes, *Israel in the Period of the Judges*, London 1974; C. H. J. de Geus, *The Tribes of Israel*, Assen and Amsterdam 1976, especially ch. 2.

3

Treaty and Covenant

THE study of the Old Testament covenant traditions during the century or so since the publication of Wellhausen's *Prolegomena* in 1878 falls conveniently into four main phases. As we have seen, a generation of controversy, stimulated by Wellhausen's work, was followed by a period of widespread agreement on essentials. The third phase began in the mid-1950s and introduced into the discussion hitherto unexplored evidence from a study of ancient Near Eastern inter-state treaties which, it is maintained, shed considerable light on the origin, nature, and form of the covenant traditions and texts in the Old Testament. The fourth and current phase began in the 1960s and represents a sharp reaction to the two preceding ones. It argues that the covenant traditions were a late development in Israelite religion and were as yet unknown to the prophets of the eighth century. Thus, Wellhausen's conclusions have, in essence, found fresh advocacy. In addition, there is renewed discussion of the meaning of the word *berīt*.

This current phase will be the subject of my next chapter. In the present chapter I turn to the third phase, the relevance of the so-called suzerainty or vassal treaties. Such has been the impact of the evidence adduced from this material that it has yielded a literature which is even more extensive than that of either of the two preceding periods surveyed above, and it is beyond the scope of this book to offer a detailed survey of it. Fortunately, much of it has been conveniently surveyed in other recent works[1] so that a brief, but I hope comprehensive, sketch of the main developments will suffice here, after which I shall offer some critical observations on the analogies drawn during this phase between treaties and the covenant between Yahweh and Israel.

---

[1] See, for example, D. J. McCarthy, *Old Testament Covenant: A Survey of Current Opinions*, Oxford 1972. His *Treaty and Covenant*, second edition, Rome 1978, offers an extensive bibliography.

I

In an article published in 1950 E. Bickerman made a passing reference to treaties between Hittite kings and their vassals as providing an analogy to the covenant relationship between Yahweh and Israel.[2] But it was not until 1954 that G. E. Mendenhall, taking up the observation made by Bickerman, drew fuller attention to what he believed to be close parallels between these Hittite treaties and the nature and form of the Sinai covenant.[3] Adopting one of the main conclusions of the preceding period of covenant-studies, he emphasized the socio-religious and institutional nature of the Sinai covenant in Israelite origins and history. Since, as research had demonstrated, Israel did not emerge in the genealogical manner described in the Pentateuch, it can only have been the covenant relationship of the tribes with Yahweh and with each other that constituted the basis of 'solidarity' among them. 'The difficulty in the past', he wrote, 'has been in arriving at any concept of a covenant which would bind together the tribes and also adequately form a foundation for the normative conception that in this event Yahweh became the God of Israel.' (p. 51.) This difficulty, Mendenhall argued, is overcome once it is realized that the type of covenant which operated was modelled upon the Hittite suzerainty treaty whereby a great king bound his vassals to faithfulness and obedience to himself and at the same time ordered relationships between the vassals themselves as subjects of the one over-lord. Further and significantly, this particular treaty-form was contemporary with Israelite origins in the late Bronze Age (*c.* 1400–1200 BC) and is not known at a later period.

Though the form of these treaties was evidently not rigidly fixed, an examination of them reveals that the following six elements were almost always present: (1) a *preamble* identifying the suzerain and listing his titles and ancestry; (2) a *historical prologue* recording previous relationships between the suzerain and his vassal and stressing the beneficent acts which the Hittite monarch had wrought in times past on behalf of the vassal; (3) the treaty *stipulations* binding upon the subject nation. Mendenhall drew particular attention to a number of characteristic laws, amongst them, for example, the requirement that the vassal is not to enter

---

[2] 'Couper une alliance', *Archives d'Histoire du Droit Oriental*, 5, 1950–1, pp. 133–56.
[3] 'Covenant Forms in Israelite Tradition', *BA* 17, 1954, pp. 50–76.

into foreign relationships outside the Hittite empire, the prohibition of any misdeeds against other peoples under the sovereignty of the suzerain, and the command that the vassal must appear once a year before his Hittite overlord. (4) Provision for *the depositing of the treaty document in the vassal's temple* and for *the periodic reading of it*—the subject state was to be constantly reminded of its obligations to the imperial authority; (5) *a list of gods as witnesses*, including the gods of both the suzerain and the vassal; amongst them are mentioned the (deified) mountains, rivers, springs, sea, heaven and earth, the winds and the clouds; (6) *curses and blessings formulae*: the weal or woe of the vassal depended upon his loyalty to the suzerain.

Turning to the Old Testament, Mendenhall argued that the form of the Hittite suzerainty treaty is reflected in the covenant tradition from the earliest period. He drew particular attention to the decalogue which, in an earlier, terser form he ascribed to Moses, and to Joshua 24. Thus the decalogue in its opening clause 'I am Yahweh who brought you forth from the land of Egypt' is akin to the historical prologue in the treaty-form, whilst the laws which follow represent the covenant stipulations of Yahweh as divine overlord. He pointed to Exodus 24: 3–8 as indicating a ritual whereby the covenant was formally ratified, an alternative rite being that described in Exodus 24: 9–11. He acknowledged that neither the decalogue nor the Sinai pericope as a whole reflects all the elements of the treaty-form; missing, for example, is the provision for the depositing of the covenant document in the sanctuary, and the list of witnesses as well as the formulae of blessings and curses. But these are evidenced elsewhere in the 'Mosaic traditions'. Thus provision for periodic pro-clamation of Yahweh's law as well as an accompanying declaration of blessings and curses for obedience or disobedience were a persistent element in Israel's legal tradition (cf. Deut. 28; 31: 10–13). The depositing of the 'tables of the law' in the sacred Ark (Deut. 10: 1–5; 1 Kgs. 8: 9) reflects one of the elements in the treaty-form. The listing of gods as witnesses, characteristic of the treaties, could of course have found no place in the monotheistic religion of Israel, but Mendenhall pointed to such texts as Deuteronomy 32: 1 and Isaiah 1: 2 (cf. Mic. 6: 1 f.) in which 'heaven and earth', 'mountains' and 'hills' are summoned as witnesses to Israel's relationship with Yahweh.

Subsequent years saw further elaboration and refinement of Mendenhall's basic thesis by other scholars. Thus K. Baltzer, who had evidently arrived at his conclusions independently of Mendenhall, traced the form in question from its earliest appearance in the Old Testament down to its occurrence in Jewish and early Christian writings.[4] W. Beyerlin elaborated Mendenhall's thesis, supplementing it with fresh insights and drawing significant conclusions from it concerning the historical origins of the covenant traditions and their transmission in Israel's cult.[5] For example, the recognition that the model of the Hittite treaty-form had been employed for expressing Yahweh's covenant with Israel meant that the ratification of the covenant proper in the covenant festival was preceded by a historical retrospect of Yahweh's saving actions in history. Thus G. von Rad's separation of the Sinai tradition from the exodus-settlement tradition was now shown to have been wrong, it was claimed, whilst A. Weiser's view of the relationship of these traditions with each other in Israel's festal cult was vindicated in a new and compelling manner.[6] Or again, adopting the view that the laws of the decalogue in its original form were, on the analogy of the treaties, Yahweh's covenant stipulations, A. Phillips argued that this explains the precise nature of these commandments: the fact that they governed the relationship between Yahweh as overlord and his vassal Israel explains why breach of them was a capital offence, since such breach threatened the very existence of Israel as Yahweh's covenant community; that is, the *Urdekalog* was Israel's 'criminal code'.[7]

II

The publication, subsequent to the appearance of Mendenhall's essay, of treaty texts from elsewhere in the ancient Near East, notably the Sefire treaties from Syria and the vassal treaties of Esarhaddon,[8] broadened the

---

[4] *Das Bundesformular*, WMANT 4, Neukirchen–Vluyn 1964; E. trs. *The Covenant Formulary*, Oxford 1971.

[5] *Herkunft und Geschichte der ältesten Sinaitraditionen*, Tübingen 1961; E. trs. *Origins and History of the Oldest Sinaitic Traditions*, Oxford 1965.

[6] Beyerlin, in particular, was concerned to argue this. For a brief survey see my *Exodus and Sinai in History and Tradition*, pp. 33–47.

[7] *Ancient Israel's Criminal Law*, Oxford 1970.

[8] See, for example, J. A. Fitzmyer, *The Aramaic Inscriptions of Sefire, Biblica et Orientalia* 19, Rome 1967; D. J. Wiseman, *The Vassal Treaties of Esarhaddon*, London 1958. For further bibliography see McCarthy, *Treaty and Covenant*,[2] pp. 309–11.

basis for a comparison of Old Testament covenant texts with the treaty-form. Whilst it enabled scholars to elaborate further some of Mendenhall's briefly stated conclusions, important modifications were also made, as we shall see.

In his comprehensive study, first published in 1963,[9] D. J. McCarthy, surveying both the Hittite and the newly published materials from elsewhere, noted some significant variations between the treaties but was nonetheless able to point to a basic unity:

Everywhere the basic elements are the same: the provisions are imposed under oath and placed under the sanction of the divine witnesses invoked. And this divine guardianship is invariably made more vivid through the curses which represent (and effect) the dreadful fate of an eventual transgressor. Hence the essential elements of the form: stipulations, the god lists or invocations, and the curse formulae which are invariably found in the treaties from Eannatum of Lagash to Esarhaddon of Assyria. (p. 122)

Applying this finding to the covenant texts in the Old Testament, McCarthy rejected Mendenhall's view that the earliest of these texts displayed the influence of the treaty-form. Instead, he found evidence of a gradual development from an older notion of covenant (Exod. 24: 1–11) centring on ritual to one in which a covenant made by verbal affirmation and pledge comes to the fore and which in turn was followed by a covenant understood and made after the manner of the suzerainty treaties. The treaty-form comes to full expression in *Urdeuteronomium* which, following many commentators, he regarded as having comprised substantially chapters 4: 44–26: 19 plus chapter 28 of the present book of Deuteronomy. In this central discourse of the book there are the following treaty-like elements (p. 186): (1) *Mise-en-scène* —normal opening for 'treaties-turned-speeches' (4: 44–9); (2) historical-parenetic prologue (5–11); (3) stipulations (12: 1–26: 15); (4) invocation-adjuration (26: 16–19); (5) blessings and curses (28: 1–46(69)). Not only does this central discourse display the structure of the treaties, it also takes up many details from the treaty tradition: for example, the command to love the Lord, 'a strange sort of thing to command but one at home in the treaties'; the insistence on an exclusive service of Yahweh, 'which is straight from the world of the treaties'; and perhaps the characteristic phrase 'hearken to

---

[9] References here are to the second edition, 1978.

the voice (of Yahweh)', the use of the verb *yāda ⁶* in the sense of 'recognize (as Lord)', and the designation of Israel as Yahweh's 'special possession' (*s̆gullāh*). 'Vocabulary thus joins with structure to define the genre of the Central Discourse.' (pp. 186 f.)

In drawing attention to the use of treaty vocabulary in Deuteronomy, McCarthy called upon a number of studies which identified the use of such vocabulary in the Old Testament and which may conveniently be outlined at this stage.

(1) W. L. Moran and others trace the concept of the love of God in Deuteronomy to a treaty background.[10] Particular emphasis is laid on the nature of this love as one that can be 'commanded', and above all as a love which is expressed in loyalty and service, in an unqualified obedience to the law. Such 'commanded' love of subject for overlord is evidenced in ancient Near Eastern texts from the early second millennium down to the first millennium BC. For example, Esarhaddon commands his vassals to 'love' his successor Assurbanipal: 'You will love as yourselves Assurbanipal'. Pointing to various other parallels between Assyrian treaties and Deuteronomy, Moran claims that 'we may be virtually certain that deuteronomic circles were familiar with the Assyrian practice of demanding an oath of allegiance from their vassals expressed in terms of love' (p. 84). It is to this source, Moran argues, rather than, as is frequently suggested, to the preaching of Hosea that the concept of the love of God in Deuteronomy is to be traced (pp. 77 f.). Prompted by Moran's suggestion, McCarthy and F. C. Fensham have argued that even the 'father–son' imagery used of Yahweh's covenant relationship with Israel or with the Davidic king is also to be understood against the background of the use of this same imagery in treaty contexts from the second to the first millennium BC.[11] The term 'slave' (*⁶ebed*), when used in a covenant context, had also a treaty background, it is maintained.[12] Yet another word designating Israel's special, covenantal relationship with Yahweh,

[10] 'The Ancient Near Eastern Background of the Love of god in Deuteronomy', *CBQ* 24, 1963, pp. 77-87. Cf. McCarthy, 'Notes on the Love of God in Deuteronomy and the Father–Son Relationship between Yahweh and Israel', *CBQ* 27, 1965, pp. 144-7.

[11] McCarthy, *CBQ* 27, 1965, pp. 144 ff.; Fensham, 'Father and Son as Terminology for Treaty and Covenant', in *Near Eastern Studies in Honor of William Foxwell Albright*, ed. H. Goedicke, Baltimore and London 1971, pp. 121-35.

[12] Cf. Fensham, pp. 132, 134; McCarthy, *Treaty and Covenant*,² p. 161 note 8.

the word *s̆gullāh* 'special possession or property' (Exod. 19: 5; Deut. 7: 6; 14: 2; 26: 18; Ps. 135: 4), is likewise found to have been at home in the treaties; like Ugaritic *sglt*, it was employed 'to distinguish a special relationship of the sovereign to one of his vassals'.[13]

(2) Following Moran's suggestion that the term *ṭbtˀ* in the Sefire treaties designates 'the amity estalished by treaty',[14] several scholars have argued a similar meaning for the word *ṭōb* and variants of it in the Old Testament.[15] Thus, according to A. Malamat the word *ṭōbāh* in 2 Samuel 7: 28 is the 'terminological indication' of Yahweh's covenant with David's dynasty here.[16] The same covenantal connotation of this word and its variants is found with reference to Yahweh's covenant with Israel in Jeremiah 33: 9, 14 and Hosea 3: 5; 8: 3.[17]

(3) A treaty background for the meaning in certain contexts of the word *yādaˁ* 'know' has been argued on the analogy of Hittite *šak*- and Accadian *idû* 'know' as designating 'mutual legal recognition on the part of suzerain and vassal'.[18] This technical sense of *yādaˁ* has been proposed for its usage in Genesis 18: 19 where God says of Abraham 'for I knew him', that is, 'recognized him as my legitimate servant'. The same meaning is given for the word in Exodus 33: 12 (of Yahweh's 'knowing' Moses), in 2 Samuel 7: 20 (of Yahweh's 'knowing' David) and in a 'derived and exaggerated' use of Yahweh's 'knowing' Jeremiah, that is, 'recognizing' him as his 'agent', 'functionary' in Jeremiah 1: 5.[19] Its usage with reference

---

[13] M. Weinfeld, *Deuteronomy and the Deuteronomic School*, Oxford 1972, p. 226 note 2. See also H. B. Huffmon and S. B. Parker, 'A further Note on the Treaty background of Hebrew *YADA ˁ*', *BASOR* 184, 1966, pp. 36 f.; McCarthy, *Treaty and Covenant*,[2] p. 162 note 10.

[14] 'A Note on the Treaty Terminology of the Sefire Stelas', *JNES* 22, 1963, pp. 173–6. Cf. D. R. Hillers, 'A Note on Some Treaty Terminology in the Old Testament', *BASOR* 176, 1964, pp. 46 f.

[15] For example, McCarthy, '*bˁrît* in Old Testament History and Theology', *Biblica* 53, 1972, p. 114; M. Fox, 'ṬŌB as Covenant Terminology', *BASOR* 209, 1973, pp. 41 f.; I. Johag, '*Ṭôb*. Terminus technicus in Vertrags- und Bündnisformularen des Alten Orients und des Alten Testaments', in *Bausteine biblischer Theologie. Festgabe für G. J. Botterweck*, ed. H.-J. Fabry, BBB 50, Cologne–Bonn 1977, pp. 3–23.

[16] 'Organs of Statecraft in the Israelite Monarchy', *BA* 28, 1965, p. 64.

[17] Cf. Fox, p. 41 f.

[18] See, for example, Huffmon, 'The Treaty Background of Hebrew *YADA ˁ*', *BASOR* 181, 1966, pp. 31–7, and Huffmon and Parker, op. cit.   [19] Huffmon, p. 34.

to 'covenant recognition' of Israel by Yahweh has been proposed for Hosea 13: 5 and Amos 3: 2, and with reference to Israel's 'recognizing Yahweh as its (sole) God' in Jeremiah 24: 7; 31: 34; Hosea 2: 22; 4: 1; 5: 4; 8: 2; 13: 4.[20]

(4) The claim of suzerains upon the exclusive loyalty and subservience of their vassals, characteristic of the treaties, has been seen as the prototype of the corresponding claim of Yahweh upon Israel's exclusive worship and service in the first commandment of the decalogue.[21] As an extension of this, it has been suggested that this same feature, the loyalty of vassal solely to his overlord, may have been the ultimate source for the development of the notion of Yahweh as a 'jealous' God as well as of the belief in the incomparability of Yahweh in the Old Testament.[22]

(5) Curse formulae in Old Testament texts, notably in Deuteronomy 28, have been regarded as the result of direct borrowing from lists of such curses in treaty documents.[23] It has been argued, for example, that Deuteronomy 28: 20–57 is materially dependent upon an Assyrian *Vorlage*.[24] Verse 23 in the same chapter and, because of their content and the sequence of the curses listed, vv. 26–35 have been regarded as being directly derived from the vassal treaties of Esarhaddon.[25]

(6) The vassal treaties have been regarded as the source or background of the nature and content of Yahweh's *rīb* 'lawsuit' with Israel, exemplified in a number of texts in the Old Testament (e.g. Deut. 32; Isa. 1: 2–3, 10–20;

---

[20] Ibid., pp. 35 ff.

[21] Cf. Beyerlin, *Herkunft und Geschichte*, p. 63; E. trs. p. 53.

[22] Fensham, 'Clauses of Protection in Hittite Vassal-Treaties and the Old Testament', *VT* 13, 1963, pp. 133–43, esp. pp. 138 ff.

[23] See, for example, Weinfeld, pp. 116 ff.; 'Traces of Treaty Formulae in Deuteronomy', *Biblica* 41, 1965, pp. 417–27; Fensham, 'Malediction and Benediction in Ancient Near Eastern Vassal-Treaties and the Old Testament', *ZAW* 74, 1962, pp. 1–9 and 'Common Trends in Curses of the Near Eastern Treaties and *Kudurru*-Inscriptions Compared with Maledictions of Amos and Isaiah', *ZAW* 75, 1963, pp. 155–75; D. R. Hillers, *Treaty Curses and the Old Testament Prophets, Biblica et Orientalia* 16, Rome 1964; R. Frankena, 'The Vassal-Treaties of Esarhaddon and the Dating of Deuteronomy', *OTS* 14, 1965, pp. 123–54.   [24] Cf. Frankena, pp. 144 ff.

[25] See the discussion in Weinfeld, *Deuteronomy and the Deuteronomic School*, pp. 116–29. Cf. Wiseman, p. 88; R. Borger, 'Zu den Asarhaddon-Verträgen aus Nimrud', *ZA* 54, (N.F. 20), 1961, pp. 191 f.

Mic. 6: 1–8; Jer. 2: 5–13).[26] The appeal in such passages to 'heaven and earth' ('mountains and hills', 'foundations of the earth' in the Micah passage) as witnesses to Yahweh's complaint against his people has been regarded as a particularly striking connection with the treaties in which the (deified) heaven and earth, mountains, springs, etc. are invoked as witnesses to the making of treaties. The origin of the form of the 'lawsuit' has been traced by J. Harvey not directly to the treaties themselves but to letters of accusation from a suzerain to his vassal accusing him of infidelity to the treaty agreement.[27]

To return to McCarthy's work, the treaty-form exemplified in the central discourse of Deuteronomy is found also, he maintains, in the material in the framework to it, which derives from the Deuteronomistic historian (*Treaty and Covenant*, [2] pp. 188 ff.). Chapter 4: 1–40 is 'a complete unit which reflects in miniature the covenant form which is that of Dt as a whole' (p. 194). The same is true of Moses's speech in 28: 69–30: 20, whilst a further example, again from the Deuteronomistic historian, is provided by Joshua 23.

Although it was not until the composition of *Urdeuteronomium*, which McCarthy dates to the period between the fall of Samaria and the reign of Josiah, that the covenant found fullest expression on the analogy of the treaty-form, the way had been prepared by a number of earlier texts which, it is argued, are the product of theological reflection on the nature of the covenant relationship between Yahweh and Israel. These texts are Exodus 19: 3b–8, Joshua 24: 2–28, and 1 Samuel 12, described by McCarthy as 'literary-reflective' texts. They already manifest a shift from the older tradition of covenant centring on rite to covenant by pledged word, that is, to the formulation of the covenant in terms of a treaty (pp. 206 ff.). These texts

seek to make explicit something of the nature of the relationship which was symbolised in the traditional cult. They seek to define the relation symbolised verbally. More, they will exhort the people to fidelity to this relationship. And

---

[26] See, for example, Huffmon 'The Covenant Lawsuit in the Prophets', *JBL* 78, 1959, pp. 285–95; G. E. Wright, 'The Lawsuit of God. A Form-Critical Study of Deuteronomy 32', in *Israel's Prophetic Heritage*, ed. B. W. Anderson and W. Harrelson, London 1962, pp. 26–67.

[27] *Le plaidoyer prophétique contre Israël après la rupture de l'alliance. Étude d'une formule littérataire de l'Ancien Testament*, Studia 22, Paris–Montreal, 1967.

they will cement that fidelity by eliciting an explicit response to the God who is present to the people, an acclamation, a pledge of that fidelity. So they turn to the word, exhortation and dialogue, using a powerful rhetoric (p. 291).

These texts are best described as proto-Deuteronomic, the earliest of them being 1 Samuel 12 apart from the more strictly Deuteronomic additions which have been made to it.

III

In their essentials, McCarthy's conclusions on the treaty background of Deuteronomy have received the support of M. Weinfeld, who has added some further detailed comparisons.[28] Without being drawn into the discussion of the possible different redactional layers in the growth of Deuteronomy, Weinfeld finds that the book has preserved the classic structure of the political treaty as evidenced during the ninth to the seventh centuries BC. By contrast, those formal elements which alone give the treaty its binding judicial validity and which are well represented in Deuteronomy—the blessings and curses (cf. Deut. 28), invocation of witnesses (cf. Deut. 4: 26; 30: 19; 31: 28), the oath imprecation (cf. Deut. 29: 9–29), the deposit of the treaty/covenant text in the sanctuary (cf. Deut. 10: 1–5; 31: 24–6), periodic readings of the text (cf. Deut. 31: 9–13), and duplicates and copies of the text (cf. Deut. 17: 18–19; 31: 25–6)—are lacking in the Sinai pericope and in Joshua 24 (p. 66).

In nature and content the list of curses in Deuteronomy 28 points to the Assyrian and Sefire treaties of the first millennium and not to the Hittite treaties of an earlier period. The latter contain only a short and generalized curse formulation, whilst the list in Deuteronomy 28 reflects the longer and more elaborate curse formulations of the later treaty texts. Such are the parallels between many of the curses contained in Deuteronomy 28 and curse formulae in the treaties of Esarhaddon—particularly striking in this connection is Deuteronomy 28: 26–35 (pp. 116 ff.)[29]—that the list in Deuteronomy 28 must have been 'drafted by scribes who were chiefly influenced by Assyrian treaty formulae' (p. 126). Weinfeld also maintains that the mixed and repetitive nature of the curse list in the treaties of Esarhaddon provides grounds for regarding

---

[28] *Deuteronomy and the Deuteronomic School*.
[29] See also his discussion in *Biblica* 41, 1965, pp. 417–27.

the curse list in Deuteronomy as a unity and not, as is frequently maintained, the result of separate redactions (pp. 128 f.).

Other alleged parallels between the treaties and Israel's covenant traditions are also supported and argued by Weinfeld. Thus, the 'stipulation of undivided allegiance' characteristic of the treaties and finding general expression by the term 'love', as W. L. Moran has suggested, is found to be paralleled in the demand for Israel's exclusive loyalty to Yahweh: 'This expression [i.e. love of vassal for suzerain], then, which served a political need in the ancient Near East, came to serve a religious need in Israel.' (p. 81.) Or again, the concept of the kingship of God, at home in Israel from an early time (cf. Jud. 8: 23; 1 Sam. 8: 7; 10: 19), also contributed to the concept of Israel as the vassal of Yahweh the king so that 'the relations between the people and their God had to be patterned after the conventional model of relations between a king and his subjects, a written treaty'.[30] This in turn explains, according to Weinfeld, the presence in Deuteronomy of many terms which originated 'in the diplomatic vocabulary of the Near East', for example, 'to go after others', 'to turn to others', 'to serve others' (in Deuteronomy 'to go after other gods' etc.); 'to love'; 'to cleave to'; 'to fear'; 'to swear'; 'to hearken to (or obey) the voice of'; 'to be perfect with (blameless before) him'; and 'to act in truth'. According to Weinfeld, all are encountered in the diplomatic letters and state treaties of the second and first millennia BC, and especially in the vassal treaties of Esarhaddon', and 'found their way into Deuteronomy (and eventually into Deuteronomic literature) as terms expressing religious loyalty' (pp. 83 ff.). A chapter such as Deuteronomy 13, warning against any seditious attempt to draw allegiance away from Yahweh, is 'permeated by an atmosphere of conspiracy of the sort that characterizes the political sphere' (p. 91).

Weinfeld points to two features of Deuteronomy which might appear to militate against understanding it as having been modelled upon treaties of the first millennium BC. The first is that Deuteronomy includes a prologue with a marked historical content, a feature which is characteristic of the Hittite treaties of the second millennium but not of the Assyrian treaties of the first millennium BC. But this, Weinfeld suggests, may be due simply to a gap in the information we have about Assyrian treaties. In

---

[30] See also his 'Covenant', *Encyclopaedia Judaica*, 1971, vol. 5, p. 1019.

any case, from neo-Assyrian 'royal grants' it appears that Assyrian kings did avail themselves of the literary pattern of the 'historical prologue'. The absence of such a prologue in the treaties may have been a matter of principle: 'the Assyrian emperor who saw himself as king of the world seems to have felt that it would have been both unnecessary and humiliating to justify his demand for loyalty by referring to his gracious acts on behalf of the vassal in the manner of the Hittite kings' (p. 68). This assumption

may also explain the lack of blessings in the Assyrian treaty. The Hittites felt it necessary not only to justify their demands for loyalty but also to give promises of help in time of danger, as well as to bestow divine blessings for loyal service. The Assyrians neither gave promises to the vassal nor bestowed blessings but, on the contrary, increased and expanded the list of threats and curses in order to terrorize him (p. 68).

A further significant difference between Deuteronomy and the treaty-form concerns its central law code which is dedicated to civil, cultic, and criminal law. Although functionally it is equivalent to the stipulatory section of the treaties, it is very different in substance: the objective of the treaty was to ensure the vassal's loyalty and not, as in Deuteronomy, to impose upon him a system of laws (p. 148).

According to Weinfeld, this is explained by seeing a coalescence in Deuteronomy of two originally distinct types of covenant, on the one hand a 'covenant of law' and on the other a 'covenant of vassalship', that is, the treaty-form. The former is represented by such old-Babylonian law codes as those of Hammurabi, Ur-Nammu and Lipit-Ištar and, from a still earlier period, the text relating the reform of Urukagina from the third millennium BC, each of which displays some of the features of the treaty-form. Of particular relevance is the reform of Urukagina which was sanctified by an agreement with the god Ningirsu and describes the liberation of the people from oppression and slavery by the proclamation of the law.

This latter type of covenant, the 'law covenant', can be discerned in the oldest Sinaitic tradition (Exod. 24: 3–8): 'Moses, like Urukagina, was the lawgiver *par excellence* who made a covenant with God stressing the observance of laws.' (p. 151.) It was not, as in the 'covenant of vassalship', concerned with the recognition of the sovereignty of Yahweh; the latter is presupposed. By contrast, however, 'Joshua's covenant (Josh. 24) concerns itself primarily with the establishment of an unequivocal relationship with Yahweh, while the law mentioned there (v. 25) has only secondary importance' (p. 152). That is, this covenant, the 'Shechem covenant', belongs to the category of the 'covenant of vassalship'.

The mixture of covenant and law in Deuteronomy is therefore pre-Deuteronomic and was thus already available to its author. His achievement was to enrich 'the covenant theme by introducing all the elements of the vassal treaty, while he blurred the covenantal pattern by putting it into a homiletic setting. Unlike the treaty, Deuteronomy is not a legal document but an oration. The structure of the speech follows a legal pattern, but its style is that of a sermon. The author of Deuteronomy had in mind the covenantal pattern in the form in which it had been lying before him in the tradition and in the manner in which it was generally formulated in his time. Nevertheless he presented the materials in a style that is free from rigid adherence to formality' (p. 157).

IV

Turning to various criticisms of the comparisons which have been drawn between suzerainty treaties and the covenant texts of the Old Testament, I draw attention first to an important conclusion which McCarthy arrived at, namely, his rejection of the view of Mendenhall and others that the influence of the treaty-form can be seen in the Sinai pericope in Exodus 19: 1-24: 11 or, more exclusively, in the decalogue in Exodus 20 (*Treaty and Covenant*,[2] esp. ch. 12). The decalogue—McCarthy has in mind with Mendenhall, Beyerlin, and others an *Urdekalog* consisting of only commands and prohibitions which can be isolated in the present form of the text in Exodus 20 and Deuteronomy 5—lacks curses and blessings formulae which were a constant feature of the treaties. As for its opening clause, this cannot seriously be regarded as a 'historical prologue' in the strict sense of that found in the Hittite treaties. Rather, it serves to designate the speaker and is properly understood as a continuation of the theophany described in Exodus 19. As for the Sinai pericope as a whole, at first glance it might seem to display the treaty-form: with its parenetic and historical introduction (ch. 19), its proclamation of laws (20: 1-23: 19), blessings and curses (23: 20-33), and its ratification of the covenant (24: 1-

11). But the resemblance is more apparent than real; a more critical scrutiny dispels the initial impression:

(1) Exodus 19 has an entirely different character from the historical prologue in the treaties. It is concerned primarily with Yahweh's theophany which serves to evoke the reverence and fear of the people on which basis their obedience to the divine will is pledged. The only historical reference in the chapter is in v. 4, which, even apart from the probability that it is (with the remainder of vv. 3b–8) a secondary insertion, is scarcely sufficient to warrant the description of this chapter as a 'historical prologue'.

(2) The promises and threats in Exodus 23: 20–33 are not strictly related to the preceding laws but are concerned with obedience to the angel who is to lead the people into the promised land. Further, this section too is very probably a secondary addition to the pericope.

(3) The manner of ratifying the covenant in Exodus 24: 1–11 where, according to widespread agreement, two originally independent traditions are preserved, is foreign to the treaties. In vv. 9–11 the covenant is ratified by means of a meal eaten on the mountain in the presence of God. As such it symbolizes the 'community' between Yahweh and his people. Such a rite points to a background in Bedouin culture where it would have been a means of taking the weaker into the family of the stronger, 'a reassuring gesture on the part of the superior toward the inferior and not a pledge of the latter' (p. 254). But the 'ratification of alliance by rite rather than by oath, and the gesture of superior to inferior rather than vice versa, these things are uncharacteristic of the treaty tradition' (p. 254). The same is true of the alternative tradition in vv. 3–8, the communion sacrifices and blood rite. They are analogous to the treaties in so far as they seek to produce brotherhood and fellowship: 'But in the treaties, at least among the Hittites, it is the word which effects the desired end; at Sinai it is sacrifice.' (p. 256.)

These rites in Exodus 24: 1–11 give the Sinai covenant its special meaning: 'More than a matter of agreement it is a question of adoptive kinship. Israel is not only subject of Yahwe, but His adopted family. And so the laws are not the terms of a treaty but the conditions covering continued union in the family.' (p. 295). The tradition in Exodus 24: 9–11, which McCarthy regards as the most ancient of the Sinai covenant traditions, exemplifies most clearly this 'non-verbal' ratification of the covenant by rite. Rite also predominates in vv. 3–8. But the latter is a more complex fragment of tradition and is later than the tradition in vv. 9–11:

In the old, simpler form there is no hint of an expression of the divine will. The people were received in the holy place. In the more complex form the divine will is heard and the people subscribe to it. There is obviously development here from a tie with implicit definition by custom to one with a more carefully worked out, explicit definition. But the feeling of a quasi-familial bond remained constant. (pp. 268 f.)

The symbolism in vv. 3–8 is richer than that in vv. 9–11; in the former an 'Israel settled on the Land long enough to assimilate elements of Canaanite sacrificial ritual without forgetting its nomadic past when special importance was attributed to blood . . . developed at some sanctuary a ceremonial in which sacrifice and blood rites are used to give making covenant with Yahwe deeper significance' (p. 268). It was not a creation of either J or E. It presupposes the double revelation of the law characteristic of the secondary development of the E narrative, since it knows not only of the proclamation of the decalogue, which belonged to the earlier form of the E narrative, but also of the Book of the Covenant which was a later addition to that narrative. Nor can it have been a Deuteronomic composition, since its emphasis upon covenant by rite contrasts with the Deuteronomic emphasis upon covenant by pledged word. It is, McCarthy suggests, pre- or proto-Deuteronomic (p. 269).

Although I disagree with McCarthy's understanding of the traditions in Exodus 24: 1–11 (see below, chapters 5 and 8), his criticisms of the view that the treaty-form has influenced either the decalogue or the Sinai pericope as a whole are well taken, and have come to be widely accepted.

But what of the view that this form has influenced the authors of Deuteronomy? To come straight to the point, it may be asked whether, as in the case of the Sinai pericope which only superficially resembles that form, the alleged parallels between Deuteronomy and the treaty-form too are more apparent than real. Some *prima facie* evidence justifying this question arises from even a cursory reading of the book. It is not a legal document in the sense that the treaties are. It is not treaty-like in its manner of presentation; rather, it is a valedictory speech of Moses, an extended oration in homiletic style. Its laws deal with many matters not strictly pertinent to the suzerain-vassal relationship. It embodies a collection of laws (the decalogue) in a position uncharacteristic of the treaties, that is, at the beginning of a prologue rather than after it. The fact that the book contains no less than two prologues is again unlike anything to be found in the treaties. Conspicuous by its absence, if Deuteronomy is to be regarded as reflecting the suzerainty treaty and its terminology, is the designation of Yahweh as king[31]—all the more so since Weinfeld argues that an old established doctrine of the kingship of Yahweh in Israel contributed to the concept of Israel as the vassal of Yahweh.

Prominent features of the book such as these make it clear that its authors were certainly not simply making a literary imitation of the treaties. Whilst acknowledging this, neither McCarthy nor Weinfeld regards any of these features as seriously detracting from the evidence of the influence of the treaty-form upon the book. For Weinfeld such features are for the most part to be explained in terms of the flexibility employed by the author of Deuteronomy who 'presented the materials in a style that is free from rigid formality'. There may be a certain amount of 'blurring' of the treaty-form, and the various elements of it may not have been arranged in an order which befits a treaty text. But all the elements are present and find expression in virtually every section of the book. It is, incidentally, for this reason that Weinfeld, in his discussion of the nature and authorship of Deuteronomy, regards it as unnecessary to discuss the various stages of redaction through which the book has gone, even though he acknowledges that a process of literary growth has been involved. The same working method and the same covenantal or treaty-like concerns are manifest in all strata of the book, from the earliest to the latest.[32] McCarthy too allows for flexibility in the authors' use of the treaty-form, and finds that to a great extent the way in which the book as we have it differs from the treaty-form is due to the way in which it has developed from its original core (5–26 + 28), which firmly manifests that

---

[31] Opinion is divided on whether the mention of 'a king' in Deuteronomy 33: 5 refers to Yahweh or to an earthly king. In any event it belongs to a passage which is widely regarded as a late interpolation into the book.

[32] *Deuteronomy and the Deuteronomic School*, p. 66 note 1.

form, through subsequent stages of supplementation chiefly at the hands of the Deuteronomistic historians.

Nevertheless, these differences between Deuteronomy and the treaty-form surely indicate that its authors were not concerned with producing, whether in form or style or contents, simply a literary and theological replica of the treaties, and this in itself warrants the question I posed above, that is, whether such resemblances as there are between the book and the treaties may not after all be more apparent than real, the result, perhaps, of a conjoining of materials, at various stages of redaction, which gives the impression of the form and elements of the treaties but which was not at all motivated by a desire to use the treaty-form and its various constituents.

A preliminary illustration of what I mean may be found in the case of the opening section of Deuteronomy (chs. 1–3) in which Weinfeld finds (*a*) a preamble after the analogy of the treaty-form (1: 1–6a), and (*b*) a treaty-like historical prologue (1: 6b–3: 29).[33] Superficially the material looks as though it conforms to these elements of the treaty-form, but its contents fit no such description. The primary concern of these three chapters is not at all with Yahweh's historical actions on behalf of Israel, but with the journey and fortunes of the Israelites after they left Horeb. They thus set the historical scene for Moses's subsequent teaching of the law, but they do not constitute a treaty-like prologue to the law. What was so forcefully argued by Noth and subsequently by many others remains a strong probability,[34] namely, that these chapters are intended as an introduction to the Deuteronomistic history, and that it is as part of that larger corpus and not simply as a prologue to Deuteronomy itself that they are properly understood. Their attitude to the history they record and to the law is characteristic of the Deuteronomistic history; as A. D. H. Mayes has put it, they 'do not on their own account belong with the law; they do not lead up to it or introduce it. Rather they lead up to and introduce the history of Israel which as a whole stands under the law.'[35]

[33] Ibid., p. 66.

[34] *Überlieferungsgeschichtliche Studien*, Tübingen 1943; E. trs. *The Deuteronomistic History, JSOT* Supplement Series 15, Sheffield 1981. For a recent discussion see A. D. H. Mayes, *The Story of Israel Between Settlement and Exile: A Redactional Study of the Deuteronomistic History*, London 1983, pp. 22–7.

[35] *Deuteronomy*, New Century Bible, London 1979, p. 42.

Compared with this, the central sections of the book—the prologue (5–11), the laws (12–26), and the list of blessings and curses (28)—would seem to offer more plausible evidence of the influence of the treaty-form. Yet this too may be seriously doubted.

Of crucial importance for the comparison between Deuteronomy and the treaty-form is chapter 28. Indeed, in significant ways this chapter has to bear much of the weight of that comparison. It is here that Weinfeld finds the most direct and striking evidence of the dependence of the authors of Deuteronomy upon contemporary Assyrian treaties. By contrast, he acknowledges that the history-like prologue in Deuteronomy is not firmly attested in those treaties, and concedes that the law section in chapters 12–26 'is very different in substance' from the stipulatory section in such treaties. As a result he is forced to fall back upon the argument that this law section is nevertheless 'functionally equivalent' to the stipulatory section in the treaties.[36] The chapter is equally significant for McCarthy who, unlike Weinfeld, has little to say about the manifest differences between the stipulatory section in the treaties and the law section in Deuteronomy:

Specifically, the blessing and curses are of the sort found in the treaties from Mesopotamia and Syria, and for that matter in a wide range of ancient documents. The very introductory formula 28, 1, and especially the negative formulation in 28, 15 ... reproduce closely the form in which certain treaties put their curses. The precision of the formulation and the fact that it is found in Hatti, in Assyria and in Israel make it reasonable to believe that we have to do with an established legal formula associated with the treaty tradition. *Its use in Dt is a sure sign that the central portion of the book was indeed conceived of as a covenant.*[37]

Three main features of this chapter have been regarded as evidence that its author(s) consciously modelled it on the analogy of treaty lists, in particular on treaties from the first millennium BC: (1) the mixture of traditional materials which it contains is characteristic of curse lists in these treaties; (2) the sheer length of the list of curses compared with the much shorter list of blessings, and thus the heavy emphasis upon curse rather than blessing, is likewise characteristic of these treaties; (3) there are close resemblances between some formulations in the chapter and extant curse lists, notably in the vassal treaties of Esarhaddon.

---

[36] *Deuteronomy and the Deuteronomic School*, p. 148.
[37] *Treaty and Covenant*,² pp. 172 f. (the italics are mine).

I shall comment on (3) later. As to (1) and (2), their validity depends to a considerable extent upon regarding the chapter as a unity or substantially a unity: in conscious imitation of a treaty list, an author has assembled a typical mixture of curses and in composing his long list has emphasized the threat of curse. Clearly, however, if the chapter grew stage by stage from an originally shorter core at the hands of a succession of redactors, the case for seeing the chapter as having been consciously modelled upon the treaty lists would be markedly weakened: the length of the list and the mixture need not necessarily, on this understanding of the composition of the chapter, be due to conscious imitation of a treaty list, and the emphasis upon curse rather than on blessing might be explained on other grounds, for example, that these redactors worked at a time in Israel when curse rather than blessing was the order of the day.

In view of this, it is essential that the question of the unity of the chapter be established on internal grounds, that is, without prior appeal to the treaty lists, since this latter procedure would patently be an argument in a circle: the treaty lists cannot be appealed to for proof that Deuteronomy 28 is a unity, and then Deuteronomy 28, established as a unity on this basis, appealed to as evidence that its authors were influenced by the treaty lists.

An examination of the arguments of Weinfeld, D. R. Hillers, and McCarthy reveals that in effect the treaty analogy is the controlling factor, or largely so, in arriving at their conclusion for the unity of the chapter, or, in the case of McCarthy, its substantial unity. Thus Weinfeld argues that the very basis of the 'supposition' that the chapter developed in separate stages 'is destroyed ... by an examination of the Esarhaddon treaty', and proceeds to show how this substantiates the view that Deuteronomy 28 is a unity.[38] Like the Esarhaddon treaty list, he argues, Deuteronomy 28 too is a composite literary creation, 'but—as Hillers has already indicated—"not because of late redactional activity but because the scribes have combined a variety of traditional curses"'.[39] 'It remains possible', Hillers states, 'that later additions are present in Deut 28, but the arguments advanced so far do not prove it. Comparison with authentic lists of treaty-curses and close examination of the poetic elements in the chapter lead to a different conclusion: Deut. 28 represents the combination

---

[38] *Deuteronomy and the Deuteronomic School*, pp. 128 f.
[39] Ibid., p. 129.

and reworking by a single author of traditional curses known to him. It is composite, but not as the result of later scribal insertions. No part of it need be dated any later than the rest of Deuteronomy. The lists of curses of the Esarhaddon treaty, Sefire I, and the Ashurnirari treaty seem to be of this nature also. They give the impression of being composite, not because of late redactional activity, but because the scribes have combined a variety of traditional curses.'[40]

McCarthy provides an examination of the structure of the chapter and defends its unity with the possible exception of vv. 47-68. With this exception, however, his conclusion, no less than that of both Weinfeld and Hillers, is to a marked extent controlled by the treaty analogy, so that what most commentators have seen as evidence of different stages of literary growth from an original core—changes in style, repetitions, evidence of *vaticinium ex eventu*—is ultimately accounted for by appeal to the analogy of the treaty list genre: 'The genre is the model for the peculiarities of Dt 28: imbalance of blessings and curses, repeated introductions and conclusions, repetitions, and changes of style. In the Assyrian treaties and at Sefire such things form part of a single composition using traditional materials. They are not the result of accretion or repeated redactions.'[41]

Commenting on the approach of both Weinfeld and Hillers to the literary problems of Deuteronomy 28, Mayes correctly states:

it is undoubtedly true that extra-biblical texts exhibit within the framework of a single text a variety of styles and a degree of repetition. However, one may not transpose this observation immediately to the biblical context. The situations are different: in the one case a treaty text dependent on a ceremony for which the text was composed; in the other a narrative framework incorporating passages which have at most an indirect relationship to any ceremony.[42]

Appearances can be deceptive, as McCarthy himself has demonstrated in the case of the Sinai pericope in Exodus 19-24. Here its general lay-out appears to exhibit the treaty-form, but a closer examination reveals that it has not at all been influenced by this form. Deuteronomy merits the same approach: 'In so far as the literary contexts of Deuteronomy and the extra biblical treaties are ... independent, the literary criticism of

---

[40] *Treaty Curses and the Old Testament Prophets*, p. 40.
[41] *Treaty and Covenant*, ² p. 176.   [42] *Deuteronomy*, p. 349.

Deuteronomy must in the first instance proceed quite independently of the treaties.'[43]

When such an independent, internal analysis of Deuteronomy 28 is undertaken, however, whereby the same sort of criteria are applied to it as are applied to other chapters and sections of the book, it appears that a complex process of growth in several stages has taken place in its formation. That is the conclusion of the great majority of comentators, even though they differ in details.[44]

The chapter falls into three main sections: vv. 1–46, 47–57, and 58–68, the first comprising conditional blessings and curses, the second the announcement of curses, and the third conditional curses.[45] It is widely accepted that vv. 58–68 are a secondary, concluding addition, displaying literary affinities with the latest parts of Deuteronomy and with other late literature.[46] A majority of commentators regard vv. 47–57 as having been added secondarily to the first section, from which it differs in form, by means of the bridging passage vv. 45 f. There is general agreement too that not all of what remains, vv. 1–44, is from a single hand, though analyses of it vary in detail. In his recent close analysis of it, Seitz, for example, followed by Mayes, argues that vv. 23–6, 29–34, 36 f., and 41 f. derive from the editor responsible for the addition of vv. 47–57.[47] A good case has been made for regarding the original core of the first section as having centred on vv. 3–6 and 16–19: a brief list of 'blessed shall you be' formulations (vv. 3–6), possibly derived from a cultic setting,[48] has in turn been the model for the composition of a corresponding list of 'cursed shall you be' formulations (vv. 16–19), and a framework provided to relate the resulting blessing–curse list to the Deuteronomic law, the subsequent gradual expansion of the chapter then following.[49] An alternative possibility, suggested again recently though not for the first time, is that the blessings section in vv. 1–14 is itself a secondary addition, composed to counterbalance an original core of curses in vv. 16–19.[50]

[43] Ibid., p. 34.

[44] For recent surveys see J. G. Plöger, *Literarkritische, formgeschichtliche und stilkritische Untersuchungen zum Deuteronomium*, BBB 26, Bonn 1967, pp. 130 ff.; G. Seitz, *Redaktionsgeschichtliche Studien zum Deuteronomium*, BWANT 93, Stuttgart, Berlin, Cologne, Mainz, 1971, pp. 254 ff.   [45] Cf. Seitz, pp. 261 ff.

[46] Ibid., pp. 298 ff.   [47] Ibid., pp. 289 ff. Cf. Mayes, *Deuteronomy*, pp. 350 f.

[48] Seitz, pp. 271 ff.   [49] Seitz, pp. 268 ff. Cf. Mayes, *Deuteronomy*, p. 350.

[50] H. D. Preuss, *Deuteronomium*, Erträge der Forschung 164, Darmstadt 1982, pp. 155 f.

When such a process of growth is acknowledged, then neither the length of the list nor its heavy emphasis upon curse, nor the mixture it embodies can be regarded as the planned work of a single author seeking to emulate the long lists in contemporary treaties, with their similar mixture and emphasis. The end result may look like such treaty lists, but neither in origin nor in its subsequent expansion was it consciously intended as such. If the blessing-curse series in vv. 3–6 and 16–19 with a framework was the first stage of this list, it cannot have been the intention of its author to emulate the treaty lists of the first millennium, from which it differs in both form and content, and in any event the presence of blessings alongside curses is totally lacking in the Assyrian treaties of this period, and is only very minimally represented in those from Sefire. If, on the other hand, the blessings are a secondary addition, this too only indicates that those who contributed to the expansion of the original core of curses in vv. 15–44 were not endeavouring to emulate the treaty lists.

The intensification of the curse element can be more readily explained by the historical circumstances in which the chapter was developed, that is, the closing years of the kingdom of Judah, when the threat of curse was seen to hover more and more ominously over the nation and then fell catastrophically upon it in the events of 597 and 587 BC. Consequently and understandably, because this woeful judgement which came to pass must have been forewarned—even foretold (cf. vv. 45–57)—the threat which had accompanied the giving of the law was sharply augmented, in both length and severity; Israel's crime was thus made to fit the pre-ordained punishment, and so the punishment fitted the crime.

Weighed against these considerations, the resemblances between some formulations in Deuteronomy 28 and extant treaty lists, notably those in the Esarhaddon material, cannot in themselves be regarded as evidence that the chapter as a whole was consciously composed on the model of the treaty-curse list. Rather, we must see such formulations as having been among a diversity of traditional materials employed in the gradual expansion of the list. No more significance than this need be attached to them. Different matters of urgency were driven home by curse formulations, not only treaties, but also, for example, boundary stones, or law codes. To this extent Deuteronomy shares with treaties, boundary stones, and law codes a curse list; but that is far from saying that it sought to imitate the form of any one of them.[51]

To return to the prologue of Deuteronomy, it is surely a weakness when Weinfeld, conceding that the marked historical element in this material is unattested in the Assyrian treaties, has then to fall back upon the suggestion that this may be due to a gap in the information we have about these treaties, and it is little improvement on this when Mayes, for example, who also notes the difference between the prologue in Deuteronomy and the Assyrian treaties, attempts to explain it in terms of a rather vague 'treaty tradition'.[52] The weakness is that one begins with the view that Deuteronomy is modelled upon the treaty-form (or, as Mayes believes, came to reflect it at a secondary stage of editing) and then has to explain why it is nonetheless quite different from it in two key sections, the prologue and the central legal section.

With regard to the latter, the central legal section, Weinfeld, as noted above, concedes that it is very different in substance from the stipulatory section in the treaties, but argues that it is nonetheless 'functionally equivalent' to the latter. This, however, simply begs the question whether the authors of Deuteronomy did, in fact, compose their book on the analogy of the treaty-form. Once again the argument is circular: Deuteronomy was modelled on the treaty-form, therefore the law section in it is 'functionally equivalent' to the stipulatory section in the treaties. This concluded, the patent differences between the laws in Deuteronomy 12–26 and the treaty stipulations are explained by recourse to the yet more elaborate view that two originally separate forms—the 'law covenant' and the 'vassal covenant'—have been combined in Deuteronomy.

V

A further question can be raised at this point: so far as Israelites in general would have been familiar with suzerain–vassal relationships, would such an analogy for their relationship with God have had any appeal of an apt or desirable nature, especially when Assyrian suzerains had subjugated and despoiled the land and people? Notwithstanding all the references in the treaties to the 'love' of suzerain for vassal and of vassal for suzerain, to

---

[51] See L. Perlitt's comment, *Bundestheologie im Alten Testament*, p. 45 note 2.
[52] Mayes, *Deuteronomy*, pp. 33 f.

the suzerain as 'father' and the vassal as 'son', such relationships were surely hardly ever like that. Vassals did not as a rule 'love' those who conquered, subdued, and dominated them—there is abundant evidence for this in the history of Israel and of the ancient Near East—and the very language of intimate and familial relationships employed in the treaties reflects not the reality of the relationships, but rather the political, strategic, and economically motivated endeavour of suzerains to maintain, with the least amount of trouble, the subservience of those whom they had conquered and regarded as subject to them. To tell Israelites that Yahweh 'loves' them in the same way as a suzerain (e.g. Ashurbanipal or Nebuchadrezzar) 'loves' his vassals, and that they are to 'love' Yahweh as vassals 'love' their suzerains, would surely have been a bizarre depiction of Yahweh's love of, and commitment to, his people, and of the love and commitment with which they were called upon to respond.

Yet this is indeed the analogy which, if I understand him correctly, McCarthy has in mind when he claims that the use of the word 'love' in Deuteronomy, the command there to 'love' Yahweh, is a 'strange sort of thing to command but one at home in the treaties'.[53] The implicit understanding is that Israel is to 'love' Yahweh in the sense that a vassal 'loves' his suzerain. Similarly, as suzerains spoke of their vassals as their *sᵉgullāh* 'treasured possession', so Israel is to understand itself as the *sᵉgullāh* of its suzerain Yahweh.

The reality is surely that terms such as these and others, supposedly derived by the biblical writers from their knowledge of treaties, belonged in the first instance to familiar settings of everyday life, and needed no treaties to mediate them or give them a special nuance. There is no need to believe that the biblical authors were dependent for such terminology on anything other than these same everyday settings. The 'father–son' analogy is an obvious example, as also is such a term as *ᶜebed* 'slave, servant'. And why should it be so strange, as Moran and McCarthy contend, that love is 'commanded'? The Israelite is commanded to love his neighbour (Lev. 19: 18, 34) and the stranger (Deut. 10:19); Hosea is commanded to love a woman (Hos. 3: 1); there is the command to love wisdom (Prov. 4: 6), the command to love truth and peace (Zech. 8: 19),

---

[53] *Treaty and Covenant*,[2] p. 186.

and to love good (Amos 5: 15). Why then should the command to love
God have to be understood as a 'strange sort of thing', explicable only
when one knows suzerainty treaty usage?

Nor would the use of the Hebrew word *yāda*ᶜ have required any
semantic assistance from the Hittite *šak-* or Accadian *idû*, and it is in any
case doubtful whether such a meaning as 'legal recognition' on the part of
vassal for suzerain and *vice versa*, or 'recognize as one's legitimate agent', as
proposed by Huffmon, is admissible for the Hebrew word. In texts such as
Genesis 18: 19, 2 Samuel 7: 20, Jeremiah 1: 5, Hosea 13: 5, Amos 3: 2, where
it is used with Yahweh as subject, its meaning is something like 'know
someone for one's own', 'choose and make someone one's own', as E.
Baumann showed many years ago.[54] When used of Israel's 'knowing'
Yahweh it connotes the worship and service of God, and not something
quite so plain as 'recognize the legal rights of Yahweh', or even obedience
to Yahweh's law, even though the latter may sometimes be included in
what is intended.[55]

As for the demand for Israel's exclusive service and loyalty to Yahweh,
it is scarcely credible that the insistence upon this in Deuteronomy is, as
McCarthy puts it, 'straight from the world of the treaties'.[56] Just as
incredible is the notion that the treaty literature was the ultimate source
of the development of the concept of Yahweh as a 'jealous God' (which is
more likely to have been derived from the sphere of husband–wife
relationship, so prominent in Hosea; cf. Num. 5: 14), or the belief in the
incomparability of Yahweh, as Fensham has suggested. There is no need
to go beyond the peculiar development of Israel's own religion for an
explanation of such theological features in the Old Testament (see below,
chapter 10).

Finally, there is no need to look beyond a familiar *Sitz im Leben* in
Israelite society, the administration of justice, for the source of the
imagery of Yahweh's *rīb* 'lawsuit' with his people.[57] The only point of difference would have been the summons to 'heaven and earth', 'mountains
and hills', or the like, as witnesses, and it is only in the use of this type of
summons that any similarity with the treaties is found. Yet here again

---

[54] '*Yāda*ᶜ und seine Derivate. Ein sprachlich-exegetische Studie', *ZAW* 28, 1908, pp.
22–41 and 110–41. Cf. esp. p. 39.   [55] Ibid., pp. 40 f., 112, 113 f.

[56] *Treaty and Covenant*,² p. 186.

[57] For a discussion see R. E. Clements, *Prophecy and Tradition*, Oxford 1975, pp. 17–20.

there is no need to look to the context of international treaties for the derivation of such an element. As J. R. Boston has pointed out, the appeal to 'heaven and earth', most familiar in the 'lawsuit' between Yahweh and Israel, was employed in a variety of ways, and does not seem to have been limited to any specific *Gattung*.[58]

The conclusion to which this chapter has led is that though for a time research into the possible influence of suzerainty treaties upon Old Testament covenant texts seemed to offer striking results, in reality it has yielded little that is of permanent value. The resemblance in form between the Sinai pericope or the decalogue and Hittite treaty texts of the second millennium BC was effectively exposed by McCarthy to be merely superficial, and it turns out that the same is true of the supposed dependence of Deuteronomy upon treaties of the first millennium. As to the use in Deuteronomy of a range of terms also employed in these treaties, it is unlikely that this is due to borrowing on the part of the Deuteronomic authors from treaties; it can be much more plausibly explained as the result of mutual use by treaty scribes and Deuteronomic writers of common sources—the familiar settings of everyday life. Further, it is inherently improbable that Deuteronomic/Deuteronomistic authors in the late pre-exilic and exilic periods would have sought to draw an analogy between Yahweh's relationship with his people and that between Assyrian emperors and their vassals. Similarly, suggestions that key theological concepts in the Old Testament covenant texts—the exclusive worship of Yahweh, the notion of Yahweh as a 'jealous' God, the incomparability of Yahweh—were prompted by treaty texts must be rejected.

The attempt to relate the Old Testament covenant to suzerainty treaties may be said to represent a dead-end in the social/functional approach; the search for a model that will explain how the covenant functioned in the religious and social life of ancient Israel here over-reaches itself. But the consequence of this failure to find a satisfactory way of presenting the covenant as an *institution* has proved positive rather than negative, for it has opened up afresh the possibility of seeing it as a *theological idea*. Indeed, as I shall suggest in the next chapter, the last

---

[58] 'The Wisdom Influence upon the Song of Moses', *JBL* 87, 1968, pp. 198–202.

representatives of 'treaty' theories, such as McCarthy and Weinfeld, are already beginning to speak of the covenant as a *metaphor* drawn from the world of treaties rather than as an institution which formed the principle of cohesion among the twelve tribes of earliest Israel. Moreover, once neo-Assyrian, rather than Hittite, treaties are seen as the model it becomes, in fact, difficult to avoid this shift of emphasis, since the picture of Israel as a 'covenant community' has to be seen as an ideal no earlier than the late monarchical period, rather than as a historical fact about the political constitution of the old 'tribal league'. Once the possibility was admitted that 'covenant' was an ideal rather than a social reality, it became possible to rehabilitate an insight of Wellhausen's which the intervening years, marked as they were by the dominance of sociology over theology, had obscured. Before we have finished we shall find that what is really of value in a sociological approach can be salvaged and can, indeed, give a much sharper focus to the insight in question. But for the moment we must examine the immediate scholarly reaction to the demise of the 'treaty' theory of covenant in which Wellhausen's conviction that covenant-theology was the result, not the presupposition, of the preaching of the prophets, has found renewed support.

4

Covenant as a Theological Idea

HARD on the heels of the phase of research outlined in the preceding chapter has come another, which may conveniently be described as the fourth phase in covenant-research since Wellhausen. This current phase is represented by a number of studies which seek to reverse the conclusions widely accepted since the 1920s concerning the antiquity and nature of the covenant between God and Israel. The 'functional' understanding of the origin and purpose of this covenant, so widely favoured hitherto, and the view that it was a central feature of Israelite religion from the earliest period, are abandoned. Instead, these studies argue that the notion of such a covenant was developed to meet specifically theological needs and crises which arose at a relatively late time in Israel.

This shift, with important attendant consequences, to such an understanding of the covenant is most extensively worked out in studies by L. Perlitt and E. Kutsch, the former in his *Bundestheologie im Alten Testament* (1969), the latter in a number of articles published between 1967 and 1972, and subsequently brought together and supplemented in his *Verheissung und Gesetz* (1973). Their main conclusions are outlined later in this chapter. First, however, a number of earlier, shorter contributions which to some extent already indicate the direction which Perlitt and Kutsch take are briefly surveyed. But as a sort of preface to this I shall first draw attention to the further aspect of the investigation of the treaty-covenant analogy which I mentioned in the closing paragraph of the preceding chapter, namely, that in the course of this a shift not wholly but certainly partially similar to that mentioned above can be seen.

I

It will be recalled that G. E. Mendenhall saw the value of the use of the treaty model for Israel's covenant with Yahweh to lie precisely in the way in which it would have functioned both in the sphere of religion and also sociologically by creating, on the one hand, a bond between the tribes and Yahweh, who now became their God, and, on the other, 'solidarity' between the tribes themselves as Yahweh's 'vassals'. This same functional understanding of the use of the treaty model found support among a number of scholars who further elaborated Mendenhall's views, for example, W. Beyerlin, and was given wider currency in popular works by such scholars as J. Bright and D. R. Hillers.[1] Thus the religio-sociological understanding of the origin and nature of the Sinai covenant, already widely accepted by the time these scholars wrote, was now thought by them to have received striking confirmation from an unexpected source. Further, it was not merely that the covenant originally functioned in such a way; it became institutionalized in Israel's cult in Canaan where it continued to operate as the norm in Israel's life as Yahweh's people. It was constitutive of Israel's life as a community of tribes; it was an institution with cultic, religious, and social roles to fulfil. The treaty-form was thus not merely believed to have influenced the shape of the Sinai pericope, Deuteronomy, and other texts *qua* literary compositions; these texts also reflect the shape and content of a recurring covenant festival which itself was shaped by the constituents of that treaty-form with its historical element, its stipulations, blessings and curses, and so forth.

With the work of D. J. McCarthy, however, especially in its second edition (1978), a significant change has taken place. He adheres to the view that the earliest Sinai traditions (Exod. 24: 3–8 and 24: 9–11) conceive of the covenant as formative of Israel as the community of Yahweh, though not because they in any way depend upon the treaty-form; the eating of a covenant meal or the sharing of sacrificial blood effect the community or 'kinship' between Yahweh and his people. In the case of Deuteronomy, however, we are dealing, according to McCarthy, not with the literary deposit of an ancient cultic and institutional concept of covenant, but with a work of *theological reflection* which uses the suzerain-vassal treaty and its terminology as an *analogy* for Israel's relationship with Yahweh. Here, late in Israel's history, 'political experience and theological reflection call upon the treaty to express some profound ideas about the

---

[1] J. Bright, *A History of Israel*, London 1960, pp. 143 ff., and his *Covenant and Promise: The Future in the Preaching of the Pre-exilic Prophets*, London 1977, pp. 31 ff.; D. R. Hillers, *Covenant: The History of a Biblical Idea*, Baltimore 1969, pp. 68 ff.

people's relation to God'.[2] Deuteronomy is thus a 'theological flowering'. As such it was prepared for by earlier texts (Exod. 19: 3b–8; Josh. 24; 1 Sam. 12) which, though still bearing some marks of a more ancient cultic or ritual notion of the covenant, are to be understood as 'literary reflective texts' in which there is already a shift from covenant as an institution to covenant as a theological analogy, a didactic construct. In addition to McCarthy's statements about this, however, it may be argued that the view that the authors of Deuteronomy adapted political and diplomatic forms and language to the religious sphere of Yahweh's relationship with Israel already carries with it, *ex hypothesi*, the view that these authors had in effect abandoned earlier cultic or institutional concepts of this covenant, if such there were, and were concerned with creating an ideology. This argument clearly applies also to M. Weinfeld's work.

What prevents McCarthy from wholly making the shift from covenant as a cultic or religio-sociological institution to covenant purely as a theological and didactic analogy is that he finds ancient testimony to the former in traditions such as those preserved in Exodus 24: 1–11, in which the covenant is the means of creating a community by various symbolic rites enacting union between the parties. According to Weinfeld, Exodus 24: 3–8, which he regards as the oldest Sinaitic tradition, with its emphasis upon the commandments of Yahweh, reflects the achievement of Moses which was 'the crystallization of Israel's tribal society by means of a reform'; the purpose of the covenant Moses introduced was 'the acknowledgement of a new system of laws, which the liberation from slavery and the achievement of political independence made indispensable'.[3] The Shechem covenant tradition in Joshua 24, which Weinfeld believes to be of ancient origin, had the purpose of reaffirming loyalty to Yahweh, which had been threatened in the post-settlement period, and had the additional aim of introducing a new faith to the native Canaanite population (p. 156).

It is of some importance to note, however, that in dealing with texts such as these neither McCarthy nor Weinfeld refers to their setting in early Israel as having been an 'amphictyony'. In this they both reflect the now increasingly widespread rejection of Noth's theory of early Israel as an 'amphictyony'. The difference this makes for our investigation of the

---

[2] *Treaty and Covenant*,[2] p. 290.
[3] *Deuteronomy and the Deuteronomic School*, pp. 152, 156.

origin and nature of the covenant between Yahweh and Israel is immediately apparent, for, as we saw earlier, it was largely because scholars since the 1920s believed Israel to have originated as a tribal con-federation that they were able to agree upon the ancient function of the covenant as operative in the formation and continuing life of this 'amphictyony'. It is partly because of this change in recent Old Testament study that McCarthy is able to understand Joshua 24, which had been so crucial for Noth's theory, as a 'literary reflective text' from the mid-monarchical period. Similarly, it is because of this change that both McCarthy and Weinfeld have to postulate a different historical setting for covenant traditions such as are contained in Exodus 24: 1–11 which they still regard as ancient.

A different view is taken by G. Fohrer with whose contribution to this matter we come a step nearer to the views of Perlitt and Kutsch. In an article published in 1966[4] he first outlines various reasons for rejecting Noth's theory of an 'amphictyony', and then seeks to reassess the significance of the covenant in early Israel. Accepting Alt's view that Genesis 15 preserves the memory of a theophany to Abraham in which the patriarch's God by means of a *bᵉrīt* made a solemn promise of land and progeny to him, he argues that the *bᵉrīt* between Yahweh and Israel, as contained in Exodus 24: 3–8, 24: 9–11, and 34: 10, 27 f., was of the same type, that is, a covenant which had the effect of constituting the religion and cult of nomadic or semi-nomadic clans. By such a *bᵉrīt* the deity became related to his clients as 'father' or 'brother'. Thus by the making of a *bᵉrīt* Moses and the groups with him at Sinai/Horeb became 'the people of Yahweh' (cols. 897 ff.). The fact that all three ancient Pentateuchal sources—J (Exod. 34: 10, 27 f.), E (the decalogue in Exod. 20 and the rite in 24: 3–8) and, as argued by Fohrer, the source N (Exod. 24: 9–11)—so firmly preserve the memory of it means that we need not doubt the historicity of such a *bᵉrīt* in the pre-settlement period.

After the settlement, however, this *bᵉrīt* as the means whereby Israel became Yahweh's people became a thing of the past. It had achieved its purpose of creating a relationship between Yahweh and Israel. Now, however, not it but the deliverance from Egypt became the fundamental confession of Israel, whilst the cult fostered the relation with Yahweh.

---

[4] 'Altes Testament—"Amphiktyonie" und "Bund"?', *TLZ* 91, 1966, cols. 801–16 and 894–904.

Further, it was not this covenant but the formulation of genealogies in the post-settlement period which served to unite the tribes and consolidate their identity as 'the people of Yahweh' (cols. 899 f.). Thus, though the memory of the covenant at Sinai/Horeb was not lost, it became nothing more than a historical datum.

It remained such for several centuries until the Deuteronomic authors took up the tradition of this covenant and created it into a *theologoumenon* of fundamental importance; and so a covenant-theology emerged (col. 900). Two significant developments accompanied this. On the one hand emphasis now became focused on the covenant as that upon which Israel's continuing relationship with Yahweh was dependent, whilst on the other it no longer connoted a relationship in terms of a 'fictitious kinship' but acquired the meaning of a treaty (*Vertrag*) formulated in appropriate legal categories (col. 900).[5] It may be added that according to Fohrer it was also at this late period that divine promises made earlier to David and his dynasty were now likewise reinterpreted in terms of a *bᵉrīt* (col. 899).

Wellhausen, it will be recalled, believed that the notion of a covenant between Yahweh and Israel was a late theological idea. By contrast, the generation which followed the First World War argued that it originated in the earliest period of Israel's history and was a religio-sociological and cultic institution. Scholars such as McCarthy and Weinfeld and Fohrer in their different ways have nevertheless laid emphasis upon the specifically theological reconception of it at a late period in Israel's history. To this limited extent they concur with the view of Wellhausen and some of his contemporaries so far as it emphasized the theological significance of the covenant in this late period. With C. F. Whitley in 1963[6] Wellhausen's view was re-argued and so the course of the argument since Wellhausen began to turn full circle and was completed most notably by Perlitt and Kutsch: not only the Sinai covenant but also the Abrahamic and Davidic covenants are, these scholars argue, late and specifically theological developments.

A further way in which the current phase was prepared for can now also be briefly described. This concerns the meaning of the word *bᵉrīt*. It

---

[5] He allows the possibility of influence from suzerainty treaties, but suggests that a more likely influence on the authors came from political events of the Josianic period.

[6] 'Covenant and Commandment in Israel', *JNES* 22, 1963, pp. 37–48: 'we may doubt if there was any notion of such a covenant before Deuteronomic times' (p. 42).

will be recalled that J. Pedersen, on the analogy of the Arabic word *'ahd*, argued that *bᵉrīt* designates a 'mutual relationship of solidarity with all the rights and obligations which this relationship entailed for the parties involved'. As we have seen, this understanding of the word subsequently became widely accepted and underlies most works since then on covenant in the Old Testament, including those more recent ones concerned with possible parallels between the Old Testament covenant traditions and suzerainty treaties.

A dissenting voice was J. Begrich who in 1944 argued that originally the word designated not a bilateral arrangement between two parties but a relationship created by a stronger party who took to himself a weaker partner and made a commitment to him expressed by means of a solemn act.[7] The one in whose favour the *bᵉrīt* was made was the passive recipient of the commitment undertaken; no reciprocal pledge on his part was involved. Examples of this original meaning of *bᵉrīt* are the covenants between the Israelites and the Gibeonites (Josh. 9), Nahash and the men of Jabesh-gilead (1 Sam. 11), and Ahab and the defeated Benhadad (1 Kgs. 20: 34). It was only at a secondary stage that the word came to designate a relationship involving mutual legal rights between two parties, that is, a treaty or the like. This development took place under the influence of Canaanite legal thinking, with its desire for juridical precision and for achieving 'a just balance between the claims of one man and another'.[8]

According to Begrich, a similar development can be observed with regard to divine covenants. Thus the original sense of the word is implied in the covenant scene described in Exodus 24: 1–2, 9–11: the covenant made here by means of a meal designates Yahweh's election of Israel; there is no hint of obligations being imposed upon Israel. Or again, the covenant in 2 Samuel 23:5 designates Yahweh's solemn guarantee to David and his dynasty, that is, the election of the Davidic dynasty. On the other hand, the later, legal connotation of the word is exemplified in the tradition in Exodus 24: 3–8 and in Joshua 24: 25–7; here Yahweh's grace is made dependent upon conditions imposed upon Israel: *bᵉrīt* in these texts designates a contract or treaty.

---

[7] 'Berit. Ein Beitrag zur Erfassung einer alttestamentlichen Denkform', *ZAW* 60, 1944, pp. 1–11.

[8] p. 5, citing A. Alt, 'Die Ursprünge des israelitischen Rechts', *KS* I, p. 294; E. trs. 'The Origins of Israelite Law', *Essays on Old Testament History and Religion*, p. 96.

A. Jepsen rejected Begrich's view as being overschematized and based upon too narrow a definition of *bᵉrīt*.⁹ The fact is that although in many places those involved in the making of a *bᵉrīt* were not equals, in many others they were. In reality, however, whether the parties were equals or not did not belong to the essence of what making a *bᵉrīt* meant. According to Jepsen to make a *bᵉrīt* was to give a solemn pledge to another, to undertake an obligation towards another. It did not involve imposing an obligation upon another. When two parties mutually made a *bᵉrīt* it consisted in each taking on an obligation towards the other (p. 165). Further, and contrary to the commonly accepted view, to make a *bᵉrīt* was not necessarily to form a relationship; for example, the *bᵉrīt* which Abraham and Abimelech made with each other consisted in their mutual pledge to leave each other alone in peace, nothing more.

In most of the cases in which Yahweh makes a *bᵉrīt*, this too consisted of his making a solemn pledge, undertaking an obligation towards another. This is so in the case of the *bᵉrīt* with Abraham, with Noah, with Levi and Phinehas, and with David. The same meaning is also clear in the announcement of a *bᵉrīt* to Moses in Exodus 34: 10. Matters are different, however, in the case of the covenant with Israel after the exodus. Here it is clear that Israel is thought of as being under obligation to Yahweh, even though it is Yahweh who makes the *bᵉrīt* (Exod. 19: 5; 24: 7,8; 34: 27 f.). According to Jepsen, such a development arose from the very nature of Yahweh's undertaking or promise to Israel, 'I will be your God', for this meant 'I *alone* will be your God' and so placed Israel under an obligation to recognize Yahweh alone as God (pp. 170 ff.). Such an understanding of the Sinai *bᵉrīt* as a promise of Yahweh which nevertheless placed an obligation upon the recipient is already known to Hosea, but how long before his time it developed is impossible to say.

II

This brings us to Kutsch's work *Verheissung und Gesetz*.¹⁰ His understanding of the word owes something to the views of Begrich and Jepsen

⁹ 'Berith. Ein Beitrag zur Theologie der Exilszeit', *Verbannung und Heimkehr. Beiträge zur Geschichte und Theologie Israels im 6. und 5. Jahrhundert v. Chr., Wilhelm Rudolph zum 70. Geburtstag*, ed. A. Kuschke, Tübingen 1961, pp. 161–79.

¹⁰ In addition to his *Verheissung und Gesetz*, see '*bᵉrīt* Verpflichtung', *Theologisches Handwörterbuch zum Alten Testament*, I, ed. E. Jenni and C. Westermann, Munich and

but also differs from them in important respects. For Kutsch *b^erīt* always means 'obligation', 'duty' or the like; it does not designate the making of a relationship. He agrees with both Begrich and Jepsen that in many places it is used of an act of taking an unconditional obligation upon oneself in favour of another. But its meaning was not confined to this; it was also used of imposing an obligation upon another. He finds four uses of the word as follows:

(1) *To take an obligation upon oneself (eine Selbstverpflichtung).* Genesis 15 provides a good example. Here Yahweh takes upon himself an obligation expressed in the pledge to Abraham, 'To your descendants I give this land, from the River of Egypt to the Great River, the river Euphrates' (v. 18). There is no indication of any reciprocal obligation being imposed upon Abraham, and the unilateral nature of the commitment is confirmed by the solemn ritual which accompanies the making of the *b^erīt*. It is a ritual of self-imprecation: by passing between the halves of the slain and divided animals the one making the *b^erīt* invokes the same fate upon himself should he fail to keep the solemn obligation he has undertaken. Were it a 'pact' or 'agreement' (*Bund*) that was being constituted, we should expect both parties to undertake obligations and mutually to participate in this rite of self-imprecation. But that is not the case; Yahweh alone assumes the obligation, and he alone, represented by a 'smoking torch', passes between the pieces of the animal victims. A similar rite is performed by 'the officers of Judah and Jerusalem, the eunuchs and priests and all the people of the land' in Jeremiah 34. Here too *b^erīt* means a solemn pledge, an obligation taken upon oneself, in this instance by those who promise to set free their slaves and who, should they fail to meet this obligation, invoke a curse upon themselves by passing between the pieces of a slain and divided calf (v. 8).

(2) *To impose an obligation upon another (eine Fremdverpflichtung).* Jeremiah 34 provides an example of this also. The obligation to free the slaves is

Zürich 1971, pp. 339–52; 'Gottes Zuspruch und Anspruch. b^erīt in der alttestamentlichen Theologie', *Questions disputées d'Ancien Testament. Méthode et théologie*, Bibliotheca Ephemeridum Theologicarum Lovaniensium 33, Leuven and Gembloux 1974, pp. 71–90; *Neues Testament—Neuer Bund? Eine Fehlübersetzung wird korrigiert*, Neukirchen 1978; 'Bund', *Theol. Realenzyklopädie*, vol. 8, New York and Berlin 1980, pp. 397–410.

imposed upon those involved by the king who, we are told (v. 8), was the one who 'made a *bᵉrīt* with all the people to proclaim an act of freedom for the slaves'. Thus, though it is Zedekiah who makes the *bᵉrīt*, he is not said to have been a party to the obligation undertaken; rather he imposes this obligation upon those named. It is not therefore a matter of a 'pact' between king and people, but of one placing an obligation upon another who 'entered into the *bᵉrīt*' (v. 10).

In this same chapter in Jeremiah Kutsch finds yet another example of *bᵉrīt* with the meaning 'to place an obligation upon another'. Verse 18a refers to those who have 'broken my (Yahweh's) *bᵉrīt*', which Kutsch takes as referring not to the *bᵉrīt* made on this particular occasion but to that made with Israel's ancestors 'on the day I brought them out of Egypt' (cf. vv. 13 f.). Here in vv. 13 f. and in 18a *bᵉrīt* designates the obligation which Yahweh imposed upon the Israelites.

A further example of *bᵉrīt* with this connotation is provided by Ezekiel 17 where the victorious Nebuchadrezzar makes a *bᵉrīt*, that is, imposes an obligation upon his vassal Zedekiah, bringing him 'under an oath'. Once again it is not a matter of a 'pact' or 'agreement'; Nebuchadrezzar himself is not said to have undertaken any obligation or to have been placed under oath. Thus the word here does not designate the relationship between overlord and vassal as such, but the stipulation placed by the former upon the latter.

(3) *The bilateral acceptance of obligations (eine wechselseitige Verpflichtung).* There are a number of examples where *bᵉrīt* designates the mutual acceptance of obligations by two parties. Thus 1 Kings 5: 26 (EVV 5: 12) records that there was peace between Solomon and Hiram 'and they both made a *bᵉrīt*'. That is, both parties were subjects of the *bᵉrīt* and both took on obligations, in this instance a non-aggression pact. Another example is provided by 1 Kings 15. Similarly, in Psalm 83: 6 the enemies of Yahweh and of his people make a pact when they share a mutual obligation to bring about the destruction of Israel. Or again, in 2 Chronicles 23: 16 Jehoiada 'made a *bᵉrīt* between himself and all the people and the king to be the people of Yahweh', that is, undertook a mutual obligation to do so.[11] It was this use of the term for the mutual acceptance of an obligation

---

[11] On the parallel passage in 2 Kings 11 see below under section (4).

by two or more parties which led to its understanding as 'alliance' or 'treaty'.

(4) *An obligation imposed by a third party (Verpflichtung durch einen Dritten).* An example of this from outside the Old Testament is contained in a text from Mari, a letter sent by one Ibal-ila to the king Zimrilim concerning various matters including affairs between the Hana people and the people of Idamaraz.[12] The relevant passage reads:

> For 'ass-slaying' between the Hana people and Idamaraz one brought a young animal and lettuce; I feared my lord and permitted no young animal or lettuce. An ass, offspring of a she-ass I myself caused to be killed; an agreement between the Hana people and Idamaraz I brought about.

By killing a donkey as a ritual of imprecation Ibal-ila made an agreement between the two peoples in question. The word here translated 'agreement' is *salīmum* = Heb. *šālōm*, so that the Accadian phrase in this letter 'I made *salīmam* between A and B' = Heb. *ʿāśāh šālōm bēn . . . ūbēn . . .* In some Old Testament texts the phrase 'to make peace with' is associated with 'to make a *bᵉrīt*' (cf. Josh. 9: 15; 1 Kgs. 5: 26). No equivalent phrase 'to make a *bᵉrīt*' is represented in the Mari text, but it nevertheless provides an analogy for understanding 'to make a *bᵉrīt*' in the sense of a third party effecting an obligation upon two other parties mutually, in this instance, a non-aggression pact.

Kutsch finds *bᵉrīt* used in this way also in Hosea 2: 20 (EVV 2: 18) where Yahweh declares: 'In that day I will make for them (the Israelites) a *bᵉrīt* with the wild beasts, the birds of the air, and creatures which creep on the earth, and I will break bow and sword and weapon of war out of the land, and will make them rest in security.' The *bᵉrīt* here is an obligation imposed upon these creatures in favour of the Israelites whom they will do no more harm. It is not an agreement made between these creatures and the Israelites mutually. Though the substance is the same, *bᵉrīt* in Ezekiel 34: 25 connotes not an obligation placed by Yahweh upon the wild beasts, but is one undertaken by Yahweh himself to rid the land of

---

[12] For this and the quotation below see M. Noth, 'Old Testament Covenant-making in the light of a Text from Mari', *The Laws in the Pentateuch and other Studies*, pp. 108–17 (for the quotation pp. 108 f.); E. trs. from 'Das alttestamentliche Bundschliessen im Licht eines Mari-textes', *Gesammelte Studien zum Alten Testament*, second edition, pp. 142–54 (esp. p. 143).

such beasts (cf. Lev. 26: 6). That is, *berīt* in this text has the same connotation as in (1) above. Different again in this connection is the *berīt* with
'the stones of the field' and 'the wild beasts' in Job 5: 23 where it designates
the obligation placed by man upon these not to harm him. That is, *berīt* is
used here in the sense given in (2) above.

The use of *berīt* in the sense of a third person imposing an obligation
upon one party in favour of another is attested, according to Kutsch, in 2
Kings 11 where, differently from the parallel passage in 2 Chronicles 23
(see above under (3)), Jehoiada makes a *berīt* between Yahweh and the
king and people in which, as the context indicates, it is a matter of
imposing an obligation upon the king and the people 'to be Yahweh's
people'. Once again, it is not a matter of making a pact or agreement
between Yahweh and those mentioned.

Kutsch seeks to substantiate his view that *berīt* means basically
'obligation' with various other observations:[13] for example, (*a*) that in a
number of texts 'to make a *berīt*' is paralleled by 'to swear an oath' or 'to
make someone swear an oath' (cf. Josh. 9: 15; 2 Kgs. 11: 4; Ezek. 16: 8; Ps.
89: 4; Ezra 10: 5; etc.); and (*b*) that in a number of texts *berīt* is paralleled by
'oath' (Ps. 105: 8–11 ― 1 Chron. 16: 15–18; in Deut. 4: 31; 7: 12; 8: 18 *berīt* is
used like the word *šebūʿāh* 'oath' in such texts as Gen. 26: 3; Num. 30: 3;
Deut. 7: 8; Josh. 9: 20); (*c*) that in some texts it is paralleled by such words
as *tōrāh* 'instruction' (Hos. 8: 1, Ps. 78: 10), *ḥuqqīm, ḥuqqōt* 'statutes' (2 Kgs.
17: 15; Ps. 50: 16; cf. Isa. 24: 5), *ʿēdōt* 'ordinances' (2 Kgs. 17: 15; Pss. 25: 10;
132: 12), *piqqūdīm* 'precepts' (Ps. 103: 18), *ʾimrāh* 'word (of Yahweh)' in the
sense of 'command' (Deut. 33: 9); (*d*) that 'to make a *berīt*' can mean to take
a 'curse' (*ʾālāh*) upon oneself in the event of failure to honour a *berīt* (Gen.
26: 28; Deut. 29: 11, 13; Ezek. 16: 59; 17: 18 f.).

According to Kutsch, the prepositions employed with the phrase 'to
make a *berīt*' to some extent reflect the different connotations of the word.
Thus, *kārat berīt le* 'to make a *berīt* to/for someone' in the majority of
instances is used for taking an obligation upon oneself in favour of
another, whilst, on the other hand, when used with *ʿim* 'with' in most
instances it connotes imposing an obligation upon another. Evidently,
however, the preposition *ʾēt* can replace either of these. With regard to
the familiar expression 'to make a *berīt* between (*bēn*) A and between (*bēn*)
B', it can designate a mutual obligation, and so an 'agreement' (*Bund*), but

---

[13] *Verheissung und Gesetz*, pp. 18–26.

in some cases it is also used when an obligation is being undertaken uni-laterally or imposed upon another.

From this contextual investigation of the meaning of *bᵉrīt* Kutsch turns to a discussion of the etymology of the word and then discusses the question of the meaning of the word *kārat* in the familiar phrase *kārat bᵉrīt*. At this point it will be convenient to mention various views on these and related issues and to make some observations on them.

III

(1) *The etymology of bᵉrīt*. As far as I am aware, the following are the main views which have been advanced on this subject:

(*a*) That it derives from the root *bārāh* I 'eat', from which comes the nouns *biryāh, bārūt* 'food'. Morphologically a substantive *bᵉrīt* from this root can be posited on the analogy of *šᵉbīth* from *šābāh* and other similar formations. Thus derived, *bᵉrīt* would have had the semantic develop-ment 'food (eaten by those making a covenant)' > 'covenant', the word acquiring metonymously the meaning of the effect achieved by the action performed (the eating of a common meal). Needless to say, such a deriva-tion has been seen as support for understanding *bᵉrīt* as 'agreement', *Bund* in German, *alliance* in French. That covenants were made by eating a common meal which effected fellowship between those involved (cf. for example, Gen. 26: 28–30) is seen as further support for such a derivation. Amongst recent scholars, this etymology is favoured by, for example, L. Köhler and F. Auer.[14]

(*b*) That it derives from a homonym of this root, *bārāh* II 'to see', 'to look at' > 'to look at with favour', hence 'to choose' > 'to decide', and so to a substantive *bᵉrīt* (the morphology being the same as in (*a*) above) 'decision', 'ordinance', 'decree', 'obligation'. This is the derivation favoured by Kutsch,[15] though it was proposed already by some

[14] L. Köhler, 'Problems in the Study of the Language of the Old Testament', *JSS* 1, 1956, pp. 3–24 (esp. pp. 3–7); F. Auer, 'Das Alte Testament in der Sicht des Bundesgedankens', *Lex tua veritas, Festschrift für H. J. Junker*, ed. H. Gross and F. Mussner, Trier 1961, pp. 1–15 (esp. pp. 3 f.).

[15] *Verheissung und Gesetz*, ch. 2. Cf. L. Wächter, 'Die Übertragung der Beritvorstellung auf Jahwe', *TLZ* 99, 1974, cols. 801–16, and (tentatively) M. Görg, 'Etymologisch-semantische Perspektiven zu *bᵉrīt*', *Bausteine biblischer Theologie. Festgabe für G. J. Botterweck*, BBB 50, ed. H.-J. Fabry, Cologne—Bonn, 1977, pp. 25–36.

nineteenth-century scholars. Kutsch finds the root in question behind the word *bᵉrū* in 1 Samuel 17: 8 where the Philistines ask the Israelites to send out a warrior to do combat with Goliath. The LXX here reads ʼεκλε ξασθε 'choose' and on this basis most commentators have suggested emending the obscure *bᵉrū* to *baḥᵉrū* from *bāḥar* 'to choose'. Kutsch, however, supports the Massoretic reading on the grounds that the existence of a Hebrew word *bārāh* 'to see' is supported by the existence of the cognate Accadian *barū* 'to see'. In 1 Samuel 17: 8 the word would have the sense 'choose' (cf. the similar semantic extension of *rāʼāh* 'to see' to 'to choose, acquire' in Genesis 22: 8). The development to the meaning 'decide', 'determine' with a substantive *bᵉrīt* meaning 'that which is decided', hence 'decree', 'obligation', would be the same as for *ḥōzeh/ḥāzūt* in Isaiah 28: 15, 18 where these two words are synonyms for *bᵉrīt* and, according to Kutsch, derive from *ḥāzāh* 'to see' by a semantic development such as that suggested for *bārāh* II 'to see' above.

(*c*) That the word derives from an Accadian word *birtu* 'clasp, fetter'. Thus understood, *bᵉrīt* designates the 'binding together' of two or more parties, hence 'binding agreement', *Bund*, and the like. This too was suggested by some nineteenth-century scholars, for example R. Kraetzschmar.[16] Amongst recent scholars it is accepted by, for example, Weinfeld and O. Loretz.[17]

(*d*) That it derives from the preposition *birīt* 'between' in Accadian. This suggestion was made by Noth on the basis of the letter from Mari referred to above where, it will be recalled, Ibal-ila records that he brought about 'an agreement *between* (*birīt*) the Hana people and Idamaraz'.[18] As a substantive derived from this proposition, *bᵉrīt* would thus have meant originally 'a between', 'a mediation' whence it became the usual word for 'agreement', *Bund, alliance*, etc. (See below under 2(*c*).)

---

[16] *Die Bundesvorstellung im Alten Testament*, pp. 244 ff.
[17] O. Loretz, 'bᵉrīt "Band-Bund"', *VT* 16, 1966, pp. 239–41; M. Weinfeld, 'Bᵉrît—Covenant vs. Obligation' (a review of Kutsch's *Verheissung und Gesetz*), *Biblica*, 56, 1975, pp. 120–8, and 'bᵉrîth', *Theologisches Wörterbuch zum Alten Testament*, vol. I, ed. G. J. Botterweck and H. Ringgren, Stuttgart, Berlin, Cologne, Mainz 1973, cols. 781–808 (esp. 783 f.), E. trs. *Theological Dictionary of the Old Testament*, vol. II, Grand Rapids 1975, pp. 253–79 (esp. p. 255).
[18] In the article cited in note 12 above.

(*e*) To these a novel suggestion recently advanced by G. Gerleman must now be added.[19] He argues that the Hebrew words *bar, bārāh, bārar, bᵉrīt*, which are or begin with a morpheme constructed from the consonants *br*, are noun and verb formations from an original biconsonantal stem *br* which provided a core-meaning 'to separate'. He draws attention to many similarly formed lexemes in Syriac which proceed semantically from this same core-notion, and then argues that the four Hebrew words in question are similarly motivated. Thus, the homonyms usually proposed for *bar*: 1. 'son'; 2. 'corn'; 3. 'pure'; 4. 'open field', and for *bārāh*: 1. 'to choose'; 2. 'to eat', as well as for *bārar*: 1. 'to eliminate'; 2. 'to sharpen', are in reality not homonyms but semantic expansions of this original core-notion. For example, *bar* = 'corn' as a collection of *separate* grains (or grain as *separated* from the straw and chaff?), *bar* = 'pure' as that which has been *set apart*, kept untainted from other things, *bar* = 'open field' as distinct from inhabited territory, whilst *bar* in Proverbs 31: 2 and Psalm 2: 12, where it is usually translated 'son', is not this but, in the case of the former, refers to that which '*distinguishes* or *sets apart*' Lemuel as king from others, and in the case of the latter is also '*separateness* (from others)' in the sense of being 'blameless, innocent' (p. 27). Or again, *bārāh* = 'to choose', that is, 'to *separate* or *select* something from amongst others', and 'to eat', that is, 'select food to eat'. Similarly, *bārar* = 'purge out, drive out', as indicated by, for example, Ezekiel 20: 38, whilst in Isaiah 49: 2 (cf. Jer. 51: 11), it is used not for a 'sharpened' arrow but for an arrow 'specially chosen', as the LXX βέλος ἐκλεκτόν indicates.

According to Gerleman, *bᵉrīt* developed from this same core-notion. To make a *bᵉrīt* is to give someone a *Besonderheit*, 'something special', that is, 'a special privilege, advantage, benefit'. Thus when God makes a *bᵉrīt* in favour of David, he grants David and his dynasty a special privilege or benefit. Or again, in Jeremiah 32: 40 Yahweh's 'eternal *bᵉrīt*' is the imparting to Israel of the special benefit that he will never again turn away from them. In still other texts Yahweh's *bᵉrīt* with Israel is the imparting to them of his special law, for example the decalogue. By extension, the recipient of a *bᵉrīt* as something specially imparted to him acquires a special status in the eyes of the one who makes the *bᵉrīt*.

---

[19] 'Die "Besonderheit". Untersuchung zu *bᵉrīt* im Alten Testament', *Studien zur alttestamentlichen Theologie*, Heidelberg 1980, pp. 24–37.

(2) *kārat bᵉrīt*. Just as controversial as the word *bᵉrīt* itself has been the discussion of the derivation and original connotation of this phrase which occurs about eighty times in the Old Testament. Once again, as far as I am aware the main suggestions have been as follows:

(*a*) Widely favoured is the view that *kārat bᵉrīt* originally described the rite performed for the establishing of a covenant. Here reference is made particularly to the ritual described in Genesis 15 and Jeremiah 34: animals are slain and divided in pieces, the party (or parties) making the *bᵉrīt* solemnly passes between these pieces and thus, it is usually suggested, takes an oath of self-imprecation that the same fate of these victims would befall one who abrogates the *bᵉrīt* now being made. An alternative suggestion is that *kārat* refers to 'the cutting up and distribution of the flesh of the victims for eating in the sacrifice of the covenants'.[20] The 'cutting' is thus seen as having originally referred to the victims slain and divided for the purpose of establishing a covenant, so that *kārat bᵉrīt* could be understood as an ellipsis for 'to cut (animals for the purpose of making) a *bᵉrīt*'; that is, *bᵉrīt* is not the object proper of *kārat*, which would have been the animals slain, but the result achieved by means of the rite. Associated with this is yet another suggestion—to mention a further proposed derivation of *bᵉrīt* itself—that *bᵉrīt* derives from a root *bārāh* 'to cut' (an Arabic cognate with the same meaning is cited in support of this), so that *kārat bᵉrīt* meant originally 'to cut a cutting'. Finally, where *bᵉrīt* has been derived from *bārāh* 'to eat', *kārat bᵉrīt* has been understood to have meant originally 'to cut up food (for the purpose of making a covenant)'.[21]

(*b*) Rejecting suggestions such as these, Kutsch has argued that *kārat* in addition to having the meaning 'to cut' can also mean 'to decree' (*bestimmen, festsetzen*), and cites in support *gāzar* 'to cut' > 'to decree' (cf. Job 22: 28), and especially the Aramaic *gzr* which is well attested with the same meaning.[22] In this connection he draws attention to the Aramaic phrase *gzr ᶜdn* in a treaty text from Sefire which he understands to mean 'to establish an ordinance'. The Hebrew phrase *kārat bᵉrīt* is the direct equivalent of this phrase and its meaning is the same. Understood in this

---

[20] So BDB, p. 503, col. B.
[21] Cf. for example, Köhler, pp. 6 ff.
[22] *Verheissung und Gesetz*, ch. 3; cf. Weinfeld, *Theologisches Wörterbuch zum Alten Testament*, I, col. 787; E. trs. p. 259.

way, Kutsch sees this phrase as bearing out his proposed understanding of *bᵉrīt* as 'obligation', 'duty', and the like.

(*c*) According to Noth, the Mari text already referred to provides the key to understanding the original of *kārat bᵉrīt*.[23] It is possible, he suggests, that the Accadian preposition *birīt* acquired an adverbial sense so that we may suppose the existence of a formulation like *ḥayaram ḳatālum birīt* 'to slay an ass in between'. Then the word *birīt* would have taken on substantival meaning in the sense 'a between', 'a mediation', so that it would have become necessary to introduce the parties to the covenant by means of a separate preposition. The result in Hebrew would have been *kārat bᵉrīt bēn . . . ūbēn*. We may add, with further reference to 1(*d*) above, that Noth believes that the word *bᵉrīt* itself had its origin in this very expression *kārat bᵉrīt*.

(*d*) Finally, there is the view of Gerleman. From what has been said of his understanding of *bᵉrīt* itself as 'something specially set apart' and hence 'special privilege, benefit', it is not difficult to see that for him the verb *kārat* 'to cut off' when used with this word poses no problem. As something which is separated as special, *bᵉrīt* forms a natural object of this verb 'to cut off'. It may even be, he suggests, that *kārat bᵉrīt lᵉ* 'to cut off a *bᵉrīt* for someone' originally described the visible handing over of something, for example a share of 'booty' or part of an inheritance, as a 'special benefit' (i.e. a *bᵉrīt*). From this the phrase *kārat bᵉrīt* became conventionalized to mean 'to grant someone an advantage, a privilege' (*jemandem einen Vorzug, ein Privileg gewähren*).

(3) *Synonyms for bᵉrīt.* Identification of these has depended upon the particular semantic range posited for *bᵉrīt* itself. Thus, understanding it either as an obligation taken upon oneself or imposed upon another, Kutsch, as we noted earlier, finds parallels to it in such terms as *šᵉbū'ah, tōrāh, ḥuqqīm/ḥuqqōt, piqqūdīm, 'imrāh, 'ēdōt, 'ālāh.* Weinfeld, on the other hand, whilst agreeing with Kutsch that *bᵉrīt* is basically 'obligation, liability', argues that since 'any settlement between two parties is conditioned by good will or some kind of mutual understanding which enables the conclusion of an agreement',[24] various words designating such

---

[23] Op. cit., pp. 147 f.; E. trs. pp. 112 f.
[24] *Theologisches Wörterbuch zum Alten Testament*, I, col. 785; E. trs. p. 257.

friendship and mutual understanding must also be included as synonyms of *bᵉrīt*. Accordingly, in addition to the various synonyms proposed by Kutsch, he includes words such as *ḥesed* 'steadfast love', *ṭōbāh/ṭōbōth* 'good', *šālōm* 'peace', *'aḥᵃwāh* 'brotherhood'.

IV

J. Barr has made a number of important observations about suggestions such as these, and has also drawn attention to striking features of *bᵉrīt* from a semantic point of view.[25]

With regard to the etymology of the word, he pertinently points out that two questions have to be distinguished here: (*a*) whether this or that etymology is correct as a matter of the prehistory of the word, and (*b*) whether, whichever one may be regarded as correct, it has any real value for understanding the semantic function of the word as employed by speakers and writers in ancient Israel.

Just how doubtful it is that the etymology of the word is of any help for understanding its semantic function can be seen from two directions. First, the variety of views listed above itself indicates how unreliable the choice of an etymology is. In fact, none of them is without difficulty. Thus, the view that the word originally meant 'food' suffers from the difficulty that *bārāh* 'to eat', *biryāh, barūt* 'food' appear to have been restricted to food eaten by the sick or by those who lament or mourn (2 Sam. 3: 5, 7, 10, 35; 12: 17; 13: 5, 6, 10; Ps. 69: 22; Lam. 4: 10); *bᵉrīt* shows no link with such an associative field. Or again, as Barr points out, the derivation from *bārāh* 'to see', 'to decide' is perilously founded upon the textually uncertain text 1 Samuel 17: 8,[26] depends for identification upon the

---

[25] 'Some Semantic Notes on the Covenant', *Beiträge zur Alttestamentlichen Theologie, Festschrift für Walther Zimmerli zum 70. Geburtstag*, ed. H. Donner, R. Hanhart, R. Smend, Göttingen 1977, pp. 23–38.

[26] The LXX renders all sorts of words containing *br* with 'choose, choice', the source of such a notion possibly being the late sense 'choose, select' of the verb *brr* in Chronicles (cf. BDB. p. 141, col. A. See Barr, 'The Typology of Literalism in Ancient Biblical Translations', *Nachrichten der Akademie der Wissenschaften in Göttingen. I. Philologisch-Historische Klasse*, Nr. 11, 1979, pp. 279–325 (cf. esp. p. 321)). In view of this it might be argued that the LXX translator of 1 Samuel 17: 8 had the same consonantal text in front of him as the MT. But (*a*) this does not necessarily mean that the MT reading is therefore correct; the Hebrew text may have been copied incorrectly before the time of the translator; and (*b*) the very fact that the LXX renders all sorts of *br*-words with 'choose, choice'

cognate Accadian *barū*, and has doubtful support from *ḥozeh/ḥozūt* for which an alternative root to *ḥāzāh* 'to see' has been proposed.[27] Two difficulties stand in the way of deriving it from the Accadian *birtu* 'clasp, fetter': first, that, again as Barr points out, the semantic associations of this word in Accadian seem to be generally unfavourable; 'it is used very largely for the tying up of kings in fetters of bronze and the like, and there is a long step from this to the Hebrew *bᵉrīt*, which has almost entirely favourable semantic associations' (p. 35). Second, that its collocation with *kārat* would be difficult to explain; there are limits, as Barr comments, 'to the extent to which idiom can suppress the literal sense of terms, and semantically it is not easy to accept that "to cut a clasp or fetter" could easily become a normal expression meaning "to make a clasp or fetter"' (p. 34). The alternative Accadian derivation—from *birīt* 'between'—though not to be ruled out as impossible,[28] is not without difficulties. Noth, as mentioned above, suggested the possibility that this preposition generated a substantive 'a between', 'a mediation'. What is attested as related to it is a noun *birītu* meaning any piece of land or area between anything else, in-between terrain, alley (between houses) balk (between fields and gardens), terrain surrounded by water, peninsula, island, spur of land; territory or property held in common by neighbours (as for example, a party wall of a house, or a border ditch).[29] But it is not employed in the sense of 'agreement', 'contract' or the like, as in Hebrew, nor does it occur in collocation with any verb meaning literally 'to cut', as in the Hebrew idiom *kārat bᵉrīt*. Semantically, it seems well removed from the associations of the Hebrew

means that we cannot be sure that the Hebrew *bᵉrū* has the sense 'choose'. In view of the extreme rarity and obscurity of this word, its unexampled locution, and the fact that 'choosing' in the imperative is normally done with *bāḥar*, it remains the case that the MT may be in error here.

[27] 'Some Semantic Notes on the Covenant', pp. 24 F. For the alternative derivation of *ḥozeh/ḥāzūt* see G. R. Driver, 'Studies in the Vocabulary of the Old Testament. VI', *JTS* 34, 1933, p. 381; 'Linguistic and Textual Problems: Isaiah i–xxxix', *JTS* 38, 1937, p. 44; 'Problems in Job and Psalms Reconsidered', *JTS* 40, 1939, p. 391; '"Another Little Drink"—Isaiah 28: 1–22', *Words and Meanings, Essays Presented to David Winton Thomas*, ed. P. R. Ackroyd and B. Lindars, Cambridge 1968, p. 58.

[28] That such a derivation does not (contrary to Weinfeld's view) involve a tautology with the Hebrew *bēn* 'between' is pointed out by Barr, p. 34.

[29] Cf. *The Assyrian Dictionary of the Oriental Institute of the University of Chicago*, B vol. II, Chicago 1965, pp. 252 ff. (The word *birtu* 'clasp, fetter' is here also related to *birīt* 'between'.)

*b*ᵉ*rīt*, and neither as a preposition nor as a noun with such a meaning did it evidently find its way into Hebrew where it might lend any transparency to *b*ᵉ*rīt*. If either should be judged the etymon of the latter word, it surely belongs to the remote pre-history of this word (on this see further below).

Gerleman's hypothesis of the monogenesis of lexemes with such dissimilar semantic functions as *bar, bārāh, bārar, b*ᵉ*rīt*, each of which has then to be regarded as polysemous, is at best hypothetical. The alleged basic association or semantic link he finds between them—the core-notion of 'separateness'—is surely rather tenuous and is arrived at only by something of a *tour de force*. There is clearly a wide semantic disparity between, for example, *bar* 'pure, clean' and *bar* 'open field, open countryside', or between *bārāh* 'to see' (if such a verb existed in Hebrew) and *bārāh* 'to eat', and it remains more likely that such lexemes are homonyms (different words with the same form) rather than polysemes (single lexemes with different meanings).

The fundamental difficulty with Gerleman's hypothesis—this brings us by a slightly different route to the main observation made by Barr in this connection—is that, although the suggestion that a (presumably proto-Semitic) biconsonantal root *br* ultimately lies behind such lexemes as *bar, bārāh, bārar, b*ᵉ*rīt* is not in itself impossible, it would tell us something only of the prehistory of these lexemes and would therefore not be a reliable guide to their semantic function and range in Hebrew as it was spoken and written in biblical times. The fact is that words can and do lose their motivation, open up a wide gulf from their root and from other words with the same root, and become opaque. Hence the identification of a core-notion behind these lexemes, even if correct, is no more likely to provide effective information about their semantic function in Hebrew than, say, the identification of *templum* as the etymon of 'contemplate' sheds any useful light upon the semantic function of this word in English or relates it with the associative field of 'temple' which derives from the same etymon. All the evidence suggests that for those who used it *b*ᵉ*rīt* was an opaque word; there is no evidence for the inherently improbable opinion that any one in Israel would have drawn the remotest connection between it and, say, *bar* 'open field', so that the latter would have given some transparency to the former (or *vice versa*). It is also unlikely, as Barr points out, that such transparency would have been gained from *bārāh* 'to see' or *bārāh* 'to eat', *biryāh/bārūt* 'food', one of which is textually uncertain and all of which are rare and semantically remote from the known functions of *bᵉrīt* and its associative field in the language. The same would be the case if it were decided that *bᵉrīt* derived from an Accadian *birtu* 'clasp, fetter' or *birīt* 'between', neither of which appears to have found its way into Biblical Hebrew whence it could have provided a semantic link with and thus transparency for *bᵉrīt* in the mind of those who used the word. Like Gerleman's proposed core-notion or etymon *br*, such an Accadian origin would have belonged to the prehistory of *bᵉrīt* and would shed scant light on the functional semantics of the word in Biblical Hebrew.

In short, it seems that *bᵉrīt* was a thoroughly opaque word, a *brutum factum* of the language, as Barr aptly puts it, and, as he later adds, from 'the point of view of semantic analysis, we might do better if we supposed that *bᵉrīt* is a primitive Hebrew noun, no more "derived" from anything else than is *ʾāb* "father", and that it had never had any other meanings than those which we find in the Old Testament' (p. 35).

With regard to the phrase *kārat bᵉrīt*, the literal value of *kārat* is stated in Jeremiah 34: 18. But, as Barr points out, what is striking is that this occurs only here. Even Genesis 15, which likewise describes the cutting and dividing of animals, makes no play of the literal sense of this verb. Thus, whatever the original sense of this verb in its collocation with *bᵉrīt*, this phrase became conventionalized, so that its normal semantic value is best represented simply by 'to make a *bᵉrīt*'. The opacity of *bᵉrīt* itself is not effectively rendered less so by its collocation with *kārat* which itself appears to have been understood almost exclusively as idiomatic in this phrase. The fact that this verb could be replaced by *hēqīm* 'establish', *nātan* 'grant', *ṣiwwāh* 'command', reinforces the idiomatic usage of *kārat bᵉrīt* for which they offer a more straightforward expression.

On the semantic range of *bᵉrīt* Barr makes some further important observations. First, the word does service for a wide area which in English is covered by such terms as 'agreement', 'treaty', 'contract', 'promise', 'obligation': 'provided that the incident is to be described with some real solemnity and with powerful religious sanctions, it seems that all of these may come under *bᵉrīt*, and indeed perhaps they must, for there seems to be no other bordering and distinguishing term under which they might fall, if a specific terminological distinction is to be made' (p. 31). Secondly, *bᵉrīt* does not appear to have had any synonyms properly speaking. The only exceptions are the rare *ḥozeh* and *ḥāzūth* (Isa. 28: 15, 18) and *ᵃmānāh* (Neh. 10: 1; 11: 23). But contrary to the opinion of, for example, Weinfeld, terms like *šᵉbū ͨāh*, *ͨālāh*, *tōrāh*, *ḥesed*, etc. are not synonymous with *bᵉrīt*, but are best described as belonging to its associative field. The fact that sometimes terms like *tōrāh* and *ᵓālāh* are found in parallelism with *bᵉrīt* shows only some kind of compatibility between them and it, not that they are synonyms. The correct test of synonymity, that is, consistent and reversible replaceability of one word by another, indicates this. For example, *tōrāh* can in some contexts replace *bᵉrīt*, but certainly not in others: that David and Jonathan made a *bᵉrīt* cannot be restated as 'David and Jonathan made a *tōrāh*'. And similarly, there are many places where *tōrāh* cannot be replaced by *bᵉrīt*. Nor is the value of *bᵉrīt* covered by terms like *ᵓālāh* or *šᵉbū ͨah*. It seems that the making of a *bᵉrīt* involved the taking of an oath. But the process cannot be reversed, so that the mere taking of an oath constitutes the making of a *bᵉrīt* (cf. Barr, p. 32).

Just as *bᵉrīt* itself does not appear to delineate between the various distinctions indicated by English terms such as 'agreement', 'treaty', 'contract', etc., so also its collocation with *kārat, hēqīm*, etc. appears not to demarcate one kind of *bᵉrīt* from another. The phrase *kārat bᵉrīt*, for example, is used whether the *bᵉrīt* is between equals or between superior and inferior or between God and man. Further, this phrase is used whether *bᵉrīt* designates an obligation taken upon oneself or imposed upon another or assumed by two parties mutually. As for the particular prepositions employed (*ͨim, ᵓet, lᵉ, bēn … bēn*), none is used with sufficient consistency to warrant a correlation between it and one kind of *bᵉrīt*.[30]

But though, as these considerations indicate, *bᵉrīt* does service for what in English requires a number of different terms, it seems, again as Barr points out, to be rather restricted in the sort of contexts in which it is used. He classifies these as follows (p. 33): (i) the making, keeping, breaking, leaving, remembering and forgetting of a *bᵉrīt*; (ii) the material or visible signs, vehicles, or embodiments of the *bᵉrīt*: the ark, the book, the tables, the blood; (iii) the duration of a *bᵉrīt*: it appears that a *bᵉrīt* was made 'forever'; there are no examples in the Old Testament of a *bᵉrīt* being made for a limited period only.

---

[30] See Barr, p. 33. Cf. J. Scharbert, '"bᵉrît" im Pentateuch', *De la Tôrah au Messie* (Studies in honour of Henri Cazelles), ed. M. Carrez, J. Doré, P. Grelot, Paris, 1981, p. 164.

V

In the light of these various observations some further comments are in order concerning Kutsch's work, which is the most thorough study of *bᵉrīt* since Kraetzschmar's monograph some ninety years ago. Kutsch correctly seeks to determine the meaning of the word from its various contexts in the Old Testament. In doing so, however, he is guided by a desire to find a common denominator of the different uses of the term, and his conclusion, as we have seen, is that this common denominator is 'obligation'; this he finds to be the 'basic meaning' (*Grundbedeutung*) of *bᵉrīt*, and from this he is then able to move on to identify other terms such as *šᵉbūᶜāh, tōrāh, ḥuqqīm/ḥuqqōt*, etc. as its parallels. But the discovery of such a common denominator shows only that it was simply that: one particular feature that was of the essence of making a *bᵉrīt*, and it is a mistake to proceed from this, as Kutsch does, to the conclusion that *bᵉrīt* can then be represented simply by 'obligation', as though a *bᵉrīt* consisted simply of this and this exhausted the semantic content of *bᵉrīt*. The fact that the word itself, as we have seen, refrains from mapping out the various distinctions which Kutsch draws between one kind of *bᵉrīt* and another, that it has no synonyms (with the rare exceptions mentioned above), that it is restricted in the sort of contexts in which it is used, militates strongly against the oversimplified and somewhat bald reduction of it which Kutsch's view proposes when he insists that it always and only means 'obligation'.[31]

For these reasons also it is difficult to accept Kutsch's suggestion, if I understand him correctly, that the use of *bᵉrīt* in contexts where it is a matter of a bilateral arrangement is a secondary usage of its 'basic meaning' which, it seems, he believes to have been originally limited to the unilateral acceptance or imposition of an obligation.[32] It is partly if not largely on these grounds that he excludes the element of 'relationship' which is usually associated with the word.[33] Once again, however, it has

---

[31] See the comment by Barr, p. 37.

[32] *Verheissung und Gesetz*, p. 12 note 65, pp. 92, 174, 203–5.

[33] Against Kutsch on this, see, for example, W. Eichrodt, 'Darf man heute noch von einem Gottesbund mit Israel reden?' *TZ* 30, 1974, pp. 193–206; H. Lubsczyk, 'Der Bund als Gemeinschaft mit Gott. Erwägungen zur Diskussion über den Begriff "bᵉrit" im Alten Testament', *Dienst der Vermittlung*, Erfurter Theologisches Studien 37, Leipzig 1977, pp. 61–96; J. Scharbert, op. cit. P. Kalluveettil, *Declaration and Covenant*, Rome 1982, from

to be said that the word itself does not delineate the distinction which Kutsch makes between a unilateral *bᵉrīt* and a bilateral *bᵉrīt*. It is the context alone which determines this, and if, with Kutsch, we are to ascertain the semantic range of *bᵉrīt* not from its etymon, whatever that may be, but from its usage, then it is difficult to see how, as it seems, he can regard the bilateral connotation of the word as a secondary or exceptional use of it. Rather, the conclusion to be drawn is surely that the semantic content of the word was such that it could be used indifferently for unilateral and bilateral arrangements. Its well-attested association not only with words like *tōrāh, šᵉbū ʿāh*, etc. but also with terms like *šālōm, ḥesed*, etc. offers further evidence of this. It seems that in this respect Kutsch has not adhered sufficiently strictly to his own avowed procedure of determining the meaning of *bᵉrīt* from its contexts and has allowed a definition of what it means, arrived at from some of its usages in the Old Testament, to govern what he finds it to mean in other, different contexts. The reality appears to be that paradigmatically *bᵉrīt* covers a wider area than any of the individual terms which Kutsch, Weinfeld and others regard as its parallels or synonyms (*tōrāh, šᵉbū ʿāh, ḥōq, ḥesed*, etc.) and cannot simply be reduced to any one of them.

Just how the word should be represented in, say, English will of course depend upon its context, which will usually provide sufficient informa-tion to enable a choice to be made between such convenient indicators as 'treaty', 'pact', 'agreement', 'solemn promise', 'obligation', etc. But what of the familiar term 'covenant', especially when used of God's *bᵉrīt* with Israel, with Abraham, etc.? I do not know how this word is used in other English-speaking countries today, but in the United Kingdom itself it is most widely employed in the context of pledging a certain amount of money to a charity. Used in this sense, that is, as a solemnly binding pledge, presumably it would be acceptable in those contexts where *bᵉrīt* has to do with such a binding pledge or promise. Currently it is also used within the ecumenical movement in the case of different denominations attempting to agree on matters which will enable them to bring about some sort of unity. Used in this sense 'covenant' has the meaning of 'agreement' upon which a new relationship can be founded. Given such

an extensive investigation of secular covenants in the Old Testament also argues that covenant conveys a primary idea of relationship. Unfortunately Kalluveettil's book came into my possession too late for consideration here.

current usages of the word, it may be retained among the range of words which may be used for translating *bᵉrīt*.

VI

On the basis of his investigation of the meaning *bᵉrīt*, Kutsch argues that it is nowhere employed in the sense of an agreement (*Bund*) between Yahweh and Israel, Yahweh and Abraham, etc., but only of either (*a*) Yahweh's self-obligation, that is, his promise to another, or (*b*) an obligation imposed by Yahweh upon another.

Kutsch finds its use in the former of these two senses to connote Yahweh's solemn promise in the *bᵉrīt* with Noah (Gen. 9: 8–17), with Abraham (Gen. 15: 18; 17: 2, 4, 7–8, 19, 21), and with all three ancestors (Exod. 2: 24; 6: 4–5; Lev. 26: 42, 45; Deut. 4: 31; 7: 12; 8: 18; Ps. 105: 8, 10; Neh. 9: 8), with David (2 Sam. 23: 1–7; Jer. 33: 21; Ps. 89; Isa. 55: 3; 2 Chron. 13: 5; 21: 7), and with the priesthood (Num. 18: 19; 25: 12 f.; Jer. 33: 21; Mal. 2: 4 f., 8). It has the same meaning in many other texts (e.g. Gen. 6: 18; Lev. 26: 9, 44 f.; Deut.7: 9; 1 Kgs. 8: 23; Jer. 14: 21; Ezek. 16: 8; Pss. 78: 37; 106: 45; 111: 5, 9; Dan. 9: 4; Neh. 1: 5; 9: 32). But none of these texts, he argues, is early; even Genesis 15 is no earlier than the late seventh century BC (he suggests that its background is the period 625–609); Psalm 89 also derives from the late monarchical period, whilst 2 Samuel 23: 1–7 ('The last words of David'), he argues, is from the mid-sixth century.

As used of an obligation imposed by God upon Israel—and therefore of his law, whether the law in general or a specific law—he again finds it extensively attested. This is especially so in the Deuteronomic/Deuteronomistic literature and in the Sinai narratives in Exodus (19: 3b–8; 24: 3–8; 34: 27, 28). He finds it also with this meaning in passages in P (Gen. 17: 9–14; Exod. 31: 16); in the Holiness Code (Lev. 26: 15); in several prophetic books including Isaiah (24: 5; 56: 4, 6), Jeremiah (11: 1–17; 22: 9; 31: 31–4; 34: 13, 18). Ezekiel (16; 17; 44); Hosea (8: 1), as well as in a number of Psalms (25: 10, 14; 44: 18; 50: 16; 78: 10; 103: 18; 132: 12), and in Proverbs (2: 17).

Once again Kutsch finds no ancient testimony to this use of *bᵉrīt* in the theological sphere; none of the many texts employing it can be dated with any certainty earlier than the seventh/sixth centuries BC. Stylistically and in content the texts using the word in the Sinai narratives in Exodus (19:

3b–8; 24: 3–8; 34: 27, 28) display the influence of the Deuteronomic/ Deuteronomistic literature of this period. Deuteronomy 33: 9b, 10, frequently cited as ancient evidence, likewise must be regarded as late: in v. 10, for example, *tōrāh* is paralleled by *mišpāṭīm* and is thus used not in its older sense of an individual priestly 'instruction', but of God's revealed will in general, that is, in the same way as Deuteronomy as a whole is designated Yahweh's *tōrāh*. Vv. 9b, 10, if not the entire section vv. 8–11, are not pre-Deuteronomic (*Verheissung und Gesetz*, pp. 71 f.). Or again, though the story of Achan in Joshua 7 is certainly of early origin, the description of his crime in terms of a breach of the covenant (vv. 11, 15) is from the hand of a Deuteronomistic redactor: the phrase *ʿābar bᵉrīt* 'transgress the covenant' occurs almost entirely in the Deuteronomic/ Deuteronomistic and related literature (Deut. 17: 2; Josh. 23: 16; Jud. 2: 20; 2 Kgs. 18: 12; Jer. 34: 18); the same is the case with the use of *ṣiwwāh* 'command' with *bᵉrīt* (Deut. 4: 13; 28: 69; Josh. 23: 16; Jud. 2: 20; 1 Kgs. 11: 11; elsewhere only Ps. 111: 9) (p. 75). As many commentators have suggested, Hosea 8: 1 is a secondary addition. For Kutsch, as earlier for Wellhausen (and now also for Perlitt, see below), it is especially indicative of the lateness of the theological use of *bᵉrīt* that none of the prophets prior to Jeremiah and Ezekiel employed it, and, he suggests, even if Hosea 8: 1 were regarded as authentic, this solitary text would carry little weight and would not effectively alter the overall conclusion to be drawn from the evidence.

Some further points made by Kutsch may also be briefly summarized here. First, contrary to the usual view, he argues that Joshua 24 does not narrate the making of a *bᵉrīt* between Yahweh and Israel; rather, it is Joshua who makes the *bᵉrīt* with the assembled Israelites, that is, places them under an obligation to serve Yahweh alone (v. 25)—it is a *bᵉrīt* made between the Israelites themselves, not between them and Yahweh (pp. 64 f.). The same is the case with the *bᵉrīt* made by Josiah in 2 Kings 23: 3, which is a *bᵉrīt* whereby both the king and the people undertake an obligation to serve Yahweh (pp. 165 f.).

Secondly, Kutsch (pp. 146 ff.) rejects the widely held view that expressions stating the relationship between Yahweh and Israel—'you shall be my people and I will be your God' and the like—are summaries of the 'covenant relationship' (*die Bundesformel*). In those texts where such expressions are accompanied by the term *bᵉrīt* it is either (*a*) an indication of Yahweh's *bᵉrīt*, that is, his solemn promise to Israel 'you shall be my people and I will be your God' (Gen. 17: 7; Lev. 26: 45; Ezek. 34: 25; 37: 26), or (*b*) the relationship between Yahweh and Israel which *results from* Israel's loyalty to the *bᵉrīt* with Yahweh, that is, Israel's obligation to serve and obey him (i.e. this relationship is not the *bᵉrīt* itself, which never means 'relationship' or 'agreement' (*Bund*). Cf. Exod. 19: 5; Deut. 29: 11 f.; Jer. 11: 3 f.; 31: 31-4).

Third, concerning the theological significance of the use of *bᵉrīt*, Kutsch, as already indicated, rejects any suggestion that it is a matter of an agreement (*Bund*) between God and his people, as though they were equal partners (p. 149). Rather, its use on the one hand to express Yahweh's promise to Israel and, on the other, Israel's duty to Yahweh, meant theologically that in 'a twofold way God comes to his people: in his grace and with his law, as one who bestows his gift and who also commands. Each finds its expression in the notion of *bᵉrīt*, which can designate both God's promise and also his demand' (p. 152).

Finally, since *bᵉrīt* is never used in the sense of relationship, an agreement between Yahweh and Israel, it follows that there never was a festival in Israel centring upon this, that is, a 'covenant festival' or 'renewal of the covenant festival' at the feast of Tabernacles. Quite apart from the fact that the Old Testament nowhere refers to such a festival (*ḥag habbᵉrīt**), the texts which are most often cited by scholars as evidence of it do not yield the support claimed from them. The most frequently cited text in this connection (Deut. 31: 9-13) is an exilic text, and, even though it associates the reading of the law with the festival of Tabernacles, it stipulates that this is to be carried out every seventh year, and it does not seem likely that this is a rearrangement of what in the pre-exilic period was an annual event. No ancient cultic ordinance lies behind this text, which must rather be seen as the attempt of the Deuteronomist to procure an audience and a hearing for the Deuteronomic law.[34] Other texts do not provide any firm evidence that assemblies at which a *bᵉrīt* was made took place, as widely claimed, at the festival in question (2 Kgs. 11: 17; 23: 3; 2 Chron. 15: 10-15; 29: 10; Neh. 8:1-12; 10: 1-40). One such assembly appears to have been held at the festival of Weeks (2 Chron. 15: 10-15) (p. 167). No evidence of a regularly recurring festival is attested in these texts. Nor does Joshua 24, so frequently referred to in this con-

---

[34] p. 162 (following Perlitt; see below).

nection, provide such evidence. It has nothing to do with an 'agreement' between Yahweh and Israel or with the renewal of such an agreement or relationship; no breach of a *bᵉrīt* is presupposed; there is no solemn proclamation of Yahweh's will, and no theophany, both of which, it is usually claimed, were central to this alleged festival. Neither an ancient historical event nor a festival tradition lies behind this chapter; it is a narrative composed in the mid-seventh century BC or perhaps later; it describes an act of self-obligation by Joshua and the Israelites to serve Yahweh, an obligation founded in Yahweh's saving deeds on Israel's behalf (pp. 168 ff.).

VII

Whilst Kutsch's study of the word *bᵉrīt* is the most thorough since Kraetzschmar's monograph in 1896, Perlitt's book *Bundestheologie im Alten Testament* is the most detailed presentation yet of the view that Israel's covenant traditions are the product of a late period in its history and arose in response to various theological needs and crises. His procedure is to begin where the theological use of *bᵉrīt* is most expansively and intensively employed, that is, in the literature of Deuteronomy and the Deuteronomistic corpus of the seventh and sixth centuries BC, whence he moves to other texts to determine whether it was used in earlier periods, and if so in what ways, or whether in fact its theological appropriation and usage is a product of the late period in which it is most in evidence.

Perlitt's is a work which inevitably loses much in being summarized; such is the close and detailed argumentation (not to mention its vigour and indeed passion) that the substance of this book is the book itself. I offer the following outline of his main conclusions with the promise that more detail will be provided in the discussions of some key texts in ensuing chapters.

(1) The Deuteronomistic historian wrote against the background of the destruction of Judah in 586 BC, as well as of the earlier collapse of the Northern Kingdom in 721 BC, and of the ensuing exile; his task was to explain theologically the ruin of the two kingdoms. If at that time there were those who in their consternation appealed to 'Abraham' and 'David', the Deuteronomist responded with 'Moses'; for him history could in this

hour be written only from the standpoint of the (unfulfilled) conditions upon which Yahweh's gifts had been bestowed. To this end he prefaced his work with 'the book of the law'. At the same time, however, he took up the term *bᵉrît*, already employed in those sections of Deuteronomy which he inherited (substantially chapters 5–26, 28) for Yahweh's promise (Deut. 7; the *bᵉrît* with the ancestors) and for Israel's obligation (Deut. 5; the *bᵉrît* at Horeb), which he used almost exclusively in this latter sense and thus of Yahweh's law, here the codified 'book of the law' which he also designated 'the book of the covenant' (cf. Deut. 29: 20, 26; 2 Kgs. 23: 2, 21). Thus in many texts the terms *bᵉrît* and *tōrāh* are reciprocal, identical and interchangeable.

As an all-embracing term for Yahweh's law, the term *bᵉrît* is intensively used by the Deuteronomist for his purposes of explaining the disaster which had now befallen Israel. As signifying above all Yahweh's exclusive demand upon Israel (the *Hauptgebot*), breach of the *bᵉrît* is seen most characteristically in Israel's worship of 'other gods', whilst its use also explains why Israel, to whom Yahweh by his *bᵉrît* with the ancestors had promised the land, has now been deprived of this land: the one *bᵉrît* had been fulfilled; the other had not, and so in the destruction of the land and in the exile Yahweh, who both promises and fulfils, is justified. Most especially, however, by his understanding of *bᵉrît* and what it entails the Deuteronomist reinterpreted the significance of the law: whereas in earlier Deuteronomic preaching the law was given for Israel's prosperity (cf. Deut. 6: 20 ff.; 16: 15), the Deuteronomistic generation experienced 'the book of the law' in its power to bring curse, and the Deuteronomist's usage of *bᵉrît* served to highlight this. The curse of the law had been unleashed because the *bᵉrît* had been broken. Thus for the Deuteronomist blessing and curse were no longer alternative possibilities for Israel: blessing belonged to the past and curse to the present; it is only in late exilic additions such as Deuteronomy 30: 1 ff. that this calamitous situation is left behind (p. 46).

In a number of passages this 'book of the law' is described as having been known to Israel from Moses to Josiah, whether as the basis of various covenant scenes (Deut. 29; Josh. 23; 2 Kgs. 23) or as the presupposition of the preaching of the prophets throughout the generations (2 Kgs. 17: 7–23), whilst from outside the Deuteronomistic corpus though clearly in relation to its theology of covenant, Jeremiah too is presented as having proclaimed what had thus been known to Israel since Moses (Jer. 11: 1–17): 'What had been enjoined upon the fathers was to be held sacred by the sons, that is, the demand of the obligation to Yahweh signified by the term *bᵉrīt*.' (p. 15) In this, however, Israel had failed, and the history which the Deuteronomist wrote is therefore a history of the violation of ordinances and of broken covenants. As described in Deuteronomy 29 and Joshua 23, these covenant scenes are transparently formulated for a future which is now present; thus the curse announced in Deuteronomy 29: 21–7 and Joshua 23: 13–16 is no longer just an alternative to blessing still possible for Israel, but a curse which has already been realized, whilst not even the piety of Josiah was able to reverse the judgement which overarched his reign from that of Manasseh into the situation in which the Deuteronomist wrote (cf. 2 Kgs. 23: 26).

'In this Deuteronomistic theology there is no more joy. The times of joy in and through Yahweh had been squandered. The Deuteronomist reflected in a time when teeth had been set on edge. The terms *bᵉrīt* and *tōrāh*, which had earlier signified promise and benevolent instruction, now signified the codified law by which Israel had been brought under judgement.'(p. 46)

Did the Deuteronomist point to any hope for Israel's future? The appeal to Yahweh's *bᵉrīt* with the ancestors represents but the 'minutest seed of hope' (Deut. 29: 11 f.); apart from this 'the secret things belong to Yahweh our God' (Deut. 29: 28). But what of the promise to David, so prominent in the Deuteronomistic history and expressed specifically as Yahweh's *bᵉrīt* with the house of David in 2 Samuel 23: 1–7? Does not this major theme in this corpus point, as G. von Rad suggested,[35] to the presence of 'gospel' alongside 'law' in the purpose of the Deuteronomist?

(2) According to Perlitt, no. The Deuteronomist knew of no *bᵉrīt* with David, but only of a promise which stood over against, and had only the effect of retarding, the judgement which breach of Yahweh's *bᵉrīt* with Israel had now finally brought. Such a promise could have been 'gospel' but since the Judaean kings forsook the law and with it the way of

---

[35] 'Die deuteronomistische Geschichtstheologie in den Königsbüchern' *Deuteronomium-Studien*, FRLANT 58, second edition, Göttingen 1948; E. trs. 'The Deuteronomistic Theology of History in the Books of Kings', *Studies in Deuteronomy*, London 1953, ch. 7.

obedient David, the promise itself fell through. The report of Jehoiachin's release in 2 Kings 25: 27–30 is no sufficient revocation of this. The so-called 'Last Words of David' (2 Sam. 23: 1–7) are a late addition to the Deuteronomistic history and were composed no earlier than the middle of the sixth century BC. Nor, incidentally, do any of the other texts, including Psalms 89 and 132, which refer to a *bᵉrīt* with David, represent ancient tradition; the former is no earlier than the death of Josiah, whilst the latter is post-Deuteronomistic. In short, the notion of Yahweh's *bᵉrīt* with David is a late redefinition and intensification in terms of a *bᵉrīt* and oath of what had earlier been expressed merely as a promise (2 Sam. 7.)

(3) In the pre-Deuteronomistic sections of Deuteronomy, *bᵉrīt* is used for (a) the covenant with the patriarchs, and (b) the covenant centring upon the decalogue at Horeb (Deut. 5). Of these, only the former belonged to the earliest material in the book; the latter is either a late Deuteronomic or early Deuteronomistic addition. Behind the former stands Genesis 15 which, contrary to the prevalent view since Alt's work, is not from the Yahwist but is a 'proto-Deuteronomic' formulation from early in the seventh century BC. As such, it represents, in the wake of the destruction of the Northern Kingdom and the threat this posed for Israel's continued occupation of the land, a late intensification, by means of a *bᵉrīt* and oath, of what had hitherto been expressed simply as a promise (cf. Gen. 12: 7). Texts in the pre-P material in the Tetrateuch which reflect this oath sworn by Yahweh to the patriarchs (e.g. Gen. 24: 7; 26: 3; 50: 24; Exod. 13: 5, 11) are similarly 'proto-Deuteronomic'.

(4) The original book of Deuteronomy probably began at 6: 4. Chapter 5, narrating the making of a *bᵉrīt* at Horeb centring upon the decalogue and thus representing Israel's obligation to Yahweh, was added at a stage between this original book and the work of the Deuteronomistic historian. Here as elsewhere in the Deuteronomic/Deuteronomistic corpus Horeb is a geographical 'catchword' for Yahweh's command understood as his *bᵉrīt* —a use of this word quite different, therefore, from its use to describe his promise to the patriarchs. It is clear, however, that the decalogue is not the *ad hoc* creation of the author of this chapter. The fact that the decalogue is formulated in the you-singular as against the surrounding framework which employs the you-plural form of address

indicates that this author has taken up an already independently formulated series of laws. This independent existence of the decalogue is further attested by the fact that it could also be inserted into the Sinai pericope in Exodus 19: 1-24: 11. Does this mean that the association between the decalogue and the making of a *bᵉrīt* is due to the author of this framework material in Deuteronomy 5, or was the decalogue in itself understood as the expression of Yahweh's *bᵉrīt*?

Perlitt argues that the decalogue is a creation of the Deuteronomic or 'proto-Deuteronomic' circle. Formally two different types of material have here been secondarily combined: on the one hand an opening speech of Yahweh in the first person singular (vv. 6-10), on the other hand a series of commands or prohibitions in which Yahweh is referred to in the third person singular (vv. 11-21). The original *Sitz im Leben* of these commands or prohibitions was community instruction, whether carried out by parents, elders or teachers. But the 'combination of prohibitions with a speech of God marks a stage in the history of the growth of the decalogue which is identical with a shift in *Sitz im Leben*. What had once been the responsibility of parents, teachers, elders, was now secondarily attached to an overriding theological conception in which the prohibitions "have been subordinated to the legitimising and protecting authority of Yahweh and his covenant"'.[36] All, that is, has been subordinated to one fundamental command: that Yahweh alone is to be Israel's God, and this command against the worship of other gods is 'the primary "covenant stipulation" of the Deuteronomic covenant theology as a whole' (p. 98).

We must suppose, Perlitt argues, that since the decalogue found no place in the original book of Deuteronomy but then acquired the decisive place it now has at a subsequent stage in the literary growth of the book, in the meantime it had become more and more important and was finally presented as the content of a *bᵉrīt* between Yahweh and Israel at Horeb. To this end also the earlier tradition of Yahweh's theophany at Sinai was used. Thus Horeb, the place of Yahweh's command, and Sinai were brought together, and with this covenant and theophany. (The incorporation of the decalogue in the JE Sinai material in Exodus 19: 1-24: 11 also took place at this stage.) It was at this stage in the history of the growth of

---

[36] p. 90, citing G. J. Botterweck, 'Form- und überlieferungsgeschichtliche Studie zum Dekalog', *Concilium*, I, 1965, p. 395.

Deuteronomy that the term *bᵉrît* acquired its new and more comprehensive legitimation, no longer understood only from the promise to the patriarchs but now and from now onwards increasingly as Yahweh's command.

(5) Two further matters arising immediately from Deuteronomy are discussed by Perlitt: (*a*) the origin of the so-called 'covenant formula' with its basic ingredients 'Yahweh is the God of Israel and Israel is the people of Yahweh' (Deut. 26: 17-19; 29: 12); and (*b*) the evidence adduced from Deuteronomy 31: 9-13 for a recurring covenant festival associated with the feast of Tabernacles in pre-exilic Israel.

With regard to (*a*), in its full reciprocal form (that Yahweh is the God of Israel and Israel the people of Yahweh) the formula is not attested before the Deuteronomic/Deuteronomistic period[37] with the exception of Hosea 2: 25. But this latter did not derive from a 'covenant tradition' of which Hosea was heir and to which he here appeals, but arose solely from Hosea's own preaching. It may be claimed, therefore, that the theological preparation for the formula was made by Hosea, but it was not until much later that it acquired wider currency, beginning with the Deuteronomic/Deuteronomistic circle (Deut. 26: 17-9 and 29: 12 are both probably from the Deuteronomist historian) whose basic theology of the relationship between Yahweh and Israel it sums up.

With regard to (*b*), Deuteronomy 31: 9-13 is from a Deuteronomist who has here drawn out the final consequence of Deuteronomy's own fiction of itself as a speech of Moses: Moses had not only spoken; he had also written 'the book of the law'. The purpose of this passage is simply to 'secure an audience and a hearing for the Deuteronomic law' (p. 123). It knows nothing of a ceremony of covenant renewal in association with the prescribed reading of the law every seven years, the purpose of which is that the people, men, women, little ones, and the sojourner 'may hear and learn to fear the Lord your God, and be careful to do all the words of this law'.

(6) From the Deuteronomic and Deuteronomistic covenant-theology of the seventh and sixth centuries BC Perlitt moves to the prophets of the

---

[37] See R. Smend's discussion of this, *Die Bundesformel*, Theologische Studien 68, Zürich 1963.

eighth century. Neither Amos nor Isaiah nor Micah employs the term
bᵉrīt for Yahweh's relationship with Israel, and all attempts to find a
covenantal background or basis for what they preached or for elements of
what they preached is in the face of this absence of the word itself. Amos
makes no mention of the themes of Sinai and covenant, even though his
reference to the forty years in the wilderness (5: 25) would have given him
the opportunity to do so. Of Yahweh's ancient dealings on behalf of his
people, Amos mentions the exodus, the gift of the land, and Yahweh's
gracious turning to his people (2: 9; 3: 2; 9: 7), and these were recalled by
him 'exclusively for the purpose of demonstrating guilt'.[38] But he spoke
'neither of Yahweh's justice or his faithfulness, nor of his covenant or his
law'.[39] 'Amos nowhere "kindled any genuine hope", but announced the
end of Israel; such a message afforded no room to a return and appeal to a
covenant.' (p. 136.)

Matters are no different in the case of Micah and Isaiah. Micah
nowhere uses the word *bᵉrīt*, and it is inadmissible to read Micah 6: 1–8
(which is in any case a secondary addition to the sayings of the prophet) as
a 'covenant lawsuit' between Yahweh and Israel, since v. 8 does not state
'that the people should live up to the covenant obligations'[40] but expresses
a general ethic addressed to 'man' (*'ādām*). In Isaiah 28: 15, 18 the word
bᵉrīt is used of Israel's dependence upon the effectiveness of human
treaties; the ironic expression 'we have made a covenant with death' is the
prophet's way of saying that in such dependence lies death, whilst in
Yahweh alone is Israel's true security. But it is altogether too forced to
find in this an implied contrast between this 'covenant with death' and a
covenant with Yahweh which leads to life, as Galling suggested.[41] Nor can
Isaiah 1: 2 ff. be understood as a 'covenant lawsuit'. The imagery it
employs is of a father and his rebellious sons, not of Yahweh as a
'covenant partner'. To reduce all such images to expressions of a 'covenant
relationship' is at the cost of the rich and varied imagery employed in the
Old Testament for Yahweh's relationship with his people.

Superficially, matters would appear to be quite different in the case of

---

[38] p. 136, citing H. W. Wolff, *Amos*, BKAT xiv/2, Neukirchen 1967, p. 123; E. trs. *Joel
and Amos*, Philadelphia 1977, p. 102.

[39] p. 136, citing Wolff, p. 121; E. trs. p. 101.

[40] p. 137, against H. B. Huffmon, 'The Covenant Lawsuit in the Prophets', *JBL* 78,
1959, p. 287.   [41] *Die Erwählungstraditionen Israels*, p. 137.

Hosea where the word *bᵉrīt* is used five times (2: 20; 6: 7; 8: 1; 10: 4; 12: 2). Of these, however, 2: 20, the authenticity of which is in any case doubtful, has nothing to do with a *bᵉrīt* between Yahweh and Israel, whilst 10: 4 and 12: 2 are concerned with Israel's vainly made treaties with Egypt and Assyria. The making of such treaties, in which Israel sought its security, is portrayed as a betrayal of Yahweh, but there is no implication that Israel's true 'treaty' is with Yahweh; the opposite of making a treaty with other nations here is not the making of a covenant with Yahweh but making *no* treaty with such nations. The enigmatic 6: 7 (probably to be emended to read '*At* Adam they broke the *bᵉrīt*; there they were treacherous against me')[42] is similarly not a reference to a breach of a covenant with Yahweh, but to the breaking of a treaty with some other group or nation. That it is described in the second half of the verse as treachery against Yahweh is simply because such a treaty would have been made by an oath taken by Israel in Yahweh's name; breach of such an oath would thus have been not merely treachery against the other treaty partner involved but against Yahweh himself. The explicit reference in 8: 1 to Yahweh's covenant with Israel is a secondary, Deuteronomistic addition.

(7) From this silence of the eighth-century prophets concerning the covenant Perlitt moves to the Sinai narratives in Exodus 19–24, 32 and 34, and finally to Joshua 24. His conclusions, to give once again but the baldest statement of them, are as follows:

(*a*) Of the three key texts in Exodus 19–24 (19: 3b–8; 24: 1–2, 9–11; 24: 3–8), Exodus 24: 1–2, 9–11, contrary to the widely held understanding of it, does not concern the making of a covenant. Rather, it centres upon the remarkable *visio dei* granted to the representatives of Israel on the mountain. The 'community' between God and the people is here established precisely through his gracious appearance on the mountain. But it is not a 'covenant relationship'; the meal referred to in the closing statement of the passage ('they ate and drank') is not celebrated with God, as in a covenant meal, but in his presence, before him. It is not the heart of the scene described, but rather presupposes what is the centre of the scene, God's appearance, and is the expression of the joy of those who thus

---

[42] p. 142, following J. Wellhausen, *Die kleinen Propheten übersetzt und erklärt*, Berlin 1892, fourth edition 1963, *in loc.*

experienced this theophany. Of the remaining two passages, Exodus 19: 3b–8 is a secondary insertion displaying late Deuteronomistic, priestly, and prophetic currents of the exilic period. Exodus 24: 3–8 is based upon an ancient nucleus of tradition concerning the offering of sacrifices at Sinai which has been worked over by a Deuteronomistic redactor who has reinterpreted it as a covenant-making ritual.

(*b*) Contrary to the generally accepted view, Exodus 34 does not contain material which formed part of an original J account of the making of a covenant at Sinai. With chapter 32, which it in every way presupposes, it is a Deuteronomic composition from no earlier than the reign of Josiah in the late seventh century BC.

(*c*) No ancient covenant tradition or tradition of a 'covenant renewal festival' underlies Joshua 24. Rather, it is a Deuteronomic composition, the background to which is most probably the reign of Manasseh in the seventh century BC.

This completes the first part of this book, 'Covenant in a Century of Study since Wellhausen'. In the light of what has been described in the foregoing pages, it could with some aptness be alternatively described as 'Covenant in a Cycle of Study since Wellhausen', for it is to a position analogous in important respects to what he argued that recent studies such as those by Kutsch and Perlitt have returned. Our next task is a survey of the Old Testament texts themselves to enquire how justified these scholars' conclusion is that the notion of a covenant between God and Israel was coined and developed at the late stage in the pre-exilic period to which they assign it.

The key texts are Exodus 19: 3b–8; 24: 1–2, 9–11; 24: 3–8; 34: 10–28, and Joshua 24: 1–28 to which must be added, for reasons which have already become apparent, the references to a covenant in Hosea 6: 7 and 8: 1. To concentrate on these texts scarcely needs defending, for in any investigation of the origin of the covenant between God and Israel they are self-evidently most crucial of all, and it is in them, as we have seen, that most scholars have found evidence of the great antiquity and the role of this covenant in Israelite religion and society.

PART TWO

THE ORIGIN OF THE COVENANT
BETWEEN GOD AND ISRAEL

KEY TEXTS

5

'They Saw God And Ate And Drank'— A Covenant Meal At Sinai?

(Exodus 24: 1–2, 9–11)

To begin with this passage requires no explanation: since Gressmann's suggestions, noted earlier, it has been widely regarded as ancient testimony, by many the most ancient testimony, to the making of a covenant between Yahweh and Israel. Perlitt has challenged such an understanding of the passage, in my opinion effectively, and what follows is intended as further support for his view, though I differ from him in some details.[1]

I

A glance at Exodus 24: 1–2, 9–11 indicates that the introduction to vv. 9–11 is contained in vv. 1–2. Between the command given in these latter verses to Moses to ascend the mountain with those who are to accompany him and the record of their ascent in vv. 9–11, there is a description of a rite of covenant ratification (vv. 3–8). This covenant ritual at the foot of the mountain and the experience of the Israelite delegation at the top of the mountain are thus related to the final stage of the covenant ceremony as a whole in Exodus 19: 1–24: 11, forming its climax and conclusion.

We have seen, however, there is general agreement among modern commentators that vv. 1–2, 9–11 and vv. 3–8 were originally independent of one another and only secondarily combined. Verses 3–8 abruptly interrupt the obvious connection between vv. 1–2 and 9–11. It is then

---

[1] I have dealt at greater length with this passage in the following publications: 'The Interpretation of Exodus XXIV 9–11', *VT* 24, 1974, pp. 77–97; 'The Antiquity of the Tradition in Exodus XXIV 9–11', *VT* 25, 1975, pp. 69–79; 'The Origin of the Tradition in Exodus XXIV 9–11' *VT* 26, 1976, pp. 148–60. I am grateful to the publishers, E. J. Brill, for permission to include some of this material in the present chapter.

usually maintained that the two passages are different accounts of the same event, the making of the covenant at Sinai, vv. 3–8 preserving a tradition according to which it was ratified by means of sacrifice and blood rite, vv. 9–11 witnessing to a tradition according to which it was sealed by means of a covenant meal eaten by the representatives of Israel in the presence of God on the holy mountain, as the expression at the end of v. 11 ('they ate and drank') indicates.[2]

It is also widely accepted that not all of vv. 1–2 is the original introduction to vv. 9–11, and some have questioned whether they contain any of the original introduction. Certainly the last part of v. 1 as well as v. 2, in which it is commanded that Moses alone is to 'draw near to Yahweh' whilst the other members of the delegation with him on the mountain are to 'worship afar off', cannot belong to the original introduction, since in the description of what takes place on the mountain in vv. 9–11 no such distinction is made between Moses and the other participants in the event; all alike share the same experience. Vv. 1b–2 thus reflect a tradition in which the role of Moses and his special relationship with Yahweh are emphasized. To this extent they presuppose the same stage of tradition as is embodied in the remainder of the Sinai pericope where also special emphasis is placed upon the figure of Moses. But in vv. 9–11 no special role or experience is accorded Moses in the scene described. They do not even portray him as *primus inter pares*, for although he is mentioned by name alongside the anonymous seventy elders of Israel, others also are referred to (Aaron, Nadab, and Abihu). This absence of any distinction between Moses and the others with him on the mountain is clear also from v. 11 where the delegation as a whole is designated corporately as the *ʾ*ṣ*īlē b*ᵉ*nē yiśrāʾēl* 'the leaders of Israel'. This is also seen as further evidence that these verses were originally independent of vv. 3–8 in which the characteristic emphasis upon the central role of

[2] See, for example, W. Beyerlin, *Herkunft und Geschichte der ältesten Sinaitraditionen*, pp. 40–2, 44–59; E. trs. *Origins and History of the Oldest Sinaitic Traditions*, pp. 33–5, 36–48; M. Noth, *Das zweite Buch Mose, Exodus*, Göttingen 1959, pp. 157 f.; E. trs. *Exodus*, London 1962, p. 194; D. J. McCarthy, *Treaty and Covenant*,[2] pp. 264 ff.; J. P. Hyatt, *Exodus*, New Century Bible, London 1971, p. 253; T. C. Vriezen, 'The Exegesis of Exodus xxiv 9–11', in *The Witness of Tradition*, OTS 17, 1972, p. 102. Against this understanding of vv. 9–11 see the cautious comment of G. H. Davies, *Exodus*, London 1967, p. 193. Perlitt's discussion of the passage is contained in *Bundestheologie im Alten Testament*, pp. 181–90.

Moses at Sinai is found. It is probable therefore that vv. 1b–2 are a secondary expansion of the original introduction in v. 1a.

The Hebrew text of Exodus 24: 9–11 is clear and there are no major textual problems. Where the ancient versions differ from the Massoretic Text, apart from minor variations, it is largely because of questions of interpretation and not because of any textual corruptions in the Hebrew (see below). Nevertheless, in addition to some suggested emendations, several questions of interpretation and translation of the passage have arisen and must be briefly discussed.

It has been proposed that *ᵃlēh ʾel-Yahweh* 'go up to Yahweh' (v. 1) should be emended to *ᵃlēh ʾēlay* 'ascend to me', thereby removing the abrupt reference to Yahweh in the third person, since it is evidently Yahweh who is here addressing Moses and who has been addressing him in the previous chapters. It is suggesed that an original *ʾēlay* was misunderstood later to be an abbreviation for *ʾel-Yahweh*.[3] But though the reference to Yahweh in the third person here is abrupt, so also is the verse's introductory clause as a whole ('and to Moses he said'). For this reason the emendation is unwarranted. The strange beginning to the verse, from the point of view of the present context of the passage as a whole, is probably just one more indication that we have here an originally independent literary unit which has been united only secondarily with the surrounding material.

It has also been proposed that of the final clause in v. 11 *wayyōʾḵᵉlū* 'and they ate' should be deleted, and *wayyištū* 'and they drank' emended to *wayyištaḥᵃwū* 'and they worshipped', 'did obeisance'.[4] The grounds for such a suggestion appear to be the command recorded in v. 1 that the delegation which is to ascend the mountain is to 'worship afar off' (*uᵉhištaḥᵃwīthem mērāḥōq*). But the deletion of one word and the emendation of the other is altogether too drastic and finds no support in the ancient versions which are unanimous in reading 'they ate and drank'.

The *New English Bible* suggests, in a footnote, that *wayyirʾū* 'and they saw' in v. 10 was possibly originally read 'they were afraid of . . .' (with one

---

[3] So, for example, G. Beer, *Exodus*, Tübingen 1939, p. 124; Noth, *Das zweite Buch Mose*, p. 159; E. trs. pp. 196 f.; and *Überlieferungsgeschichte des Pentateuch*, p. 39 note 40; E. trs. *A History of Pentateuchal Traditions*, p. 36 note 40; Vriezen, p. 103. For evidence of the abbreviation of the Tetragrammaton to its first letter see G. R. Driver, 'Abbreviations in the Massoretic Text', *Textus* 1, 1960, pp. 119. f.   [4] Cf. Beer, p. 126.

manuscript), and translates *wayyeḥᵉzū* 'and they saw' in v. 11 with 'they stayed'. Of these, the first is unlikely. The context requires the translation 'they saw the God of Israel', for this phrase is followed immediately by a description of what was seen. In addition, it seems probable that the statement at the beginning of v. 11 ('but he did not stretch forth his hand against the leaders of Israel') presupposes the understanding of this word as 'and they saw', the meaning being that the delegation remained unharmed in spite of having seen God. Once again we may also note that none of the ancient versions lends support to a translation of the word as 'and they feared', even though the statement that the representatives of Israel 'saw the God of Israel' constituted a major theological problem for some of them (see below).

The basis for the translation of *wayyeḥᵉzū* as 'they stayed' is the theory that the verb *ḥāzāh* here is to be related to the Arabic *ḥadâ*, which in the first theme means 'was opposite', in the third 'rivalled', and in the sixth 'ran parallel', and that it is the Hebrew root from which *ḥāzeh* 'breast' derives. The South Arabian *ḥdyt* 'things that correspond', 'agreement', it is argued, evidences the same root, and the words *ḥōzeh* and *ḥāzūt* in Isaiah 28: 15, 18 which are translated in the LXX as συνθήκας 'agreements' and διαθήκην 'covenant' witness to the same root in Hebrew. Thus *wayyeḥᵉzū* in Exodus 24: 11 is taken as being from this root *ḥāzāh* = 'to be opposite', 'to be in front of' and hence 'to stay before'.[5]

Though a verb *ḥāzāh* with such a meaning may be attested elsewhere in the Old Testament,[6] it is unlikely that *wayyeḥᵉzū* in Exodus 24: 11 is to be related to it. Although there is a variant reading in the Samaritan Pentateuch,[7] all the ancient versions support the understanding of it as 'and they saw' and afford no hint of any other possible translation. There is no need to understand it in any other way than its traditional translation 'they saw'.

Some such meaning as 'leaders', 'chief men' is required for *ᵃṣîlē* in

---

[5] On this see the various articles by G. R. Driver in ch. 4, note 27.

[6] G. R. Driver, 'Studies in the Vocabulary of the Old Testament. VI', *JTS* 34, 1933, p. 381; 'Problems in Job and Psalms Reconsidered', *JTS* 40, 1939, p. 391.

[7] The Samaritan Text reads *wy'ḥzw* 'they seized', 'took hold of' (cf. A. F. von Gall, *Der hebräische Pentateuch der Samaritaner*, Giessen 1918, p. 167). But it is difficult to conceive how such a reading was understood, and it cannot seriously be regarded as a plausible alternative to the MT reading. The reading in the Samaritan Pentateuch may be due to nothing more than a scribal error.

v. 11. The Vulgate rendering of v. 11a *nec super eos qui procul recesserant de filiis Israhel misit manum suam* appears to understand the word as being from *ʾāṣal* 'to lay aside', 'set apart', and it is possible that this was further prompted by the words 'and worship afar off' in v. 1 which the Vulgate renders *et adorabitis procul*. It is possible that the LXX translation of the word as *ἐπιλέκτων* 'chosen ones' may be based upon a similar understanding of the word, hence 'those who are set apart'. More favoured is the understanding of the word as being a figurative use of *ʾāṣīl* 'side', 'corner', after the analogy of *pinnāh* 'corner' as a figurative expression for the leaders of the people in Judges 20: 2, 1 Samuel 14: 38. Alternatively, the word has been related to the Arabic *ʾaṣula* 'to be deeply rooted', 'to be of distinguished or superior origin'.[8] The names *ʾāṣēl* (1 Chron. 8: 37 f., 9: 43 f.) and *ᵃṣalyāhū* (2 Kgs. 22: 3; 2 Chron. 34: 8) are probably to be related to the same root, the first meaning literally 'eminent', 'noble', the second 'Yahweh has shown (or proved) himself to be exalted'.[9] But whether the word is to be understood in this manner or is a figurative use of *ʾāṣīl* 'side', 'corner', it is clear that it is designating those on the mountain in some way as 'leaders' of Israel.

Finally, we need note only briefly that the expression *lōʾ šālaḥ yādō* in v. 11 must be understood in a hostile sense, that is, 'he did not stretch forth his hand against the leaders of Israel' to destroy them.[10]

II

That a covenant can be ratified by eating a common meal is attested elsewhere in the Old Testament. Two clear examples of it are found in Genesis 26: 26–30 and 31: 43–50. In the former it is recorded that Abimelech and Isaac took an oath and made a covenant together to bring to an end the enmity which had arisen between them. Having thus come

---

[8] Cf. L. Köhler and W. Baumgartner, *Hebräisches und aramäisches Lexikon zum Alten Testament*, third edition, vol. I, Leiden 1967, p. 79.

[9] See M. Noth, *Die israelitischen Personennamen in Rahmen der gemeinsemitischen Namengebung*, BWANT III: 10, Stuttgart 1928, pp. 193 f., 231. Cf. E. G. Kraeling, *The Brooklyn Museum Aramaic Papyri*, New Haven and London 1953, Papyrus 7, line 44 and the note on p. 222.

[10] For a discussion of the meaning of this expression in the Old Testament see P. Humbert, 'Étendre la main', *VT* 12, 1962, pp. 383–95; J. J. M. Roberts, 'The Hand of Yahweh', *VT* 21, 1971, pp. 244–51.

to an agreement they shared a meal prepared by Isaac, and, we are told, 'ate and drank' (v. 30). In Genesis 31: 43–50 Laban and Jacob make a covenant concerning the treatment and status of Laban's daughters who are Jacob's wives, and having set up a heap of stones as a witness to their agreement, they eat together by this cairn (v. 46). It is usually argued that the ratification of a covenant by such means was because of the special bond of friendship and mutual acceptability which eating a meal was felt to create between those who shared it. Not surprisingly, therefore, the eating and drinking referred to in Exodus 24: 11 is similarly regarded as a covenant meal. Thus McCarthy writes of it as symbolizing 'the community between God and Israel', and so 'an authentic gesture of covenant making'.[11] Likewise Noth, for example, can claim: 'The fact that God lets the representatives of Israel hold a meal in his presence on the mountain indicates the making of the covenant between God and people.'[12] The final clause in the passage is therefore believed to supply the key to the interpretation of the scene described. This is emphasized even more by Beyerlin: 'Undoubtedly, there is something special about this meal: it is *for this purpose* clearly that the God of Israel orders the representatives of his people to ascend the mountain'.[13]

Beyerlin's statement is typical of the way in which commentators in general have emphasized the final clause in the passage at the expense of the significance of the material which immediately precedes it. But it is in this material, as Perlitt has rightly argued, that the nature of the scene described is to be found, so that the concentration upon the final clause in the passage is in this instance indeed a case of 'the tail wagging the dog'.

It should be noted in any case that eating and drinking in the presence of God cannot be understood as *ipso facto* the making of a covenant with God. The narrative in Exodus 18: 1–12 illustrates this. Here we are told that after the exodus the Israelites met the Midianites led by Moses's father-in-law Jethro. On hearing of 'all the good Yahweh had done for Israel', Jethro uttered a blessing to Yahweh after which he offered sacrifices and, we are told, together with Aaron and the elders of Israel 'ate bread before God'. But it is unwarranted to describe what takes place here at 'the mountain of God' as the ratification of a covenant between

---

[11]   *Treaty and Covenant*,² p. 254.
[12]   *Das zweite Buch Mose*, p. 159; E. trs. p. 196.
[13]   p. 40; E. trs. p. 33 (the italics are his).

Yahweh on the one hand and the Israelites and Midianites on the other. It has been suggested that the passage preserves the tradition of the making of a covenant between Israel and the Midianites in which Yahweh was the divine guarantor and witness.[14] But there is no mention of the making of a covenant, whether between Yahweh and those who 'ate bread' in his presence or between Israel and Midian, and there are no grounds for understanding the eating referred to here as anything other than the cultic activity of eating and drinking, rejoicing 'before God', mentioned in a number of texts elsewhere in the Old Testament, none of which can seriously be understood as descriptions of covenant ceremonies (e.g. Deut. 12: 7; 14: 26; 27: 7; I Chron. 19: 22). One should not therefore automatically assume that the eating and drinking referred to in Exodus 24: 11 is indicative of a covenant meal.

It may be objected to this that the context of Exodus 24: 9–11 within the description of the final stages of the covenant ceremony at Sinai renders the interpretation of the event recorded in terms of a covenant rite probable. But a covenant rite has already been described in vv. 3–8, so that *prima facie* one does not expect it to be followed immediately by yet another description of such a rite. It may be conceded that this in itself is not impossible; a redactor may have wished to preserve two ancient covenant traditions which he inherited. But it does open the possibility that vv. 9–11 are not concerned with such a rite but centre on something else and that the phrase 'they ate and drank' here has a connotation other than that of indicating a covenant meal. I shall return to this later.

III

Any attempt to determine the central concern of Exodus 24: 9–11 should begin with, and proceed from, what is surely its most striking feature, viz. the statement, which occurs twice in this short passage (vv. 10 and 11), that the Israelite delegation on the mountain saw God. The ease with which modern commentators accept with little or no comment this feature of this passage is in sharp contrast to the significance it had, and the problem it posed, for ancient translators and commentators for whom

---

[14] C. H. W. Brekelmans, 'Exodus xviii and the origins of Yahwism in Israel', *OTS* 10, 1954, pp. 315–24; F. C. Fensham, 'Did a Treaty between the Israelites and the Midianites Exist?', *BASOR* 175, 1964, pp. 51–4.

the statements that these Israelites on the mountain saw God demanded explanation or comment. The LXX translators already recognized the theological problem that such boldly anthropomorphic statements pose, and accordingly rendered them periphrastically. They translated 'and they saw the God of Israel' as καὶ εἶδον τὸν τόπον οὖ εἰστήκει ὁ θεὸς τοῦ Ἰσραήλ 'and they saw the place where the God of Israel stood'; whilst 'they saw God' is rendered as καὶ ὤφθησαν ἐν τῷ τόπῳ τοῦ θεοῦ 'and they were seen in the place of God'. Symmachus understands 'and they saw the God of Israel' to mean καί εἶδον ὁράματι τὸν θεὸν Ἰσραήλ 'and they saw in a vision the God of Israel'.[15] The Targums Onkelos, Pseudo-Jonathan, and Neophyti I, and the Fragment Targum interpret each of the two statements as meaning that the Israelites on the mountain saw 'the Glory' of God.

Jewish exegetes have varied between understanding the seeing of God by the Israelite delegation as a unique blessing bestowed upon them, and as a wilful and sinful act on the part of some of them. When the latter of these two interpretations is adopted, Nadab and Abihu are usually singled out as those who looked at God and thereby incurred the death penalty, a penalty later exacted (Num. 3: 4). Thus, commenting on the death of Nadab and Abihu in Numbers 3: 4, Numbers Rabbah II: 25 records that Rabbi Phinehas, taking the ᵃṣīlē bᵉnē yiśrā'ēl to refer to these two individuals alone, understood the statement that God did not stretch out his hand against them to imply that the doom of both of them had already been sealed at Sinai. Similarly, it records the saying of Rabbi Hoshaia: 'Were provisions taken up with them to Mount Sinai, as is implied by the text, *And they beheld God, and did eat and drink*? Certainly not; but it teaches that they fixed gloating eyes upon the Divine Presence, as one that stares at a person and at the same time goes on eating and drinking'.[16] It also mentions the saying of Rabbi Tanhuma: 'It teaches that they waxed haughty and stood upon their feet and fixed gloating eyes upon the Divine Presence.'

A quite different interpretation of the experience of the representatives of Israel on the mountain in seeing God is also evidenced in Rabbinic

---

[15] F. Field, *Origenis Hexaplorum Quae Supersunt; sive Veterum Interpretum Graecorum in Totum Vetus Testamentum Fragmenta*, vol. I, Oxford 1875, p. 122.

[16] *Midrash Rabbah*, translated under the editorship of Rabbi H. Freedman and M. Simon: *Numbers*, translated by J. J. Slotki, vol. I, London 1939.

literature. Thus Numbers Rabbah records the saying of Rabbi Johanan who said 'that the pleasure derived from gazing at the Divine Splendour was real nourishment; as it is written: *In the light of the king's countenance is life*' (Prov. 16: 15). Similarly, the Talmud records: 'A favourite saying of Rab was: [The future world is not like this world.] In the future world there is no eating nor drinking nor propagation nor business nor jealousy nor hatred nor composition, but the righteous sit with crowns on their heads feasting on the brightness of the divine presence, as it says, *And they beheld God, and did eat and drink*'[17]—the vision of God was like food and drink to the delegation on the mountain, and their experience was a paradigm of the life hereafter in the presence of God.

Of medieval Jewish exegetes Rashi, for example, probably following the tradition attributed in Numbers Rabbah to Rabbi Joshua of Sikin and Rabbi Levi, understands the text to mean that Nadab and Abihu as well as the seventy elders 'stared and peeped' at God and thereby incurred the penalty of death, the penalty being postponed, however, until the erection of the Tabernacle, in the case of Nadab and Abihu (Num. 3: 4), and until the murmuring at Taberah, in the case of the elders (Num. 11: 1–3).[18] On the other hand Ibn Ezra, in characteristic manner as one dedicated to expounding 'the plain meaning' (*Peshat*) of the biblical text as against the traditional Haggadic exposition (*Derash*) so typical of Rashi, understands 'they saw the God of Israel' to mean that they saw God in a prophetic vision, and he compares the statement with Isaiah's call vision 'I saw the Lord seated upon a throne' (Isa. 6: 1). The same interpretation of the text is adopted by Nachmanides who further explains that the 'leaders of Israel'—he takes these to be Nadab and Abihu and the seventy elders—did not die as a result of seeing God because they were worthy of such a unique experience.

In contrast to the manifest concern of ancient translators and commentators alike with this remarkable feature of Exodus 24: 9–11, modern commentators have for the most part either failed to see or at least underestimated its significance. Yet it is surely the most emphasized aspect of the passage as a whole. This is not simply because the statement

---

[17] *Babli Berakoth*, 17a, translated by M. Simon, London 1948. (In *The Babylonian Talmud*, translated and edited under the editorship of I. Epstein, London 1948.)

[18] Rashi takes *q*ṣē* in Numbers 11: 1 to mean *q*ṣīnīm* (*qāṣīn* = 'chief', 'ruler') and thus to be a reference to the elders as the 'chiefs' or 'rulers' of Israel.

that the delegation saw God occurs twice in so short a text, though this fact in itself is surely striking. The passage not only states twice that they saw God but also describes, even though briefly, what they saw: 'Beneath his feet there was something like a pavement of sapphire, clear as the very heavens' (v. 10). Whatever the source of this imagery,[19] it is sufficient to note here that the description further evidences the concern of this tradition with what the representatives of Israel on the mountain saw rather than with what they did.

This concern is further emphasized by the phrase which immediately follows: 'But he did not stretch forth his hand against the leaders of Israel' (v. 11a). This can only be taken to mean that although they saw God they did not suffer the normal consequences of such an experience—theirs was a uniquely privileged experience; they saw God and lived.

In view of these considerations it seems clear that the primary concern of this passage is with the unique and awful experience of the representatives of Israel in seeing God on the holy mountain of his abode: after recording their ascent, it states in the most direct manner that they saw the God of Israel, it describes what they saw, it states that in spite of such an experience they remained unharmed, and then it states again that they saw God. It is this that forms the bulk of the passage; it is upon this that all the emphasis is laid. In short, the tradition embodied in this passage is, properly speaking, a theophany tradition, a tradition of a *visio dei*, the most remarkable in the Old Testament.

IV

This brings us back to the final phrase in the passage, 'they ate and drank'. Granted that the tradition emphasizes the theophany on the holy mountain, does it also record the ratification of a covenant? After all, it may be contended, theophany and covenant are combined within the context of the Sinai pericope as a whole, and so here also does it not seem

---

[19] For a recent discussion see E. Ruprecht, 'Exodus 24, 9-11 als Beispiel lebendiger Erzähltradition aus der Zeit des babylonischen Exils', in *Werden und Wirken des Alten Testaments. Festschrift für Claus Westermann zum 70 Geburtstag*, ed. R. Albertz, H.-P. Müller, H. W. Wolff, Z. Zimmerli, Göttingen 1980, pp. 138-73. I remain convinced that the tradition preserved in Exodus 24: 9-11 is of ancient origin. Since, however, I do not consider this tradition to concern the making of a covenant, its dating need not concern us here.

likely that the tradition first of all describes a theophany and then records the making of a covenant by means of eating a meal?

In my opinion this is unlikely. To begin with, it has to be asked whether it is credible that such an important event as the making of the covenant between God and Israel would be referred to so tersely if, as is usually argued, this tradition concerns the covenant. Surely if this passage concerned the making of the covenant we should expect some more concrete reference to it, some more substantial allusion to it or treatment of it than the last two words of the passage which are so very much over-shadowed by the remarkable description of the theophany which precedes them and dominates the tradition, and after which the phrase 'they ate and drank' appears rather lame. But we look in vain through the passage for any such reference. All this indicates that the case for understanding the tradition as being concerned with the making of a covenant is weak.

How then are we to understand the phrase 'they ate and drank'? Perlitt suggests that what it refers to is quite simply a celebratory meal with which the representatives rejoice before God. The passage, summed up, would thus mean 'they saw God and rejoiced'. Such an interpretation is possible. But the difficulty of it is that elsewhere such 'eating' or 'eating and drinking' occurs in contexts where sacrifices have been offered. Appeal cannot be made in the case of Exodus 24: 9–11 to Exodus 24: 3–8, where sacrifices are recorded as having been made, since, as already indicated, this passage was originally unrelated to the tradition in vv. 1–2, 9–11.[20]

More probably, in my opinion, the phrase is to be interpreted as meaning 'they lived'. In support for this understanding of the clause are the following observations.

First, there is evidence that the expression 'to eat and drink' or 'to eat bread' or simply 'to eat' is sometimes used in the Old Testament to connote 'to live a prosperous life', 'to enjoy life' or, again simply, 'to live'.

---

[20] The Targums Onkelos, Pseudo-Jonathan and Neophyti I appear to draw a connection between the sacrifices referred to in verse 5 and the statement that the representatives of Israel 'ate and drank'. Ibn Ezra takes 'they ate and drank' to mean that 'they came down from the mountain rejoicing and ate the sacrifices which their young men had offered'. U. Cassuto, *A Commentary on the Book of Exodus*, Jerusalem 1967, p. 315 (following Ibn Ezra?) states that they ate and drank 'at the sacred meal of the peace offerings when they returned to the camp'.

For example, it is recorded that in the days of Solomon 'the people of Judah and Israel were countless as the sands of the sea; they ate and drank, and enjoyed life' (1 Kgs. 4: 20). Another example is provided by Jeremiah's words to Jehoiakim about the latter's father Josiah: 'Did not your father eat and drink and deal justly and fairly?' (Jer. 22: 15), where the context appears to indicate that Josiah 'enjoyed life, but did not omit to fulfil the solemn duties for which, as king, he was responsible'. A more pertinent text is Ecclesiastes 5: 16 where the Hebrew text is *kol-yāmāw baḥōšek yōʾkēl* (lit. 'all his days in darkness he shall eat') which must be understood 'all his days he shall live *or* spend in darkness'.[21] It is possible that another text where 'to eat bread' means 'to live' is Amaziah's command to Amos 'Seer, be off with you to Judah and there eat bread and prophesy there' (Amos 7: 12). The usual understanding of 'eat bread' here is 'earn your living'.[22] But we may note that the LXX translates 'eat bread' in this text with καταβίου 'live'.

Secondly, scholars have frequently pointed to the poetical style of this short passage, and there are some grounds for believing that the author has employed *parallelismus membrorum*. Thus v. 10a reads 'and they saw the God of Israel' which, after a brief description of what they saw 'beneath his feet', is followed in v. 11a by 'but he did not stretch forth his hand against the leaders of Israel', that is, *A* 'they saw the God of Israel': *B* they came to no harm, they survived. V. 11b forms a direct parallel to vv. 10a + 11a: *A*¹ 'They saw God' and *B*¹ 'they ate and drank', that is, 'lived'.[23]

If, contrary to the usual understanding of it as an alternative tradition to that recorded in Exodus 24: 3–8, Exodus 24: 1–2, 9–11 is rather a description of a *visio dei* vouched to Israel's representatives on the holy mountain, what is the significance of this passage as the final scene of the narrative of the making of the covenant in Exodus 19: 1–24: 11? How is it to

---

[21] See G. R. Driver, 'Problems and solutions', *VT* 4, 1954, pp. 228 f. Driver compares the Arabic expression *ʾakala ʿumurahu* (Lane) i.e. 'he completely spent his life in such and such a way', and also points to the Arabic *ʾakala rauqahu* 'he ate his life' = 'he became extremely aged' (Lane).

[22] Against this see E. Würthwein, 'Amos-Studien', *Wort und Existenz*, Göttingen 1970, p. 79 (originally published *ZAW* 62, 1949–50, p. 21), who understands Amaziah's words to Amos thus: 'So wollen die Worte in 7: 12b nur besagen: ernähre dich dort, friste dort dein Leben (das, wenn du hier bleibst, gefährdet ist).'

[23] Baroness Eileen De Ward first drew my attention to this way of understanding this text.

be understood in relation to Exodus 24: 3–8 which it now enframes? I shall return to these questions when discussing this latter passage and Exodus 19: 3b–8 which, as we shall see, is to be closely associated with it. For reasons which will be apparent later, however, I move at this stage to two other texts which have been widely regarded as ancient testimony to the tradition of a covenant between Yahweh and Israel: Exodus 34: 10–28 and Joshua 24: 1–28.

6

Apostasy and Renewal of the Covenant at Sinai
(Exodus 34: 10–28)

THE Sinai pericope in Exodus 19: 1–24: 11 is immediately followed by a narrative which in its final part is also concerned with the covenant between Yahweh and Israel (Exod. 24: 12–34: 28). The main theme of these chapters, which contain material from different sources, is the threat which Israel's apostasy in making a golden calf posed to its continued existence as Yahweh's people (Exod. 32), and the survival of its relationship with Yahweh notwithstanding this apostasy (Exod. 34). For this reason scholars usually describe this theme as one of covenant renewal. Of central importance in this narrative, and forming its literary framework, are 'the tables of stone' which Yahweh gives to Israel through Moses. Thus Moses is summoned to ascend the mountain to receive these tables upon which Yahweh has written (24: 12); upon receiving them (31: 18) he learns that during his absence upon the mountain the people have made a golden calf which they are worshipping and hailing with the cultic cry 'these are your gods, O Israel, which brought you up from the land of Egypt' (32: 1–8). On returning to the people at the foot of the mountain, Moses smashes the tables (32: 19). Subsequently he is commanded by Yahweh to prepare fresh tables upon which are to be written by Yahweh the same words which were on the first tables (34: 1); the episode as a whole ends with the record that the two tables were inscribed with 'the words of the covenant, the ten words' (34: 28).

It is only here at the end of the narrative that it is explicitly stated what was written upon these two tables. But to what does the phrase 'the ten words' refer? In its version of the same incident of the making of the golden calf, Deuteronomy leaves no doubt about this: the 'ten words' are none other than the ten commandments spoken directly by God to Israel at Horeb (Deut. 9: 7–10: 5; cf. 4: 13; 5:22); the tables upon which they are inscribed are 'the tables of the covenant' (Deut. 9: 9, 11, 15) which are deposited by Moses in 'the ark of the covenant' (Deut. 10: 1–5).

Given this, it is natural to suppose that the phrase 'the ten words' in Exodus 34: 28 likewise refers to the ten commandments which had been declared by Yahweh to Israel in Exodus 20. This would appear to be confirmed by references in the chapters immediately preceding Exodus 34 to these tables as 'the tables of the testimony' which are to be placed in 'the ark of the testimony' (25: 16, 21, 22; 26: 33, 34; 30: 6, 26; 31: 7, 18; 32: 15), terms which the Priestly author, from whom these passages derive, employed for what is described in the Deuteronomic literature as 'the tables of the covenant' and 'the ark of the covenant' respectively.

What complicates such a view, however, is that in Exodus 34: 11–27 a series of laws is given which ends with the command by Yahweh to Moses, 'Write these words, for in accordance with these words I have made a covenant with you and with Israel' (v. 27), where 'these words' clearly refers to the commandments announced in the preceding verses. How are we to reconcile this with what is then stated in the immediately following verse: 'And he was there with Yahweh forty days and nights . . . and he wrote upon the tables the words of the covenant, the ten words' (v. 28)?

I

The best known and most widely accepted solution to this problem, though not without variations in detail, received its classic presentation by Wellhausen, though he was anticipated by Goethe a century or so earlier and, it seems, even by a fifth-century Alexandrian theologian.[1] It is that before being placed in its present context by the redactor of J and E, the so-called Jehovist, the basic material in Exodus 34 was J's account of the giving of the law by Yahweh at Sinai. The phrase in v. 28 'the ten words' refers not to the decalogue of Exodus 20 but to the laws in Exodus 34: 11–26 which, though now numbering more than ten, must originally have been ten in number. This J decalogue was then termed by scholars 'the ritual decalogue', on account of its marked cultic interest, to dis-

---

[1] Goethe argued that Exodus 34 contains an alternative decalogue to that in Exodus 20 (*Zwo wichtige bisher unerörterte Fragen*, 1773, Weimar edition, xxxvii, 1896, pp. 175 ff.). See E. Nestle, 'Ein Vorgänger Goethe's über den zweiten Dekalog', *ZAW* 24, 1904, pp. 134 f. For Wellhausen's discussion see *Die Composition des Hexateuchs*, 3rd edition, Berlin 1899, pp. 85 ff.

tinguish it from the 'ethical decalogue' of Exodus 20 which was usually regarded as deriving from a later period.

Though many scholars have since rejected the view that the 'ethical decalogue' is necessarily later than the ritual laws in Exodus 34—many have argued that the decalogue in Exodus 20 and Deuteronomy 5 is based upon a much more ancient, terser composition—Wellhausen's basic insight concerning the older material in Exodus 34 is still favoured by many. As presented in more recent times by, for example, Noth, this understanding of the origin of the material in Exodus 34 is as follows.[2]

The basic material in this chapter is from J and includes the laws in vv. 11–26 (with the exception of vv. 11–13, 15–16 which are from a Deuteronomic editor) and the record of the making of the covenant in vv. 27–8.[3] In its present form and context this chapter is cast as a narrative of a renewal of the covenant which the apostasy described in Exodus 32 had broken. But this is a result of the entirely secondary linking of the original material in Exodus 34 with the narrative of the golden calf in chapter 32, a narrative which itself is a secondary addition to J and is a 'latecomer' and indeed an 'alien element' within the Pentateuchal narrative, presupposing as it clearly does the apostasy of Jeroboam I (cf. 1 Kgs 12: 26–33).[4] 'The references to the first, broken tables at the beginning of ch. 34 are inserted only loosely into the basic material of the text and can easily be separated as secondary references to ch. 32.'[5] With these and other secondary material in chapter 34 removed, what remains is none other than the original J account of the giving of the law and the making of the covenant at Sinai. This basic J material

provides the most explicit details we have in the Old Testament about the way in which this covenant is made. Yahweh's announcement in v. 10 that he now intends to make a covenant, and his closing words in v. 27 that he has now made a covenant, leave no doubt that it is here that we have the fundamental action of the covenant ... In J as it was originally written, the preparations for the theophany on mount Sinai and the theophany itself were first reported in ch. 19, and then the original J probably had some part of 24: 12–15a according to which

---

[2] *Das zweite Buch Mose*, pp. 200 ff.; E. trs. *Exodus*, pp. 243 ff.

[3] Ibid. pp. 214 ff.; E. trs. pp. 260 ff.

[4] Cf. Noth. *Überlieferungsgeschichte des Pentateuch*, p. 160; E. trs. *A History of Pentateuchal Traditions*, p. 144.

[5] *Das zweite Buch Mose*, p. 214; E. trs. p. 260.

Moses was summoned up the mountain. Ch. 34 was at first attached directly to this point.[6]

With regard to the phrase in v. 28 'the ten words', even if it is, as Noth suspects, a secondary addition, whoever placed it here must have understood the laws in vv. 11–26 to have numbered ten, though secondary additions to them make it difficult for us to discern the ten commandments as they lay before this editor.[7]

Others, however, whilst agreeing that an original J acount of the making of the covenant can be discerned in this chapter, are more uneasy about the phrase 'the ten words' and, rejecting all attempts to find an original decalogue in vv. 11–26, regard this phrase as a later addition, probably from a Deuteronomic editor, intended to interpret what was written on the tables as the decalogue of Exodus 20, nothwithstanding the confusion which the addition of this phrase in its present context creates. Amongst recent advocates of this view is, for example, B. S. Childs.[8] He sees three main stages in the development of this chapter. The basic material derived from J and contained a series of laws (allowance is made for some secondary additions in vv. 11–26 by a Deuteronomic editor) and a distinct understanding of how the covenant between Yahweh and Israel was made. In this original J account the series of laws was not conceived of as a decalogue. At a second stage the Jehovist redactor linked this J material with Exodus 32–3, introduced the motif of the broken and restored tables into chapter 34, and thus created the major theme of sin and forgiveness, breach of the covenant and its renewal. The fact that the laws in vv. 11–26 were not a repetition of those given in the Sinai pericope proper (the decalogue and the Book of the Covenant) was no problem for this redactor, since the laws in Exodus 34 'represented a convenient abbreviation of both these collections of laws on which the covenant was to be renewed' (p. 608). It was only at a still later stage that a Deuteronomic editor added the phrase 'the ten words' in v. 28 which introduced 'a distinction into the chapter which was hitherto unknown. As a result, the laws of Ex. 34 no longer matched their new framework' (p. 608).

---

[6] Ibid., p. 214; E. trs. p. 260.
[7] Ibid., p. 216; E. trs. 262.
[8] *Exodus*, London 1974, pp. 607 ff. Cf. earlier S. R. Driver, *The Book of Exodus*, Cambridge 1911, p. 365.

In contrast to this is the view first suggested, as far as I am aware, by W. Rudolph and more recently argued in detail by Beyerlin[9], which proceeds from the consideration that the phrase 'the ten words' must belong to the oldest stratum of tradition in this chapter precisely because it is impossible to derive exactly ten commandments from vv. 11–26: 'If there had been no mention of the "ten words" already present,' argues Beyerlin, 'it would never have occurred to anyone to call them "ten words" on the basis of vv. 10–26, which are a later addition and not a unity in themselves.'[10] His view is that in the earliest stage of the tradition the space now occupied by the material in vv. 11–26 was in fact occupied by the ten commandments of Exodus 20 in their earliest form. But at an early time— he leaves it open whether this was already at the stage of the formation of the Pentateuchal *Grundlage* (G) which, according to Noth, underlies the work of both J and E, or whether it took place only at the stage of the composition of J itself—the 'ethical decalogue' was displaced by the basic material in vv. 11–26. With regard to the motive for this displacement, his suggestion is as follows. The striking similarities as well as the differences between the older elements in these verses and the laws contained in Exodus 23: 12–19 render it probable that they are different recensions of a common original. The version which was worked into Exodus 34 contained vv. 14a, 17, 18, 19a, 20b, 21a, 22, 23, 26—all stipulations of a cultic-ritual nature which originally had a cultic setting and were probably transmitted in writing from the beginning. These laws, as well as those in Exodus 23: 12–19, were formulated soon after the settlement in Canaan and were directed at

upholding and promoting the indispensable aims and principles of the covenant and cult of Yahweh. Corresponding to the importance of such a law for the tribes of Israel when they settled in Canaan, not only the Book of the Covenant with its cultic regulations but also the stipulations of Exod. xxxiv. 14–26 were set in contexts which could give them a special degree of authority and emphasis. Hence, the Book of the Covenant (Exod. xx. 22–xxiii. 19) displaced the Decalogue (Exod. xx. 2–17)[11] in its rôle of *sēper habbᵉrît*, on the basis of which the Sinaitic

---

[9] W. Rudolph, *Der 'Elohist' von Exodus bis Josua*, BZAW 68, Berlin 1938, p. 59 note; W. Beyerlin, *Herkunft und Geschichte der ältesten Sinaitraditionen*, pp. 90–104; E. trs. *Origins and History of the Oldest Sinaitic Traditions*, pp. 77–90.   [10] Ibid. p. 94; E. trs., p. 81.

[11] Like many others, Beyerlin (pp. 16 f., E. trs. pp. 11 f.) argues that the decalogue originally followed Exodus 20: 18–21 and was subsequently placed before it to accommodate the incorporation of the Book of the Covenant.

covenant was made (cf. Exod. xxiv. 3-8); similarly, everything suggests that
the cultic stipulations of Exodus xxxiv supplanted the 'ten words' which were the
basis of the covenant according to J (Exod. xxxiv. 27). The maintenance of the
Sinaitic covenant in the changed situation after Israel settled in Canaan depended
on this new law being upheld. It was this conviction and not any rather clumsy,
literary editing in the Jehovistic compilation or redaction that was responsible for
the insertion of the bulk of these stipulations between Exod. xxxiv. 10aα and
Exod. xxxiv. 27, 28, to replace the original Decalogue in the Yahwistic account of
the making of the covenant.[12]

II

Perlitt has broken radically with the whole exegetical tradition since
Wellhausen which, however differently carried out in detail, finds a layer
of J material in Exodus 34: 1-28.[13] He defends the substantial unity of this
passage which he sees as having been composed along with Exodus 32
which it in every way presupposes. Both chapters are the work of a
Deuteronomic author of the seventh century, and their theological
motivation and purpose point for their background to the period of
Josiah. It was at this time that the sanctuary at Bethel was destroyed (2 Kgs.
23: 15 f.), that the prophetic narratives concerning Jeroboam's apostasy,
which Exodus 32 clearly presupposes, were composed (1 Kgs. 13; 14), and
that the dire consequences of Israel's apostasy since the time of Jeroboam
were manifest to all. Projected back to Sinai itself, since 'warning and
prohibition must of course precede the deed itself' (p. 208), Exodus 32
describes the fate which inevitably had to befall Israel because of its apostasy since the time of Jeroboam, whilst Exodus 34 describes what can still
be for the remainder of Israel, that is, contemporary Judah, if it abides by
the 'words of the covenant'; the bitter lesson of history is the pointer to
that alone in which Judah can trust for the future.

In outline, the main points of Perlitt's discussion are as follows.

(1) It is impossible to find a traditio-historical kernel for the development
of the theme of the tables of stone in the bare reference to them in Exodus
24: 12 where they are mentioned abruptly for the first time and have

---

[12] Beyerlin, p. 102; E. trs., pp. 87 f.
[13] *Bundestheologie im Alten Testament*, pp. 203-32.

evidently no source in the preceding Sinai pericope. Nor does Exodus 34 provide evidence of an original tradition concerning them, as is generally maintained especially with regard to vv. 27, 28 where it is stated what was inscribed upon them. In this chapter references to them are confined to the framework, and this framework, including vv. 27-8, is so meagre in content that it cannot properly be understood apart from the narrative in Exodus 32. Exodus 24: 12 and 34: 28 form the beginning and end of a narrative which has its focal point in Exodus 32, and it is to this chapter that we must look for the motivation of the theme of these tables of stone in the narrative as a whole.

The main concern of this chapter is with the apostasy of the making of the golden calf at Sinai, and the role of the tables of stone here is that of pressing home in a particularly dramatic manner the nature of Israel's apostate act. In short, the function of these tables in this narrative is quite simply to be smashed. Having served their purpose within the narrative in chapter 32, these tables are of little further concern for the author; it simply remained to record the manufacture of fresh tables upon which Yahweh is to reinscribe the words which had been on the first tables. That is, if I understand Perlitt correctly, Exodus 34: 1-4 is to be taken as implying the rewriting of the tables. What follows 'belongs neither upon the tables nor requires their preparation' (p. 206). The narrative in Exodus 34 originally ended with v. 27 where the tables have been 'quite forgotten'; it was a later Deuteronomistic author who, sensing a deficiency at this point and expecting some explicit reference to the reinscribing of the tables, inserted v. 28 (p. 230 note 4). The view that the content of vv. 10-26, whether as a whole or reduced to 'ten commandments', belonged upon these tables (vv. 27-8), is dependent upon the view that an originally independent J narrative of the making of a covenant is to be isolated from this chapter. But this involves an inadmissible fragmentation of the material in this chapter (see below).

(2) Since the motif of the tables of stone in these chapters is simply ancillary to the depiction of Israel's apostasy—that is, the narrative is not concerned with them in themselves—its creation is to be attributed to the authors responsible for the story of apostasy at Sinai. No part of this can be assigned to J. If this author had been responsible for an original narrative concerning these tables on which was written the law as the outcome of

the solemn encounter between Yahweh and Israel at Sinai, then we should have to ask why there is no further mention of them in the ensuing J narrative in the Pentateuch. In reality, however, the narrative as a whole belongs to a later period than the Yahwist; it presupposes the last quarter of the seventh century, the period of Josiah, when the narratives about Jeroboam's sin in making the golden calves (1 Kgs. 13; 14) were composed and when Josiah destroyed the sanctuary at Bethel (2 Kgs. 23: 15 f.). We must therefore look for the origin and formulation of the narrative of apostasy and forgiveness at Sinai to the Deuteronomic school where alone we find much greater interest in these tables (Deut. 4: 13; 5: 22; 9: 9–10: 5; 1 Kgs. 8: 9 (LXX)). It is in the Deuteronomistic literature that we are informed not only of the inscribing of the tables of stone but also of the use to which they were put: on them were written the words of the covenant and they were then deposited in the ark of the covenant by Moses. This understanding of the nature and purpose of the ark is, as is widely agreed, a distinctively Deuteronomistic development, a reinterpretation of the significance of the ark. Thus Perlitt views the use of the motif of these tables in Exodus 32 as the beginning of the development of the tradition concerning them. It was the work of a 'Levitical-Deuteronomic' circle of the late seventh century, the subject matter of what they wrote being subsequently taken up and further developed by their Deuteronomistic successors for the composition of Deuteronomy 9 f. and related texts.

(3) A serious weakness in the attempts to isolate an original J stratum in Exodus 34 is that it entails severe 'surgery' on the text. Perlitt estimates that Noth's analysis, for example, requires the excision of almost two-thirds of the material. Further, apart from the resulting mangling of what is otherwise a coherent narrative, what remains after the excision of alleged secondary material rather hangs in the air. When, for example, the references in vv. 1, 4 to the 'first tables' are deleted, the chapter begins (v. 1aα) so abruptly and without any indication of a setting that one is forced to search for a suitable starting point somewhere earlier. Noth suggests that this may be found in part of Exodus 24: 12–15a. The difficulty with such a suggestion is that what is commanded to Moses in 24: 12 is repeated in 34: 1. Such a repetition is readily understood, however, when this narrative is taken for what it is: part of the sequel to Exodus 32 where

it is already narrated that Moses, having ascended the mountain (24: 12 f.), has now descended it (32: 15). To all this may be added that such elements of Exodus 34: 1–4 as show points of contact with the J material in Exodus 19 indicate only what we should in any case expect, namely, that the author of chapter 34 knew the old description of the theophany in Exodus 19.

Perlitt likewise rejects the view that a nucleus of J material can be isolated in 34: 6–9. The excision of vv. 6aβb, 7, 9 (see Noth) not only destroys the passage from a literary point of view, but also fails to appreciate its intention and form within the overall narrative in chapters 32–4 in which it is an essential part of the 'paradigmatic drama' of sin (Exod. 32), punishment (ibid.), and forgiveness (Exod. 34: 6–9). Decisive in this respect, and not to be regarded as secondary material, is v. 9, a verse which in fact characterizes the theological context of Exodus 32–4 as a whole: like 32: 34a or 33: 1–6 or 33: 12–17, it has in view the coming (and now realized) future history of Israel; it is in reality an overview of Israel's fate from Sinai to the period in which this verse belongs, a period now also characterized by apostasy, and it focuses upon that pattern of apostasy and appeal for forgiveness which was already established at Sinai, according to the 'paradigm' of this overall narrative, and which can now again, in this late period, be operative for Israel. Structurally and theologically, this passage belongs to the same type of context as Numbers 14: 18–20 or 1 Kings 8: 30 ff., and this context is here supplied by the narrative in Exodus 32–4.

(4) In the light of this, what follows also falls naturally into place. In response to the plea in Exodus 34: 6–9 there follows Yahweh's declaration 'Behold, I make a *bᵉrît*' (v. 10). Noth's suggestion that the remainder of v. 10 is a secondary addition is to be rejected; what we expect after the plea in vv. 6–9 is just such a promise, and that is the content of the word *bᵉrît*, as Kutsch has shown. The entire course of the narrative in Exodus 32–4 serves this promise of Yahweh's faithfulness; it is the expression of his grace from which not even Israel's apostasy can deflect him. Accordingly, this promise has its proper context within the narrative of these chapters; we do not have to postulate that it once existed independently of this context as part of an original J covenant narrative, as is usually maintained.

Moreover, Exodus 34: 27 must be understood strictly alongside the declaration in v. 10: the obligation which is here (v. 27) laid upon Israel corresponds to the promise given (v. 10); both together, promise and obligation, grace and law, constitute the basis of Israel's life according to Deuteronomic theology.

(5) What of the laws in Exodus 34: 11–26? Perlitt quotes with approval Alt's view that both 'from its literary relationship to the Book of the Covenant and from its particular interest, appropriate to its formal compilation, [this collection of laws] can be seen to be a later and hetero-geneous compilation, containing priestly ordinances about cultic duties of lay-people in a greater proportion than apodeictic elements from the Decalogue of Exodus 20'.[14] Further, neither the supplementary note in v. 28bβ ('the ten words') nor the analogy of the decalogue in Exodus 20 warrants the attempts to isolate a decalogue in Exodus 34: 11–26. The many attempts to do so, with the resulting wide variations, do not inspire confidence, and in any case usually depend for their viability upon the unwarranted isolation of v. 14a ('you shall not worship another god') from its context (vv. 11–16) which is widely agreed to be from a Deuteronomic hand. Such attempts also entail a fragmentation of the text and must be rejected so long as other explanations of its origin and nature remain possible. In reality there is nothing in this series of commandments, including their specifically cultic interest, which cannot be attributed to a Deuteronomic provenance (cf. especially Deuteronomy 16 for a similar cultic interest).

III

Further studies which have appeared since the publication of Perlitt's work differ both from his analysis and from each other's, so that a lack of consensus currently characterizes the investigation of the composition and growth of Exodus 32–4. J. Halbe, for example, concentrating on Exodus 34,[15] has argued again the view that a substantial stratum of this

---

[14] Alt, 'Die Ursprünge des israelitischen Rechts', *KS* 1, p. 317 note 1; E. trs., p. 117 note 95.

[15] *Das Privilegrecht Jahwes. Ex 34, 10–26: Gestalt und Wesen, Herkunft und Wirken in vordeuteronomischer Zeit*, FRLANT 114, Göttingen 1975.

chapter derives from the Yahwist's work from the period of the united monarchy, though the Yahwist inherited its basic material from a still earlier time when most of the laws contained in vv. 10-26 constituted a statement of the 'privileges' due to Yahweh (*das Privilegrecht Jahwes*). Halbe argues that the later history of this ancient *Privilegrecht* now incorporated into Exodus 34 formed part of the background to the emergence of the Deuteronomic theology. E. Zenger, on the other hand, comes closer to the view of Perlitt, though there are still important differences.[16] There are some fragments of J and E material in Exodus 32-4, but the composition of these chapters began with the work of a Jehovist author who composed it as a programme for Hezekiah's reformation in the final years of the eighth century BC . Zenger sees this Jehovist author as the precursor of the Deuteronomic school, what he wrote subsequently being worked over in two stages by Deuteronomistic redactors and still later by a Priestly editor, though other individual fragments of tradition and further redactional additions have also been incorporated. R. W. L. Moberly, whilst allowing for a certain amount of redactional material, attempts to defend the substantial unity of these chapters, especially of 34: 1-28 of which he states: 'There is a smoothness and coherence which more likely suggests original unity than secondary modification.'[17] By contrast, H. L. Ginsberg regards 34: 10-27 as a secondary Deuteronomistic insertion into an original E narrative of the incident of the making of the golden calf; the 'ten words' mentioned in 34: 28 refer not to the decalogue in Exodus 20: 1-17 but to a decalogue which can be isolated from the stipulations in Exodus 23: 10-27 and which he names 'The First Ritual Decalogue'.[18]

IV

In my view Perlitt's discussion of Exodus 32-4 has made a number of illuminating and permanent advances for the understanding of the nature and composition of this narrative. The observations which follow are

---

[16] *Die Sinaitheophanie. Untersuchungen zum jahwistischen und elohistischen Geschichtswerk*, Forschung zur Bibel 2, Würzburg 1971.

[17] *At the Mountain of God, JSOT* Supplement Series 22, Sheffield 1983, p. 158.

[18] *The Israelian Heritage of Judaism* , New York 1982, pp. 46 f.

dependent in significant respects upon his work, but it will be seen that I do not accept his conclusions in their entirety.

(1) Whilst I accept that the primary role of the tables of stone in this narrative is as Perlitt suggests, in my view the question remains pertinent: what did its author understand to have been written upon the tables of stone?

It is difficult to accept that the author was unconcerned with this, and that his sole interest in these tables was, as Perlitt suggests, in their being dramatically smashed at the foot of the mountain. If that was the limit of his interest in them, why did he concern himself with stating that fresh tables were prepared to be re-inscribed by Yahweh? After all, one would have supposed, on Perlitt's understanding of the matter, that the destruction of them and thus their loss for ever would have been an effective way to portray the seriousness of Israel's apostasy on the occasion described. That he recorded the making of new tables to be re-inscribed with the same words as were on the first tables surely suggests that he was more concerned with what was written upon them than Perlitt allows. Further, it is surely inherently unlikely that the author would not have expected his readers to be aware of, or to infer, what was written on these tables in a unique way by God himself, by 'the finger of God'.

Zenger (p. 164) argues that in the original (Jehovist) form of this narrative these tables were not conceived of as having laws inscribed upon them. Rather, they were 'Lebens-Tafeln' upon which Yahweh registered Israel's name as his people (reference is made to Psalm 87: 6 for a similar motif). But not only has such a suggestion no evidence to support it in the narrative in Exodus; it also fails to explain why more than one table would have been required for such a purpose.

In my opinion there are no good reasons for doubting that the author of this narrative, like the priestly author to whom Exodus 24: 12–34: 35 owes substantially its final form, intended it to be understood that the two tables of stone were inscribed with the decalogue of Exodus 20 which had earlier and in a unique manner been communicated directly by Yahweh to Israel.[19] The uniqueness of the inscribing of the commandments upon these tables by God himself, by 'the finger of God' (Exod. 31: 18; cf. Deut.

---

[19] On this, see my 'The Decalogue as the Direct Address of God', *VT* 27, 1977, pp. 422–33.

9: 10), fittingly corresponded with the uniqueness of their primary delivery by the direct address of Yahweh to the assembled people: what God himself had directly spoken to his people was now also written by him.

(2) Perlitt's suggestion that the author of Exodus 34: 1–4, who in v. 1 states that Yahweh is to re-inscribe the tables, intended the reader to understand that this was carried out by Yahweh is both illuminating and valid. Had the author intended otherwise, it would have been an easy matter to describe (in v. 1) Yahweh as commanding Moses to write upon the tables, just as he describes him as having ordered Moses to prepare new tables to replace the first ones which Yahweh himself had made. That Yahweh re-inscribed the tables, and that what follows—the commandments in vv. 11–26—is to be written by Moses as something separate from the tables is what the narrative as far as v. 27 describes, and coherently so.

What, then, of v. 28? Though syntactically it appears to attribute the inscribing of the second set of tables to Moses, it is surely difficult to accept that it was deliberately intended to contradict what up to this point is a coherent narrative. If it is from the author of vv. 1–27, we should regard him as having been guilty of nothing more than a somewhat infelicitous syntax and read it as referring not to Moses as the subject of the action described, which would flatly contradict what he wrote in v. 1, but to Yahweh, and thus as being in accordance with what is stated in the latter verse. Alternatively, if v. 28 is, as Perlitt suggests, a secondary addition, its most likely source is a Deuteronomistic editor, and it is difficult to believe that a Deuteronomistic editor would have intended what was written upon the two tables of stone to be understood as anything other than the decalogue, or that he could have intended it to be understood that Moses and not Yahweh wrote upon these tables (cf. Deut. 4: 13; 5: 22; 9: 10; 10: 2, 4). Moberly (p. 103) makes a plausible suggestion as follows:

V. 28a reads naturally as the conclusion to the preceding narrative, rounding off the time of Moses' sojourn on Sinai. If Moses is the subject of v. 28b and he is fulfilling the command of v. 27, one would expect the note in v. 28a about the duration of his stay on Sinai to come after v. 28b and not before. V. 28b, coming after v. 28a, reads like an additional note, added to tie up a remaining loose end in the narrative, rather than as a continuation and fulfilment of v. 27. As such, the focus in v. 28b could have moved away from Moses, reference to whom is now complete, to Yahweh.

An alternative suggestion, partly based on this, is to regard v. 28a as completing the description of Moses's activity on the mountain, and v. 28b as an *inclusio* with v. 1 and therefore not necessarily a secondary addition.

(3) According to Perlitt, the covenant described in vv. 10–27 was composed for its present context as the expression of Yahweh's grace and Yahweh's demand after the apostasy at Sinai. His overall view is that it was this narrative which first introduced the notion of a covenant into the narratives of the events at Sinai, the description of the making of a covenant in Exodus 19: 3b–8 and 24: 3–8 being, in his view, the result of Deuteronomistic redaction subsequent to the Deuteronomic composition of Exodus 32–4, and Exodus 34: 28 being also a secondary addition from a Deuteronomistic hand.

But even if v. 28 is a secondary addition, we are still left not only with what Moses (v. 27) is commanded to write—the words of the covenant in vv. 11–26—but also with what Yahweh inscribed upon the tables of stone (v. 1), that is, as seems likely, the decalogue. Since, however, it is surely unlikely that, though the commandments in vv. 11–26 are commandments of a solemn covenant, those of the decalogue were not considered such by the author of this narrative, the conclusion must be that two covenants are referred to in this narrative: the one involving the decalogue and concluded prior to the episode described in Exodus 32–4, the other (vv. 10–27) declared in the wake of the apostasy here narrated. How may this be explained?

(4) The Old Testament describes more than one occasion of the making of a covenant involving Yahweh and Israel. Deuteronomy 28: 69 (EVV 29: 1) records the making of a covenant between Yahweh and Israel 'in the land of Moab, besides the covenant which he had made with them at Horeb'; upon completion of the settlement in the land, according to the Deuteronomist author of Joshua 24 (see below, chapter seven), Joshua made a covenant binding Israel to exclusive allegiance to Yahweh, 'and

made statutes and ordinances for them at Shechem, and . . . wrote these words in the book of the law of God' (Josh. 24: 25 f.); at a later time Josiah 'made a covenant before Yahweh, to walk after Yahweh and to keep his commandments and his testimonies and his statutes' (2 Kgs. 23: 3).

Theologically we touch here upon an understanding of the relationship between Yahweh and Israel which was one of the distinctive contributions of the notion of a covenant between them to Old Testament faith: that Israel's status as Yahweh's people was not something grounded in the nature of things, something divinely guaranteed as permanent as though inherent in a fixed cosmic order, but rather that it was constituted by Yahweh's decision and choice and no less by Israel's.[20] God chooses, but Israel too must decide and choose, and this deciding and choosing confronted Israel throughout its history, for by its very nature the notion of a covenant between Yahweh and Israel carried with it the possibility that the relationship between them could be terminated. Put differently, that Israel is the people of Yahweh is conceived of in covenant-theology as a declaration not merely of Israel's status but of Israel's vocation, and the presupposition of the covenant and its demands is an Israel which is not naturally given to fulfilling this vocation and which therefore has to be summoned ever and again to decide for Yahweh.

On this basis the covenant described in Exodus 34: 10–27 should be taken for what it is portrayed as within the overall context of the events at Sinai beginning at Exodus 19: a second covenant freshly declaring Yahweh's commitment to Israel and what this requires of Israel in the wake of the apostasy which threatened its continued existence as Yahweh's people. In its nature and content this covenant is bilateral: it arises immediately from Moses's plea in v. 9 that Yahweh would 'go in our midst' and take Israel for his 'inheritance', in response to which it declares Yahweh's commitment to Israel and the demands which this places upon Israel as his people.

(5) All this means that, without accepting the particular source-critical analysis upon which it was arrived at (as outlined in section I above), we may still understand Exodus 34: 10–27 as a renewal or reaffirmation of Yahweh's covenant with Israel. As such, it was composed for and with its present context, as Perlitt has cogently argued, and there is no need to

---

[20] See below, pp. 210, 214–7.

suppose that the space it occupies was once occupied by the decalogue of Exodus 20, as some have maintained. There are no compelling reasons for seeing it as a reworking of an earlier J narrative, a view which is further weakened by necessitating the excision of material from the passage to an extent scarcely paralleled in the case of the analysis of any other Pentateuchal text. It is a late composition, most probably, as Perlitt argues, from a Deuteronomic author: Deuteronomic style and theology are discernible in vv. 11-16;[21] v. 24 appears to know of the notion of a centralized cult, as in Deuteronomic theology, while the designation of the passover as a pilgrim-festival (*ḥag*, v. 25) is also evidence of a late date.[22]

The passage belongs to a narrative which, set within the context of the events at Sinai at the beginning of Israel's history, reflects Israel's continued rebelliousness and the judgement this merits—and, in the case of northern Israel, has incurred—but also declares Yahweh's continued grace and readiness to forgive a repentant Israel, and no less Yahweh's demand upon Israel. That is, like other descriptions of covenant-making—at Sinai in Exodus 19-24, on the plains of Moab, and at Shechem—what is portrayed as a past event is in reality a present endeavour to transform Israel from what it historically has been into what it is summoned to be: the people of Yahweh; herein lay Israel's *raison d'être* and thus Israel's hope.

(6) The Deuteronomistic authors of Deuteronomy 4-5 and of the narrative of apostasy at Horeb in Deuteronomy 9: 7-10: 5 make no mention of the covenant described in Exodus 34: 10-28; for these authors only one covenant was made at Sinai and on the basis of the decalogue alone, though they state that other 'statutes and ordinances' were communicated by Yahweh to Moses at that time for later instruction of the people (Deut. 4: 14; 5: 31). But this may be explained as a distinctively Deuteronomistic development and does not necessarily mean that earlier

---

[21] The use of the you-plural form of address in v. 13 may here be to effect emphasis and is not necessarily evidence that this verse is a secondary insertion. On this phenomenon see N. Lohfink, *Das Hauptgebot: Eine Untersuchung literarischer Einleitungsfragen zu Dtn 5-11*, Analecta Biblica 20, Rome 1963, pp. 30 f., 239 ff., 244 ff., 252 ff., and the comments of A. D. H. Mayes, *Deuteronomy*, pp. 35 ff.

[22] Cf. G. Fohrer, *Geschichte der israelitischen Religion*, Berlin 1969, pp. 90 f.; E. trs. *History of Israelite Religion*, London 1973, pp. 100 f. (Against Fohrer, however, there is no need to regard the words 'the sacrifice of the feast of the Passover' as a secondary addition.)

Deuteronomic authors could not have understood and described matters differently.[23]

Perlitt makes a good case for ascribing the composition of the narrative of apostasy and forgiveness in Exodus 32–4 to the reign of Josiah. On the other hand, others recently have plausibly argued that it derives from a Jehovist author, understood as a 'proto-Deuteronomic' author, of the time of Hezekiah, and relate the contents of 34: 10–26 to the reformation carried out by that king in the closing years of the eighth century BC.[24] A decision between these two views is not essential for our purposes here;[25] it is sufficient to conclude that Exodus 34: 10–27(28) derives from this relatively late period in Israel's history and does not provide testimony to a more ancient covenant tradition.

[23] A. Phillips, 'A Fresh Look at the Sinai Pericope', *VT* 34, 1984, pp. 46 f., argues that these Deuteronomist authors have deliberately suppressed references both to the Book of the Covenant and to Exodus 34: 10–28 in order 'to provide the only authoritative statement of the nature of Israel's relationship with her God based on their covenant theology' (p. 47).

[24] For example, Zenger, p. 164; Phillips, *Ancient Israel's Criminal Law*, pp. 169 ff.; 'Prophecy and Law', *Israel's Prophetic Tradition*, ed. R. Coggins, A. Phillips, M. Knibb, Cambridge 1982, p. 227; 'A Fresh Look at the Sinai Pericope', pp. 48 ff. Cf. C. H. W. Brekelmans, 'Éléments Deutéronomiques dans le Pentateuque', *Recherches Bibliques* 8, Bruges 1967, pp. 77–91.

[25] My acceptance of the pre-exilic origin of Exodus 34, which, as argued above, presupposes the presence of the decalogue in the Sinai pericope, entails a revision of my conclusions in *VT* 27, 1977, p. 431, in that there I argued that the decalogue was inserted in Exodus 20 by a P editor of the exilic or early post-exilic period.

7

A Covenant at Shechem
(Joshua 24: 1–28)

No text has been more significant in the discussion of the origin and nature of the covenant between Yahweh and Israel than Joshua 24, with its record of the making of a covenant by Joshua at Shechem upon the completion of the conquest and settlement of the land. The location of this ceremony at Shechem, the evident importance of Shechem in early Israelite history, and, most notably, the references associating a deity named *ba'al bᵉrīt* or *'ēl bᵉrīt* with the Canaanite sanctuary there (Jud. 8: 33; 9: 4, 46) were at one time believed to be evidence that the notion of a covenant between Yahweh and Israel originated at Shechem. The tradition of the making of a covenant at Sinai was believed to be a secondary development dependent upon this more ancient Shechemite tradition.[1] For various reasons such a view was unable to sustain itself, especially in face of the conviction which became widely accepted that at least a nucleus of historicity underlies the tradition of the making of a covenant at Sinai in the pre-settlement period.[2] Nevertheless, Joshua 24 was by no means overshadowed by this, and with the publication in 1930 of Noth's work on early Israel the view gained widespread support that this passage preserves the memory of the formation of an Israelite 'amphictyony' by means of a covenant made by Joshua and the representatives of the tribes at Shechem. It was also generally maintained that the passage reflects not simply a once-for-all event but also a recurring festival which centred upon the renewal of this covenant between the tribes and Yahweh. Thus, for the understanding of the covenant as originally an 'institution' rather than a 'theological idea' Joshua 24 has been of paramount importance.

---

[1] See the works cited in ch. 2 note 8.

[2] For a review and discussion see R. E. Clements, 'Baal-Berith of Shechem', *JSS* 13, 1968, pp. 21–32.

I

The fact that the passage displays unmistakable affinities with the language and style of the Deuteronomic literature was not regarded as a difficulty in arriving at such a conclusion: an earlier nucleus of material had been secondarily edited by a Deuteronomic or Deuteronomistic hand and placed in its present context. Perlitt begins his own discussion of the text with two observations concerning this.[3] First, it is methodologically inadmissible, since it is prompted not by the text itself but by an understanding of a historical situation exterior to the text, to postulate a pre-Deuteronomic basic stock here and then proceed to eliminate other elements as Deuteronomic 'glosses', and in any case analysis will show that what remains after the deletion of Deuteronomic material is so meagre as to be of no further use, least of all for reconstructing events of the pre-monarchical period. Secondly, sounder method requires that we begin with the text as we have it and seek to determine whether in language, form, and content it is a unity with a discernible historical and theological motivation and setting in the period to which its Deuteronomic language naturally points. Only if it should turn out that the passage is not such a unity would an alternative setting for the tradition have to be sought. The main points of Perlitt's discussion are as follows.

(1) Joshua 24: 1–28 has no narrative connection with its context, but has been secondarily inserted into it. Thus the assembly of the people which is mentioned in v. 1 has been summoned without that described in chapter 23 having come to an end; and whilst in 23: 14 Joshua announces his imminent death, which is recorded in 24: 29, 24: 15 with its reference to his future worship of Yahweh implies the continuation of his life.

(2) To regard this passage as a 'narrative' is a misconception. The specifically narrative elements (vv. 1, 25 f., 28) are nothing more than a framework providing the setting for a monologue by Yahweh placed on the lips of Joshua (vv. 2–13) and a dialogue between Joshua (vv. 14 f., 19 f., 22 f.) and the people (vv. 16–18, 21, 24). Any attempt to analyse the passage

---

[3] *Bundestheologie im Alten Testament*, p. 240.

from a literary-critical point of view cannot make any appeal to a distinction between actions described and speeches recorded, for the action of Joshua in v. 25a ('so Joshua made a covenant for the people that day') is not related to what is described in v. 1 but to the preceding dialogue between himself and the people, and to the vow which they implicitly make there which is explicitly ratified with the making of *bᵉrīt* in v. 25. The *bᵉrīt* here is not a covenant (*Bund*) with Yahweh, but the formal expression of Israel's solemn pledge or oath of loyalty to Yahweh (pp. 260–70). This is the content of the *bᵉrīt* here: to worship Yahweh alone. It is not a question of the ordering of Israel's daily life, nor the way in which they are to serve Yahweh; it is Yahweh as the sole object of their service which is the centre of attention here. For this reason vv. 25b, 26a ('and he made statutes and ordinances for them at Shechem; and Joshua wrote these words in the book of the law of God') are probably from a still later Deuteronomistic hand. They point to a period in which the *bᵉrīt* could no longer be envisaged without a legislative content and so to the period when the Deuteronomic preaching had itself become literature. In its original, pre-Deuteronomistic form the passage probably ended with 25a, 26b, 27; vv. 25a and 26b belong together in both content and syntax, and v. 27 presupposes both of them: the people's oath of loyalty is witnessed to by this stone at Shechem. Verse 28 brings the episode to an end, but it is questionable whether it belonged to the pre-Deuteronomistic text. The way in which it is taken up and filled out in Judges 2: 6 suggests that it was added by the Deuteronomistic editor who placed the passage as a whole in its present context.

(3) The scene described in this passage cannot seriously be considered to derive from a cultic *Sitz im Leben*. The choice here placed before Israel, for or against Yahweh, and the sort of dialogue which is described as having taken place renders such a view impossible. No cultic tradition lies behind v. 15; it is unthinkable that in its festival cult Israel could have been thus addressed: 'If it does not please you to serve Yahweh, choose this day whom you will serve' (pp. 244, 259). Similarly, v. 19a ('you cannot serve Yahweh, for he is a holy God') renders the view that the scene described depicts the taking of a vow in a cultic setting absurd, whilst as a preparation for the concluding of a 'treaty' with Yahweh such a statement would be as suitable as using oil to put out a fire (p. 244).

(4) Joshua 24 is not a description of the initiation of groups into the worship of Yahweh. On the contrary, its urgent parenetic tone, its depiction of the challenge from other gods, its appeal for Israel's undivided loyalty to Yahweh, all betray a background in which the worship of Yahweh has been long known but can no longer be taken for granted and as a matter of course. What the worship of Yahweh means here is presupposed; it is not a question of what kind of service is to be rendered him, but whether he alone is to be the object of Israel's worship. What may the background to such a situation have been?

(5) Perlitt finds the key to this in the striking references, unique to this passage, to 'the gods whom your fathers worshipped beyond the river' (vv. 2, 14, 15). Here we have no mere historical allusion to what once was; the 'of old' in v. 2 is matched by the 'and now' of v. 14 which with its appeal to 'put away' the worship of these gods means that such worship is a present reality in Israel. It is from 'beyond the river' that this threat now endangers Israel's life, 'beyond the river' where the Assyrians live and whose gods have been installed for worship here and now in the midst of Israel:[4] 'For this only one period comes into consideration, the seventh century, and that is the period in which and from whose religious necessities the Deuteronomic preaching arose.' (p. 251.) It was a situation in which the gods of Mesopotamia and Palestine, here specified by 'the gods whom your fathers worshipped' and 'the gods of the Amorites' respectively, stood in opposition to Yahweh. Thus the subject matter and the purpose as well as the form and style of this passage converge in the historical setting of Assyrian domination of Israel and Judah and the rise of the Deuteronomic movement. And this renders attempts to find a different setting, with the splitting up of verses or the separation of literary layers or motifs which this involves, quite unnecessary.

(6) The passage cannot be attributed to a Deuteronomistic author of the exilic period. The choice which it lays before Israel is a real one; here we

---

[4] That this was Assyrian policy toward vassals has been recently re-argued by H. Spieckermann, *Juda unter Assur in der Sargonidenzeit*, FRLANT 129, Göttingen 1982, against, for example, J. W. McKay, *Religion in Judah under the Assyrians*, London 1973, and M. Cogan, *Imperialism and Religion: Assyria, Judah and Israel in the Eighth and Seventh Centuries B.C.E.*, Missoula 1974.

have the voice of Deuteronomic preachers who as yet do not know the judgement which was to follow the wrong choice which Israel made and which is one of the subjects of the Deuteronomistic theology and writings of a later period (pp. 245, 273–9). The *terminus ad quem* for the composition of Joshua 24 is therefore the period of Josiah. The century or so between the time of Hezekiah and Josiah, when the worship of Yahweh was in constant danger of being stifled, suggests itself as the most likely period. For a more precise setting Perlitt suggests three possiblities.

(*a*) For Northern Israel this century was characterized by loss of statehood and identity. The replacement of the name Israel by the geographically and politically restricted province of Samaria, and the replacement of erstwhile native ruling classes with foreigners loyal to the Assyrian overlord, would have driven underground an 'all-Israelite' way of thinking and a theology associated with it. What the Assyrians had introduced in the religious sphere was thus referred to in concealed fashion as the gods 'from beyond the river'. Further, the description in 2 Kings 17: 33 ('they feared Yahweh but also served their own gods') indicates the climate in which not only the newly settled foreigners but also the Israelites lived. The pronounced emphasis upon the choice before Israel in Joshua 24, as well as the pointed witness to what Yahweh alone had wrought in history on Israel's behalf, fits suitably into such a climate of uprooting, foreign rulership and religious plurality. It is possible, therefore, that Joshua 24 originated in northern Israel, in the newly constituted province of Samaria. Shechem was chosen as the location for the setting of the scene described because it had long since ceased to be politically significant, was associated with an ancient Yahweh sanctuary, and besides had not been disavowed by prophetic threats. From northern Israel the text would subsequently have found its way to Judah, perhaps at the hands of refugees.

(*b*) Alternatively, a Judaean setting for the composition of the passage is also possible. Judah had become a vassal of Assyria already in the time of Ahaz and was to remain so for over a century. The virtually complete subordination of Ahaz to the Assyrians is evidenced by his reconstitution of the temple in Jerusalem into a sanctuary for the Assyrian god Asshur (cf. 2 Kgs. 16: 10–18). Hezekiah's attempt to break with the Assyrians came to failure; vassaldom remained under Manasseh and the religious situation of Manasseh's reign would fit well as the background for Joshua 24. In such a situation Joshua 24 would have been viewed not as a call to resistance—that would scarcely have been possible—but as a sort of holding programme: 'Far be it from us to forsake Yahweh' (v. 16a). Such a situation would also explain why the imposition of the Assyrian state cult is not explicitly mentioned but is referred to cryptically as the gods from 'beyond the river'.

(*c*) A third possibility remains: the period of the downfall of Assyrian power and the actions of Josiah who not only dismantled the religious and political concessions made by Ahaz and Manasseh (2 Kgs. 23: 5), but also in so doing renounced Judah's vassaldom to Assyria. More favourable conditions than those which existed in Hezekiah's days now presented themselves; the Assyrians were probably no longer able to take effective action, and so Josiah began his march northwards to Bethel (2 Kgs. 23: 15), to the province of Samaria (2 Kgs. 23: 19), and to Megiddo (2 Kgs. 23: 29) where he met his death. But before the tragedy at Megiddo new hopes had been kindled and fanned. In such a situation Joshua 24 may have been composed with those in northern Israel in mind as its addressees; this would explain the references both to the gods here being opposed and to the particular place (Shechem) where the scene described is set. Shechem would have guaranteed dignity without lifting the veil of secrecy, which we may presume was still necessary in northern Israel at this stage; a choice of Bethel would clearly have been ruled out (cf. 2 Kgs. 23: 15), as also would the long discredited name of Samaria.

Of these three possibilities Perlitt considers the second to have most in its favour. Against the first he suggests that the Deuteronomic language and theology of Joshua 24 are already relatively too mature for such an early dating, and that if it had originated at such a time one might have expected to find some traces of its influence in the exchanges between Isaiah and Hezekiah. A difficulty with the third is that under Josiah a more overt action would have been possible than is suggested by this text. The covert reference to the Assyrian gods as the gods from 'beyond the river', as well as the unavoidable choice which Israel is here called upon to make between Yahweh and other deities, is most readily understood against the background of the reign of Manasseh in whose time there was as yet no sign of the crumbling of Assyrian power.

II

In his discussion of this passage McCarthy, whose views on its supposed treaty-like elements we noted earlier, also regards it as substantially a unity. With Perlitt too he agrees that it is to be dated earlier than Deuteronomy and the Deuteronomistic literature.[5] Beyond this, however, his conclusions are markedly different from those of Perlitt. He argues that the passage contains too many 'un-Deuteronomic' features to be regarded simply as deriving from the Deuteronomic school of the seventh/sixth centuries; the passage is best described as pre- or proto-Deuteronomic. For example, the 'stone and especially its function developed in vs. 27 is simply unacceptable to Dtistic ideas. So is the sacred tree—Dt and later traditions deplored the "high places and green trees"' (p. 223). These same features together with the location of the scene at Shechem give the tradition an 'antique setting'. This does not mean that the admittedly Deuteronomic phraseology observable in the passage is to be excised as the work of a later editor working upon an earlier text:

A style like that of Dt and Dtr does not spring fully equipped from a writer or a school. It presupposes a preparation, a development of language and thought which makes the style possible. To say the least, the 'almost Dtistic' phrases in Jos 24 are the kind of thing which show such development going on. They should be seen as relics of a stage of language which made Dtic writing possible. This is far more likely, surely, than that they are Dtistic tags added to the material by later hands which could create a masterful construction but which could not quite control their proper language. This is confirmed by the fact that the over-whelming bulk of the material is old. The 'Dtistic' elements are well integrated with it. They belong to the expression of this old material. (pp. 233 f.)

As to the historical background of the passage, McCarthy like Perlitt believes the clue to lie in the references to the gods from 'beyond the river', but he rejects all three possibilities suggested by Perlitt concerning the background to these references. Since the text is pre- or proto-Deuteronomic, it is necessary to look for an earlier setting than Perlitt suggests. In this connection he points to the use of the phrase 'beyond the river' in 2 Samuel 10: 16 where it refers to the Aramaeans, and he concludes:

[5] *Treaty and Covenant*,[2] pp. 221–34.

Now here we have a people in constant touch with Israel. Their military power and their commercial colonies (1 Kgs. 20, 34) exercised continual influence not just from outside but even from within Israel, and in ancient times it would have been as much religious as political and economic pressure. Hence the reference could relate to the kingdom of Israel at almost any time after the collapse of David's empire when Aram immediately became a menace to Israel (cf. 1 Kgs. 11, 23–25). The problem was so great that the Omrids made alliance with Tyre in an attempt to create a balance. In this light the suggestion that Jos 24 is linked with the revival of Yahwist opposition typified by Elijah is excellent. It fits the historical situation when there was influence from Aram to the east and pressure from the Baal worshippers within the land itself under Jezebel's encouragement. It makes reasonable the suggestion that the gods of the Land as well as those from beyond the River were a danger (24, 14–15). It also takes into account the relation of the pre-Dtic material with the prophetic movement which has been recognised almost since the critical study of the OT began. (p. 283.)

The background suggested by McCarthy for Joshua 24 is untenable. Whatever pressures Israel may have felt from the Aramaeans of the period which he has in mind, there is no evidence of an introduction or upsurge of Aramaean cults in Israel at that time. The narrative of the contest between Elijah and his opponents at Carmel (1 Kgs. 18) makes no mention of such cults as a threat to the worship of Yahweh; it is the indigenous cult of Baal, evidently encouraged by Jezebel, which poses the danger here. Similarly, the summary of Ahab's apostasy in 1 Kings 21: 26 refers to his worship of indigenous 'Amorite' gods, but not to specifically Aramaean cults. In the narrative of Ahaziah's sickness (2 Kgs. 1) this king's apostasy is to Baal-zebub of Ekron. Or again, the narrative of Jehu's bloodthirsty purge (2 Kgs. 10: 18–27) makes no mention of Aramaean gods and cults; as in the scene at Carmel, here too it is the indigenous cult of Baal that is the focus of concern.

It is more likely that Joshua 24: 1–28 derives from a much later period. It is very probably a secondary addition to the Deuteronomistic history, possibly indeed a very late addition.[6] In my opinion Perlitt is justified in rejecting the suggestion that it is based upon a more ancient nucleus. In addition, the narrative provides no evidence that what is described as having taken place was the initiation of Israelite groups into the worship

---

[6] For a recent discussion see A. D. H. Mayes, *The Story of Israel between Settlement and Exile*, London 1983, pp. 46–52.

of Yahweh hitherto unknown to them, much less that it was the initiation of elements of the autochthonous Canaanite population. Rather, as Perlitt correctly observes, the passage has all the appearance of having been addressed to an Israel which had long since known the worship of its national God but had also long since worshipped other gods as well.

<h2 style="text-align:center">III</h2>

I shall return to the historical background of the narrative. But first the question arises of the nature of the *bᵉrīt* described at its climax, 'Joshua made a *bᵉrīt* for the people that day' (v. 25a). Perlitt argues that it consists solely in Israel's oath of loyalty to serve Yahweh alone; it is not a 'covenant' (*Bund*) between two partners, Yahweh and Israel, but an obligation (*Verpflichtung*) placed upon Israel by Joshua ('Josua verpflichtet das Volk'; p. 263). He argues that v. 25b, which describes a broader content of the *bᵉrīt* here made, is a later interpretative interpolation, and suggests that it derives from a time when such a *bᵉrīt* could no longer be conceived of solely in terms of the first commandment but embraced a wider range of obligations. It reflects a time when the Deuteronomic preaching had already found expression in literature. The content of vv. 1–25a, he argues, is solely 'to serve Yahweh, and him exclusively'; the object of Israel's worship, Yahweh alone, is the issue here, not the regulating of daily life or even the particular kind of worship due to Yahweh. Over against this pre-occupation of vv. 1–25a, v. 25b is 'foreign matter' (*res aliena*; p. 268).

Indisputably the emphasis of the narrative is upon the exclusive worship of Yahweh. Yet even without reference to vv. 25b, 26a it may be questioned whether this is the only issue here, the sole content of the *bᵉrīt* which is made. The people's final response to Joshua in v. 24b 'Yahweh our God we will serve, and his voice [i.e. command] we will obey' already suggests a wider content than Perlitt is willing to allow to the *bᵉrīt* (cf. Exod. 19: 5 'Now therefore, if you will obey my voice indeed, and keep my covenant . . .'). Similarly, the warning in v. 19 that this 'holy God' whom 'you cannot serve' will not forgive 'your rebellion and your sins' appears to have a broader understanding of what it means 'to serve' Yahweh than Perlitt allows for vv. 1–25a. In the light of what is said in these verses (19, 24), which suggests that the concern here is more than simply the first commandment, there is no sound reason for regarding the reference to 'statute and ordinance' in v. 25b as *res aliena*, or for viewing v. 26a with its allusion to 'the book of the *tōrāh* of God' as also a secondary addition.

The making of the covenant so tersely described in v. 25a is therefore not simply an agreement between Joshua and the people, or a solemn pledge exacted by Joshua from them, to worship Yahweh and eschew the worship of other gods. More than this, it is a matter of what this God, who through his actions on their behalf has made this people his own (vv. 1–13) and is acknowledged by them to have done so (vv. 16–18), requires of them if he is to continue as their God and they as his people: their loyalty to him alone and their obedience to his *tōrāh*. He does not remain their God, come what may (cf. vv. 19–20). He has chosen, but Israel too must now choose. And this surely suggests that the covenant here is bilateral in nature: Yahweh's commitment to Israel not only in the past but for the future, and the response this necessitates of Israel.

IV

Nevertheless, the emphasis is unmistakably upon Israel's worship of Yahweh alone, and this, together with some other features of the narrative, may provide a clue to its background. The possibility may be granted that it is a Deuteronomic composition of the late pre-exilic period. But an exilic provenance is at least an equal possibility.[7] That it probably belongs to the latest stages in the growth of the Deuteronomistic history favours this. Further, though it is possible that the references to the gods 'beyond the river' are allusions to imperial gods imposed by the Assyrians upon Israel and Judah in the pre-exilic period,[8] they are equally compatible with an exilic background. At this time many Israelites found themselves back precisely 'beyond the river' where tradition located the original home of their ancestors, and where it is likely that some exiles began to adopt the worship of indigenous Mesopotamian gods. In addition, if the statement in v. 14 that the ancestors of Israel who had been

---

[7] This has been argued recently by J. Van Seters, 'Joshua 24 and the Problem of Tradition in the Old Testament', *In The Shelter of Elyon. Essays on Ancient Palestinian Life and Literature in Honor of G. W. Ahlström*, ed. W. Boyd Barrick and J. R. Spencer, *JSOT* Supplement Series 31, Sheffield 1984, pp. 139–58.

[8] Reserve is surely justified, however, about Perlitt's understanding of these references as a sort of 'code' employed by an 'underground' Yahwistic movement in the land during the period of Assyrian rule.

in Egypt worshipped other gods there is not a secondary insertion,[9] this too would point to an exilic setting: apart from Ezekiel 20 and 23, it is the only reference in the Old Testament to apostasy already in Egypt by Israel, and it is likely that the allusion in Joshua 24: 14 to such worship is dependent upon Ezekiel's more expansive and idiosyncratic portrayal of this apostasy as far back as the days of bondage.[10] The association of the scene in the narrative with Shechem does not militate against an exilic provenance, since this city was evidently still known as a place of pious Yahwistic groups in the exilic period (cf. Jer. 41: 5), and possibly was also known as a place of a venerable tradition of Yahwism.

If it is a Deuteronomistic composition of the exilic period, for what purpose may it have been intended? Some scholars argue that the Deuteronomistic authors wrote not only of judgement but also of a future for Israel beyond judgement if it turned again to Yahweh. If this is accepted, the narrative in Joshua 24: 1–28 may be related to such a 'kerygma' as an appeal to those who had undergone judgement to turn to the worship of Yahweh alone. Against this, however, the passage contains nothing to suggest a renewal of Israel's standing as the people of Yahweh beyond the judgement which it itself envisages as a possibility (cf. vv. 19–20; contrast this with, for example, Deut. 4: 29–31).

An alternative possibility, and one fully in line with a prominent theme in the Deuteronomistic history, is that the narrative is concerned with the judgement which had deservedly befallen Israel because of its faithlessness to the covenant. In the fiction of the narrative the Israel of Joshua's time is addressed as a people which can choose for or against Yahweh, and is described as having chosen him. But those to whom its author addressed himself in the much later period in which it was composed

---

[9] That it is a secondary addition is usually argued on the grounds that there is no reference to the worship of other gods in Egypt in the narration of the 'saving history' in vv. 2–13 where only the worship of other gods 'beyond the river' by Israel's ancestors is mentioned (so, for example, Perlitt, p. 257 note 1). Similarly, the appeal in v. 15 makes no mention of the worship of other gods in Egypt. Nevertheless, an important undertone of the narrative, as I shall suggest below, seems to be Israel's age-old propensity for worshipping other gods, and if this is so a reference to such worship in Egypt is by no means out of place.

[10] On Ezekiel 20 see W. Zimmerli, *Ezechiel 1*, BKAT xiii/1, Neukirchen 1969, pp. 432–59, cf. esp. p. 446; E. trs. *Ezekiel 1*, Philadelphia 1979, pp. 399–419, esp. p. 409: 'we are concerned here, as in Ezek 15, 16, with an overall radical judgement upon Israel which allows it, even in its earliest period, no place for any bright period of obedience'.

knew that Israel down the centuries had in fact chosen otherwise, and with dire consequences. Thus the remarkable statement in v. 19 'you cannot serve Yahweh' is now known in this later period to have indeed been the case,[11] and this 'holy' and 'jealous God' who 'will not forgive your rebellion or your sins' has indeed turned and 'wrought harm' upon Israel and 'consumed' it 'after having done good' to it (v. 20). Similarly, those in this later period of judgement whose ancestors are declared in the narrative to be 'witnesses against yourselves that you have chosen Yahweh' (v. 22) are witnesses against themselves as belonging to an Israel which had long since rejected Yahweh; and the stone set up by Joshua in 'the sanctuary of Yahweh' at Shechem is likewise a witness, just as it was purposed to be, against an Israel that has 'dealt falsely' with Yahweh (v. 27).

A further suggestion which I make tentatively in support of such an understanding of this narrative arises from its striking references to the worship of other gods 'beyond the river' and in Egypt. Evidently these references were not intended by the author as mere historical notices; the appeal which he places upon the lips of Joshua to 'put away' the worship of these gods means that it has continued into the period of the settlement. No less than their ancestors 'beyond the river' and in Egypt, the Israelites whom Joshua addressed at Shechem worshipped other gods—notwithstanding what Yahweh had wrought on their behalf (vv. 2–13). Further, the entry into the land had now added the temptation to extend this worship of other gods to 'the gods of the Amorites in whose land you now dwell' (v. 15). The impression conveyed by the narrative is of an Israel which had a propensity for worshipping other gods. More than this, it seems that its author allowed no room for a so-called 'honeymoon' period in Israel's relationship with Yahweh. On the contrary, in a way that is surely reminiscent of a major theme in Ezekiel's preaching, he had sought to portray Israel as having been from the very beginning of its history unfaithful to Yahweh.[12] At the assembly at Shechem there was a

[11] The same moral impotence is implied in the 'new covenant' passage in Jeremiah 31: 31–4 which probably derives from an exilic Deuteronomistic redactor of the Book of Jeremiah. This similarity between Joshua 24: 19 and the 'new covenant passage', the former openly declaring the moral impotence implied in the latter, strengthens the case for an exilic setting of Joshua 24.

[12] See Zimmerli's comment in note 10 above. Elsewhere Zimmerli has suggested that the statement in Joshua 24: 19 'you cannot serve Yahweh; he is a holy God' 'receives in

change, and Israel chose Yahweh. But the tone of the narrative, its warnings and threats, its appointing of 'witnesses' against Israel lest it forsake Yahweh, strongly suggest that its author wished this to be seen as but a brief episode of fidelity. And indeed this is how it is described (Josh. 24: 31; Jud. 2: 7, 10). In short, though this narrative describes the glad commitment of Joshua and his generation to Yahweh, its theme is in reality Israel's age-old apostasy and the judgement which this has brought upon it.

As such, it may plausibly be regarded as a Deuteronomistic composition of the exilic period[13] rather than a pre-exilic Deuteronomic 'kerygmatic' text. Its context is well chosen, for in describing the commitment of Joshua and the assembly at Shechem to Yahweh upon completion of the settlement in the land, it sets in sharp relief, and in its warnings and threats anticipates, the history of apostasy in the land recorded in the following sections of the Deuteronomistic history.

Ezekiel an uncompromising interpretation' (*The Law and the Prophets: A Study of the Meaning of the Old Testament*, Oxford 1965, p. 80). My view differs from Zimmerli's in suggesting the possibility that the author of Joshua 24 may have been influenced by Ezekiel.

[13] I cannot therefore accept Van Seter's view (p. 154) that it is the work of a 'post-Deuteronomistic Yahwist'.

8

The Covenant Ritual at Sinai
(Exodus 19: 3b–8 and 24: 3–8)

WHETHER or not the first of these two texts is of ancient origin has remained controversial. From a source-critical point of view it has been variously assigned to J with some additions from a JE redactor, or to E, or to E with some Deuteronomic additions, or simply to a Deuteronomic author.[1] With this there has also been disagreement on whether it preserves ancient tradition. Whilst some believe it to be a late Deuteronomic insertion, others find it to be a text of great antiquity. For example, H. Wildberger, who deletes the specifically covenantal clause in v. 5a as a secondary Deuteronomic addition, believes it to be the most ancient formulation of Israel's election in the Old Testament,[2] whilst J. Muilenburg, limiting the unit to vv. 3b–6, has classified it as 'a special covenantal *Gattung*', suggesting that 'it is scarcely too much to say that it is *in nuce* the *fons et origo* of the many covenantal pericopes which appear throughout the Old Testament.'[3]

With L. Perlitt I agree that it has some points of contact with Exodus 24: 3–8, and it is within the context of a discussion of this latter text that I shall draw attention to these. That Exodus 24: 3–8 belongs to the 'key texts' concerning the making of the covenant between Yahweh and Israel is obvious; the claim is justified that among such texts it is self-evidently the covenant text *par excellence*.

---

[1] A tabulation of some main analyses is provided by E. Zenger, *Die Sinaitheophanie: Untersuchungen zum jahwistischen und elohistischen Geschichtswerk*, pp. 207 f.

[2] *Jahwes Eigentumsvolk*, ATANT 37, Zürich and Stuttgart 1960.

[3] 'The Form and Structure of the Covenantal Formulations', *VT* 9, 1959, pp. 345–65 (the quotation is from p. 352).

I

Three main questions arise in the study of this passage: first, its unity; second, its antiquity; and third, the meaning of the ritual it describes.[4]

With regard to the first of these, opinion has been divided. The unity of the passage (with the possible exception of 'and all the judgements' in v. 3aβ) is accepted by, for example, S. R. Driver, O. Eissfeldt, and W. Beyerlin, who ascribe it to E,[5] by S. Mowinckel, who assigns it to his J^v source,[6] and by M. Noth who associates it with the Book of the Covenant.[7] More recently D. J. McCarthy too has defended its unity, though he regards it as deriving from a source independent of the main Pentateuchal sources whilst reflecting the same tradition represented by them (especially E).[8] Others (for example, R. Kraetzschmar, A. Dillmann, H. Holzinger, B. Baentsch, G. Beer, J. P. Hyatt) regard vv. 3aβ, 4aα ('And Moses wrote all the words of the Lord') and 7 as redactional, without agreeing to which redactor they are to be attributed, and ascribe the remaining material to E.[9] None of these commentators severs the connection between the sacrificial offerings described in vv. 4aβ–6 and the ritual described in v. 8.[10] Both Perlitt and E. Zenger, however, have severed this connection, arguing that an earlier tradition of sacrificial offering (vv. 4aβ–6 [Perlitt] and vv. 4aβ–5 [Zenger]) has subsequently been reinterpreted by a Deuteronomic redactor as a covenant rite.[11] I shall return to this later.

We have seen that since C. Steuernagel's study of this passage in 1899

---

[4] What follows, with some alterations, was first published in my article 'The Covenant Ritual in Exodus XXIV 3–8', *VT* 32, 1982, pp. 74–86. I am grateful to the publishers, E. J. Brill, for permission to include some of this material here.

[5] S. R. Driver, *The Book of Exodus*, pp. 252 ff.; O. Eissfeldt, *Hexateuch-Synopse*, Leipzig 1922, repr. Darmstadt 1962, pp. 151*–2*; W. Beyerlin, *Herkunft und Geschichte der ältesten Sinaitraditionen*, pp. 20 f.; E. trs. *Origins and History of the Oldest Sinaitic Traditions*, pp. 15 f.

[6] *Erwägungen zur Pentateuch Quellenfrage*, Oslo 1964, pp. 83 ff.

[7] *Das zweite Buch Mose, Exodus*, p. 161; E. trs. *Exodus*, pp. 198 f.

[8] *Treaty and Covenant*,[2] pp. 266 ff.

[9] R. Kraetzschmar, *Die Bundesvorstellung im Alten Testament*, pp. 79 f.; A. Dillmann, *Die Bücher Exodus und Numeri*, third edition by V. Ryssel, Leipzig 1897, pp. 284 ff. (ascribes these verses to J and the remainder of vv. 1–11 to E); H. Holzinger, *Exodus*, Tübingen 1900, pp. 103 ff.; B. Baentsch, *Exodus-Leviticus-Numeri*, Göttingen 1903, pp. 212 ff.; G. Beer, *Exodus*, pp. 125 ff.; J. P. Hyatt, *Exodus*, pp. 254 ff.

[10] Dillmann and Holzinger regard all or part of v. 8b as secondary.

[11] Perlitt, *Bundestheologie im Alten Testament*, pp. 190 ff. Zenger, pp. 75 f., 216.

the view has been widely accepted that this text preserves an ancient tradition of the making of the covenant at Sinai, the reference to the role of 'the young men of Israel' in v. 5 rather than priests being generally regarded as decisive in this respect.[12]

There has been general agreement on the significance of the blood rite described in the passage. Particular importance has been attached to the division of the blood into two halves (v. 6), one half being thrown against the altar, the other half upon the people (v. 8). By this means a *communio sacramentalis* was created between the two partners to the covenant, Yahweh and Israel, Yahweh being represented, it has frequently been maintained,[13] by the altar. In support of such an understanding of this rite reference has then usually been made to the evidence adduced by, for example, W. Robertson Smith, J. Wellhausen, H. C. Trumbull, and earlier scholars, from ancient Near Eastern and classical texts concerning a similar use of blood as a means of creating covenantal 'brotherhood' between individuals or groups.[14]

II

Perlitt has rejected the long-established understanding of this passage as preserving an ancient covenant tradition. In this he has been supported by E. Kutsch who has at the same time advanced a new interpretation of the meaning of the blood rite it describes.[15]

Perlitt argues that an earlier tradition of the offering of sacrifices, described in vv. 4aβ–6, has subsequently been worked over and recast by a Deuteronomistic redactor as a covenant ritual (pp. 190 ff.). Since his argument here depends partly upon his understanding of Exodus 19: 3b–8, we must first note his view of the origin of the latter passage (pp. 167 ff.).

Following many commentators, he regards it as a Deuteronomistic insertion which he dates to the exilic period. In support of this he draws attention to the following: the expression 'you have seen' (v. 4a) or similar

---

[12] See above, pp. 12 f.

[13] For example, S. R. Driver, p. 253; Noth, pp. 160 f., E. trs. p. 198.

[14] W. Robertson Smith, *Kinship and Marriage in Early Arabia*, Cambridge 1885, pp. 48 ff., 281; *The Religion of the Semites*, Edinburgh 1889, pp. 296 ff.; H. C. Trumbull, *The Blood Covenant*, New York 1885; J. Wellhausen, *Reste arabischen Heidentums*, Berlin 1887, p. 120.

[15] *Verheissung und Gesetz*, pp. 80 ff.

expressions (e.g. 'what your eyes have seen'), when used of what God has done on Israel's behalf, is especially characteristic of the Deuteronomist (cf. Deut. 4: 3, 9; 10: 21 f.; 11: 7; 29: 1; Josh. 23: 3); the imagery in v. 4b ('I bore you on eagles' wings') is similar to that in Deuteronomy 32: 11, another later addition to the original book of Deuteronomy; the description of Israel as Yahweh's 'peculiar possession' (*s͏ᵉgullāh*, v. 5b) is found in Deuteronomy 7: 6, 14: 2, 26: 18; in Deuteronomy also Israel is described as a 'holy people'—the fact that Exodus 19: 6 describes Israel as a 'holy nation' (*gōy qādōš* indicates not a non-Deuteronomic hand but only that its Deuteronomistic author wrote against the background of the exile when Israel found itself numbered amongst the nations (cf. the use of *gōy* for Israel in the Deuteronomistic passage Deut. 4: 6–8); the expression 'for all the earth is mine' (v. 5b) also fits an exilic background and echoes the world of Deutero-Isaiah (cf., for example, Isa. 42: 5), whilst the description of Israel as 'a kingdom of priests' echoes the Trito-Isaianic text Isaiah 61: 6 ('But you shall be named priests of the Lord'). Thus, according to Perlitt, late Deuteronomistic, priestly and prophetic currents of the exilic period run through this passage.

Turning to Exodus 24: 3–8, Perlitt finds similarities in structure and language between vv. 3, 7 and Exodus 19: 3b–8. In both passages Moses comes to the people (*wayyābō'* 19: 7a; 24: 3a), and declares to them what Yahweh has said ('all these words which Yahweh had commanded him' in 19: 7b; 'all the words of Yahweh' in 24: 3a; 'the book of the covenant' in 24: 7a); in both passages the people respond unanimously ('And all the people replied together' in 19: 8a; 'and all the people replied with one voice' in 24: 3b) pledging themselves to obey ('all that Yahweh has spoken we will do' in 19: 8a and 24: 7b; 'all the words which Yahweh has spoken we will do' in 24: 3b). On these grounds he argues that Exodus 24: 3, with which he associates v. 4aα ('And Moses wrote all the words of Yahweh'), and v. 7 are, like Exodus 19: 3b–8, from a Deuteronomistic hand (p. 192).

What of the material that remains, that is, vv. 4aβ–6, 8? From this Perlitt isolates the description of the offering of sacrifices in vv. 4aβ which he regards as an originally independent unit and which, in view of its reference to 'the young men of Israel' as having offered the sacrifices, he believes is of ancient origin (p. 196). It begins with Moses building an altar and concludes with v. 6; that is, it is a self-contained account of sacrificial offering, nothing more and nothing less, which requires no accompanying words, whether delivered orally or read. It is a mistake, he maintains, when scholars, anticipating v. 8, regard the dividing of the blood in v. 6 as a preparation for a covenant ritual. In reality, the blood as a whole has already been disposed of in v. 6, one half being thrown upon the altar, as cultic practice required, the remainder being placed in the vessels mentioned, that is, also disposed of; no one has succeeded in associating these vessels with a covenant ritual (pp. 198 f.). Further, the other half of the blood is no longer mentioned in v. 8 which refers simply to 'the blood', that is, all the blood. Accordingly, this verse, Perlitt argues, is a secondary addition construing the sacrificial offering in v. 6 as a covenant rite. Its concluding words ('in accordance with all these words') betray its dependence upon the terminology of vv. 3 and 7, and with them it too is to be ascribed to a Deuteronomistic redactor who has thus recast the old tradition in vv. 4aβ–6 to make it read as a covenant-making ceremony.

Unlike Perlitt, Kutsch regards this passage as a literary unit, no part of which is pre-Deuteronomic.[16] His understanding of the ritual described is bound up with his understanding of what the word $b^e r \bar{\imath} t$ means. In the case of Exodus 24: 3–8 it is a matter of a *Fremdverpflichtung*, that is, an obligation placed by Yahweh upon Israel (p. 87).

For the understanding of the ritual here described, like many before him he points to the analogy of such rites in ancient Arabic literature, specifically to descriptions of rituals in which the parties involved dip their hands in the blood of a sacrificial victim. But as a particularly clear example of such a ritual, which Kutsch interprets as a means of taking a solemn oath, he draws attention to a passage in Aeschylus' *Seven Against Thebes*, lines 42–8:[17]

Seven warriors, impetuous leaders of their companies, shedding a bull's blood into a black-bound shield, and touching with their hands the victim's gore, have sworn an oath by Ares, by Enyo, and by bloodthirsty Rout, that they will bring destruction on the city of the Cadmeans and ravage it by force of arms, or in death imbrue this land of ours with their blood.

Kutsch sees clear parallels between what is recorded here and what is described in Exodus 24: 3–8: in both cases the groups mentioned are

[16] Ibid. p. 89. (He excludes only the phrase 'and all the judgements' v. 3a as a secondary insertion; p. 80 note 161.)

[17] The translation here given is from H. W. Smyth, *Aeschylus*, The Loeb Classical Library, London 1922.

placed under obligation by means of a solemn act; according to Exodus 24: 7b (cf. 3b) the assembled Israelites declare 'all that Yahweh has spoken we will do, and be obedient', and Moses thereupon places them under solemn obligation; similarly the Greek commanders take upon themselves the solemn commitment to destroy Thebes. In both passages the blood of sacrificial victims is placed in containers and, again in both passages, the groups mentioned are brought into contact with this blood. The only difference is that in Exodus 24: 3–8 the obligation is placed upon the Israelites by Yahweh through the mediation of Moses (it is a *Fremdverpflichtung*), whilst in the passage in Aeschylus the warriors impose the obligation upon themselves (it is a *Selbstverpflichtung*; p. 87). As in the case of the Greek warriors, so in Exodus 24: 3–8: it is not a matter of creating a relationship (*Bund*); rather it is a matter of the Israelites being solemnly placed under an obligation (only they and not Yahweh). That is, the application of the blood of the victims in Exodus 24: 3–8 accompanies the taking of a solemn obligation, as it does amongst the Arabs and the Greeks. The rite described signified an act of self-imprecation: as the blood of the sacrificial victims has been spilt, so would the blood of those be spilt who break their obligation, that is, their oath (p. 87). What is explicitly stated in the passage in Aeschylus is implied in Exodus 24: 8.

III

In my opinion there are serious difficulties in the way of accepting either Perlitt's or Kutsch's understanding of this passage. To consider first Perlitt's view, it is at least doubtful whether he has done justice to the reference in v. 6 to half the blood of the sacrificial victims being placed in vessels. In no other text describing a similar sacrificial offering (for example, Lev. 1: 5, 11; 3: 2, 8, 13; 7: 2, 14) is the blood of the victims described as having been disposed of in such a manner, some being cast upon the altar, the remainder being placed in vessels (and then what?). Was the normal cultic requirement being contravened in the case of Exodus 24: 6? If so, why? If not, why has the author felt it necessary to add what, on Perlitt's view, would have to be regarded as a rather pedantic detail (supplied in no other text describing a similar sacrificial scene) concerning the 'disposal' of that half of the blood which had not been or could not be dealt with in the same manner as the other half, that is, thrown upon the altar?[18]

Further, why is there this apparently exact division of the blood into two equal parts? In view of the references elsewhere (e.g. Exod. 29: 12; Lev. 4: 6 f., 13–35; 5: 9; 8: 15, 23 f.) to part of the blood of a sacrifice being used for some specific purpose, whilst the remainder of it is thrown upon the altar or at its base, does it not seem likely, contrary to Perlitt's view, that here too in Exodus 24: 6 a similar use of some of the blood is envisaged, in other words, that this verse looks forward to some such action as is recorded in v. 8? This surely accounts more plausibly for the exact description of the blood being divided in half. In short, Perlitt's argument at this point is rather forced.

Zenger avoids this difficulty by maintaining that v. 6 also comes from a Deuteronomistic redactor, and that what is here described prepares the way for the ritual in v. 8, which he ascribes to the same redactor; in his view the original tradition ended with the offering of the sacrifices in v. 5. For two reasons, however, this view is unconvincing.

First, it is clear that in the narrative the offering of the sacrifices is subordinate to the blood ritual; it is upon the latter that the emphasis lies, whilst the former is but the necessary preliminary to it. Further, the separate roles of 'the young men of Israel' and Moses here described conforms to normal procedure: to the former is assigned the task of immolating the sacrificial victims, to Moses the specifically priestly task of manipulating the blood of these sacrifices upon which the emphasis lies.[19] In short, v. 6 is the necessary continuation of v. 5 and is anticipated by the latter; to regard v. 6 as a secondary addition to v. 5 is arbitrary. (An alternative suggestion, which leads to the same conclusion, is the possibility that the word *na ʿar*—used in the construct plural here—is not to be understood as 'youths' but in the sense, also widely attested in the Old Testament, of 'servants', in this context 'cultic' or 'priest's servants' (cf. 1 Sam. 2: 13–17). If this is so, what is described in v. 5 is what the subordinate

---

[18] As Perlitt himself acknowledges (p. 201), it is merely hypothetical to suggest that at some stage in the earlier history of this tradition the other half of the blood may have been intended for casting upon the 'twelve pillars' (v. 4) regarded as representing the people.

[19] Cf. R. de Vaux, *Les Institutions de l'Ancien Testament*, vol. II, Paris 1960, p. 209; E. trs. *Ancient Israel: Its Life and Institutions*, London 1961, p. 356.

cultic servants perform, whilst v. 4b—which describes the building of an altar—and vv. 6 and 8 describe the role of Moses as priest proper.)

Second, the view that v. 6, and also v. 8 with its description of a covenantal blood ritual, are the creation of a Deuteronomistic editor runs into a further difficulty. This is that the making of a covenant by such ritualistic means is not at all at home in Deuteronomic/Deuteronomistic literature, where it is by pledged word rather than by cultic rite that the covenant is ratified.[20]

For these reasons the separation of the sacrifices described in v. 6 from the use of the blood of these sacrifices in v. 8 must be rejected as being forced, whilst the covenantal application of this blood in v. 8 cannot plausibly be regarded as the notion of a Deuteronomic or Deutero-nomistic redactor.

How is the ritual in v. 8 to be understood? It does not seem to me correct to understand it on the analogy of the relationship of 'brother-hood' created between unrelated groups or individuals by means of the blood of sacrificial victims, as described in ancient Arabic literature. The Old Testament itself contains no evidence of such a use of blood for creating such 'brotherhood' between individuals or groups. For example, David referred to Jonathan as his 'brother' (2 Sam. 1: 26), but the covenant which they made with each other makes no mention of any blood ritual (1 Sam. 18: 3 f.). More significant, however, is the fact that wherever the Old Testament refers to kinship, it does so with the terminology of 'flesh and bone' but never with that of blood (cf. Gen. 29: 14; 37: 27; Jud. 9: 2; 2 Sam. 5: 1 (=1 Chron. 11: 1); 19: 12, 13; Neh. 5: 5). Evidently ancient Israel did not think of kinship in terms of blood-relationship, and this renders it improbable that the sacrificial blood in Exodus 24: 3–8 was conceived of as effecting a sort of covenantal 'kinship' between Yahweh and the Israelites.

As for Kutsch's view, there is likewise no evidence whatsoever in the Old Testament of self-imprecation rites by means of blood, and it is surely inadmissible to have to go so far afield as Aeschylus in order to understand a ritual in ancient Israel. It may be added that the context in

---

[20] This point is made by D. J. McCarthy, '*bᵉrît* in Old Testament History and Theology', *Biblica* 53, 1972, p. 117; A. D. H. Mayes, *Deuteronomy*, p. 67. (McCarthy's and Mayes's observation on this has persuaded me to revise my view in *Exodus and Sinai in History and Tradition*, p. 72, that v. 8 derives from a Deuteronomic editor.)

each case is strikingly different: in the one it is related to the preparation for war, in the other to the meeting of a cultic community with its God for a very different purpose. A sounder method requires us to attempt to understand in the first instance the ritual described in Exodus 24: 3–8 on the basis of what we know from elsewhere in the Old Testament concerning the significance and use of sacrificial blood in Israel's cult.

What does this reveal? The belief is prominent that blood is holy; that is why, for example, the blood of sacrificial victims is devoted to God. Further, blood conveys holiness to that with which it is brought into contact. Thus, for example, it is used as part of the rite whereby Aaron and his sons are hallowed, consecrated as priests (Exod. 29: 20 f.; Lev. 8: 22–30). Given this, an explanation of the ritual in Exodus 24: 3–8 readily suggests itself: half the blood is thrown upon the altar, devoted to God (cf. Exod. 29: 16, 20; Lev. 1: 5, 11; 3: 2, 8, 13; 7: 2; 8: 19, 24; 17: 6; Num. 18: 17; etc.), whilst the other half, carefully noted as having been set aside, is cast over the assembled Israelites who are thereby consecrated as Yahweh's *holy people*. Those over whom the blood of Yahweh's sacrifices is cast now belong peculiarly to him, and are thereby also solemnly commissioned to his service, just as the consecration of priests was a commissioning to the office of priest.[21]

IV

Some additional support for such an interpretation of the significance of the blood rite in Exodus 24: 3–8 may be adduced from Exodus 19: 3b–8. Perlitt has drawn attention to several similarities in both structure and terminology between this passage and 24: 3–8. Childs too has noted an important relationship between them: chapter 24 'brings to completion the sealing of the covenant which had been first announced in 19: 3. The repetition of the people of the same response (19: 8 and 24: 3, 7) marks the beginning and end of one great covenant event'.[22]

A further way in which these two passages may be related is as follows. Exodus 19: 6a states that Israel as God's covenant people will be to him 'a

---

[21] Cf. E. Ruprecht, 'Exodus 24, 9–11 als Beispiel lebendiger Erzähltradition aus der Zeit des babylonischen Exils', pp. 165 f.

[22] *Exodus*, pp. 502 f.

kingdom of priests and a holy nation'.[23] If Exodus 19: 3b–8 as a whole is an anticipatory summary and interpretation of the nature and basis of the covenant,[24] it may be suggested that the statement in 19: 6a was intended by its author as an interpretation of Exodus 24: 3–8; that is, the author of 19: 3b–8 understood Israel's status among the nations in a similar way to that of the author of Isaiah 61: 6 ('you shall be named priests of the Lord and ministers of our God') and saw Exodus 24: 3–8 as a record of Israel's consecration and commissioning as such.[25] Thus, what is set out in programmatic manner in Exodus 19: 3b–8 is finally completed in 24: 3–8 where Israel gives its pledge of obedience to the words of the covenant and is then, as the author of Exodus 19: 3b–8 took it, constituted as Yahweh's 'kingdom of priests and a holy nation'. By such means Exodus 24: 3–8 has been interpreted as the solemn commissioning of Israel as a holy nation, obedient to God's will and functioning among the nations in the manner that a priesthood functions in a society[26]—a theologically striking understanding and extension of the ritual described in 24: 3–8.

Further possible support for such an understanding of this ritual may be gained from Exodus 24: 9–11 which I discussed earlier. Although, as was there noted, from a traditio-historical point of view this latter passage was originally probably unrelated to the event described in vv. 3–8, they have been brought into close relationship with each other by an editor, so that vv. 9–11 with their (editorially expanded) introduction proper in vv. 1–2 enframe the covenant rite in vv. 3–8.

The remarkable contents of vv. 9–11 and its redactional relationship with the description of the covenant ceremony in vv. 3–8 suggest that it is intended as a description of the very crowning of the covenant ceremony which has finally conveyed Israel to Yahweh as his holy people. The

[23] As Childs (pp. 367, 374) points out, the various parallelisms in Exodus 19: 5–6 render questionable the suggestion by some scholars (e.g. W. L. Moran, 'A Kingdom of Priests', *The Bible in Current Catholic Thought*, ed. J. L. McKenzie, New York 1962, pp. 7–20) that the phrase 'a kingdom of priests' does not refer to the totality of Israel but only to part of it, the priesthood, and that this phrase is to be understood in some such way as 'a royalty of priests'.   [24] See Childs, pp. 360 f.

[25] See also Ruprecht, pp. 165 f. (I had not seen Ruprecht's suggestion concerning this when I wrote the article mentioned in note 4 above. My view there expressed and here repeated was first prompted by Kraetzschmar (pp. 84 f.) who, though he does not himself make this observation, links Exod. 19: 6 with 24: 3–8 and notes the similarity of the rite described in the latter with that in Exod. 29: 20 f., Lev. 8: 23 f.)

[26] Cf. Childs, p. 367.

otherness of God is not infringed; the description of the *visio dei* is notice-
ably restrained. Yet the contrast with Exodus 19 is unmistakable. In the
latter the people are forbidden on penalty of destruction even to touch the
mountain; an unsanctified people is to prepare itself for the coming of
God: there is the ritual cleansing of clothes, and the order to abstain from
sexual relationships. In Exodus 24: 9–11, by contrast, the representatives of
this now consecrated people are invited to ascend the holy mountain,
there to behold God. The statement that no harm befell them, that God
'did not stretch forth his hand against the leaders of Israel', serves to
emphasize further the contrast: there is no terror here, such as is expressed
in Exodus 19, but only the brightness of God's presence to the eyes of
these representatives of his holy people. There could be no more decisive
a portrayal of God's drawing-near to his people than this; there could be
no more vivid a sign of their acceptance by him than what is now granted
them through their representatives.[27] With the making of the covenant,
which involved Israel's solemn pledge to Yahweh and its consecration as
his holy people, Israel's election is completed.

V

When were Exodus 19: 3b–8 and 24: 3–8 composed? With regard to the
former, the presence of Deuteronomic vocabulary is generally acknowledged. There are, however, several non-deuteronomic features in the
passage. Its depiction of Israel as a 'kingdom of priests' and with this the
implied concept of the role of Israel as a priestly nation witnessing to the
holiness of Yahweh among the nations has no background in Deuteronomic theology. D. Patrick, who regards the passage as part of a narrative
framework attached to the Book of the Covenant when the latter was as
yet an independent source, dates it to the ninth century BC.[28] But it is, in
my view, difficult to accept that the universalistic role of Israel as
Yahweh's 'kingdom of priests' and his 'holy nation' witnessing among the
nations was conceived of as early as this period. More plausibly, the
passage reflects the emergence of such a concept in prophecy from the

---

[27] It is possible that originally the tradition preserved in Exodus 24: 9–11 referred only
to the seventy elders as the representatives of Israel. (See my 'The Antiquity of the Tradition in Exodus XXIV 9–11', *VT* 25, 1975, p. 78.)

[28] 'The Covenant Code Source', *VT* 27, 1977, pp. 145–57.

exilic period onwards. Thus, as Perlitt observes, with Israel's vocation 'you shall be to me a holy nation' may be compared Ezekiel 36: 23 'When they see that I reveal my holiness through you, the nations will know that I am the Lord, says the Lord God', whilst Israel's status as Yahweh's 'kingdom of priests' is close to Isaiah 61: 5 'you shall be named priests of the Lord and ministers of our God'. The combination of Deuteronomic, priestly and prophetic elements and terminology which characterizes this passage points to an author of the late exilic or perhaps even early post-exilic period.[29]

What of Exodus 24: 3–8? Steuernagel, it will be recalled, believed that it preserves a tradition of great antiquity, and his view remains widely accepted. Perlitt and Zenger, on the other hand, argue that only an ancient tradition of the offering of sacrifice underlies the passage; it was at the hands of a Deuteronomistic editor, whom Perlitt equates with the 'late Deuteronomistic' author of Exodus 19: 3b–8 and whom Zenger dates as late as the early post-exilic period, that it was reworked into a description of a covenant-making ritual. Kutsch and Ruprecht argue that the passage in its entirety is late. According to Kutsch, no part of it is pre-Deuteronomic, whilst Ruprecht (p. 167) regards it as exilic, arguing that an author living at a time when the temple had been destroyed and when the sacrificial cult had thus ceased would have found no difficulty in describing the 'young men of Israel' as having offered sacrifices, as this passage narrates. Or again, Patrick, who argues that the passage, like Exodus 19: 36–8 as understood by him, originated as part of the narrative framework of the Book of the Covenant, dates it to the ninth century BC. Thus periods as far apart as the earliest period of Israel's history, possibly even the pre-settlement period, and the early post-exilic period have been proposed as the background of Exodus 24: 3–8.

According to Zenger (p. 165), the Book of the Covenant with the addition of Exodus 23: 20–33 was inserted into the Sinai pericope by a late Deuteronomistic editor—he suggests that it belongs to a second Deuteronomistic editing of the Sinai pericope in the early post-exilic period—who at the same time reworked the narrative of the offering of sacrifices in Exodus 24: 4–5* into a covenant-making ritual. This editor, he suggests,

---

[29] Cf. also, for example, G. Fohrer, ' "Priesterliches Königum" Ex. 19, 6', *TZ* 19, 1963, pp. 359–62.

was motivated by a desire for a return to the 'ideal time' of Israel's beginnings; a similar tendency can be discerned, it is claimed, in Ezekiel.

Two considerations render Zenger's view unconvincing. First, for the reasons given above there is no sound basis for questioning the unity of this passage. The sacrifice and the following ritual are integrally related, and the making of the covenant with which the ritual is associated clearly carries with it the reading of, and the people's declaration of obedience to, the commandments. Nor need the description of the people's 'preliminary' pledge of obedience (v. 3) be regarded as redactional on the grounds that the same pledge is repeated later in the context of the covenant ceremony proper (v. 7).[30] It is difficult to see what aim a redactor would have had in mind in inserting v. 3b. For reasons which I shall suggest later, there is no need to question that the narrative from the outset contained a description of this twice-given pledge of the people in response to their twofold hearing of the commandments.[31]

Second, against Zenger's dating of the passage, it is commonly agreed that the authors of Deuteronomy itself already knew the Book of the Covenant and used it in composing their programme of reform. But though they too sought to call Israel back to the ancient will of Yahweh, declared in the 'ideal time' of Israel's beginnings, they did not simply reissue the Book of the Covenant, but went beyond its prescriptions in a number of significant respects, most notably in demanding the centralization of the cult. It is difficult to accept, as Zenger's view requires, that a later member of the Deuteronomic movement would have shown such a preference for the Book of the Covenant which in a number of ways, again most notably in the matter of the centralization of the cult, was unacceptable to his Deuteronomic predecessors. After all, Israel's apostasy which brought such judgement upon the nation, according to the Deuteronomistic history, consisted partly in the fact that the law of centralization had not been obeyed by Israel. In Deuteronomy and in the Deuteronomistic history centralization of the cult is presented as no less than a principle upon which the religious community stands or falls, and it is scarcely credible that a later Deuteronomist would have gone back on this.

Is it possible, however, that Exodus 24: 3–8 is nevertheless from an

---

[30] This represents a revision of what I earlier argued in *Exodus and Sinai in History and Tradition*, pp. 70–2.   [31] See below, p. 214.

author of the exilic or early post-exilic period, especially in view of the similarities between it and Exodus 19: 3b–8 which, as argued above, may be ascribed to just such a late author? This is the view of Perlitt who ascribes both these passages to a late Deuteronomist; only the sacrificial scene described in Exodus 24: 4aβ–6 is earlier.

What has been said of Zenger's view applies also to Perlitt's: there is no need to question the unity of Exodus 24: 3–8, and it is improbable that a Deuteronomist was responsible for the description of the covenant ritual that characterizes it. An additional objection to Perlitt's view, however, may be made on the basis of his own understanding of the contents of the Sinai pericope by the time this late Deuteronomist wrote. By this time, according to Perlitt, this pericope already included both the decalogue and the laws in Exodus 20: 22–23: 33.[32] But this entails accepting that in an earlier form of the narrative of the events at Sinai, the making of a covenant between Yahweh and his people was described as only having followed Israel's apostasy (Exod. 32–4), whilst the laws given at the most solemn moment of Yahweh's encounter with his people (the decalogue and Exodus 20: 22–23: 33) were not associated with a covenant. On Perlitt's view, it was not until a much later time that it occurred to a Deuteronomist, by means of editing the original nucleus of Exodus 24: 3–8, to constitute the laws in Exodus 20–3 as the laws of a covenant. Such a view is, in my opinion, scarcely credible. What makes Perlitt's argument at this point still less convincing is that he believes the decalogue to have been inserted into the Sinai pericope in Exodus contemporaneously with its incorporation, as the basis of the covenant at Horeb, into Deuteronomy sometime between the composition of *Urdeuteronomium* and the work of the Deuteronomistic historian. This means, if I understand him correctly, that although from a relatively early stage the decalogue was understood in Deuteronomy as the basis of the covenant at Horeb, it stood in the Sinai pericope for a considerable period after this without being associated with the making of such a covenant.

In my opinion, there are no convincing reasons for doubting that not only Exodus 20: 22–23: 33[33] but also its related narrative in 24: 3–8 are of

---

[32] pp. 98–102, 225 note 5.

[33] It is generally agreed that Exodus 23: 20–33 is a secondary Deuteronomic appendix to the Book of the Covenant and that this corpus has in other places been subjected to some Deuteronomic redaction. C. H. W. Brekelmans has argued that such material is

pre-Deuteronomic origin. As for the similarities between this latter passage and Exodus 19: 3b–8, they are not such as necessarily indicate common authorship. They can be readily explained as the result of the particular interest of a later author in the significance of the ritual described in 24: 3–8 which he understood in the striking manner suggested in section (IV) above.

How long before the period of Deuteronomy may Exodus 24: 3–8 have originated? Contrary to Steuernagel's well-known view, the role of the *na ᵃrē bᵉnē yiśrāᵓēl* here is not necessarily an indication that the passage is of ancient origin. As suggested above, what is described probably reflects normal cultic procedure—the immolation of the sacrificial animals by 'the young men of Israel' and the specifically priestly role of Moses, or, alternatively, the priestly role of Moses assisted by 'cultic servants'. There is nothing in this that must be of early rather than of later origin. Nor does the passage's close association with the Book of the Covenant, which derives its name from it, enable us to determine its period of origin, for the Book of the Covenant is itself not necessarily of early rather than later origin in the pre-exilic period.[34]

Although, therefore, Exodus 24: 3–8 is probably of pre-Deuteronomic origin, in itself it offers no indication of how long before the Deuteronomic period it may have originated. We seem to have arrived at an *impasse* on the question of when in the pre-exilic period the notion of a covenant between Yahweh and Israel was coined. But there remain to be discussed two texts in the book of Hosea which may help us forward, and it is to these texts that we now turn.

'proto-Deuteronomic' rather than simply Deuteronomic or Deuteronomistic ('Éléments Deutéronomiques dans le Pentateuque', Recherches Bibliques 8, Bruges 1967, pp. 77–91 (esp. pp. 84 ff.).

[34] Cf. R. Smend, *Die Entstehung des Alten Testaments*, Stuttgart, Berlin, Cologne, Mainz 1978, pp. 94–6.

9

Covenant Texts in Hosea

(Hosea 6: 7, 8:1)

OF the key texts usually regarded as testimony to the antiquity of a covenant tradition in Israelite religion, our survey has shown that neither Exodus 19: 3b–8 nor 34: 10–28 nor Joshua 24 can confidently be regarded as pre-Deuteronomic, whilst Exodus 24: 9–11, though it may be of ancient origin, is not concerned with the making of a covenant. Only Exodus 24: 3–8 may plausibly be regarded as pre-Deuteronomic, but its contents do not enable us to say how long before the Deuteronomic period it came into existence.

In view of this, it becomes all the more important to re-examine the evidence in the book of Hosea that this prophet of the eighth century employed the word *bᵉrīt* with reference to the relationship between Yahweh and Israel. The texts in question are 6: 7 and 8: 1. Is the first of these, contrary to Perlitt's view, concerned with a covenant between Yahweh and Israel, and is the second, again contrary to his conclusion, an authentic saying of Hosea? If so, what conclusion may be drawn from these two references in Hosea concerning the appropriation of the word *bᵉrīt* into the theological sphere of God's dealings with Israel?

I

Since, in contrast to 6: 7, 8: 1 unambiguously concerns a covenant between Yahweh and Israel, it might seem desirable to begin with it. Since, however, on the other hand, the authenticity of 8: 1 has frequently been doubted, whilst that of 6: 7 cannot seriously be questioned,[1] it is preferable

---

[1] See L. Perlitt, *Bundestheologie im Alten Testament*, p. 143 note 2. The obscurity of the verse tells against its being from a glossator, and it can scarcely be from a Deuteronomic editor, since nowhere in the Deuteronomic literature is there any reference to the treachery here referred to. See also J. Day, 'Pre-Deuteronomic Allusions to the Covenant in Hosea and Psalm lxxviii', forthcoming in *VT*.

to begin with the latter. If it can be shown that it does concern such a covenant, it may in turn contribute something to the discussion of whether 8: 1 derives from Hosea or is a secondary insertion.

The boundaries of the unit to which 6: 7 belongs have been much disputed. Following H. W. Wolff, I am persuaded that it cannot be regarded as the beginning of a unit, since the opening *uᵉhēmmāh* 'but they' would be without antecedent.[2] There is much to be said for regarding v. 4 as the beginning of a new unit.[3] Its opening rhetorical questions make a natural beginning. What precedes (vv. 1–3) has all the appearance of an originally independent unit; in form it is strikingly similar to Lamentations 3: 40 f. and may plausibly be regarded as an adaptation by Hosea of the *Aufruf zur Volksklage* ('Summons to Community Lament')[4] with which it shares the same function. The *ᶜal kēn* 'therefore' which begins v. 5 relates this verse to v. 4; there is a change from the second person singular to the third person plural in v. 5, but such a change is attested elsewhere in Hosea (cf. 2: 18–19; 4: 15; 5: 13) and is no ground for regarding v. 5 as originally unrelated to v. 4. The word *ḥesed* in v. 6 relates this verse to what is said in v. 4. There follows a 'catalogue of sins' (vv. 7–9; v. 10 is possibly a generalizing conclusion to the unit as a whole) contrasting Israel's behaviour with what Yahweh desires as stated in v. 6.

If such is its original context, v. 7 may plausibly be interpreted as referring to a transgression of Yahweh's *bᵉrīt* with Israel. In favour of such an interpretation would also be the presence of the word *ḥesed* in v. 6, a word which certainly belongs to the associative field of *bᵉrīt*. The phrase 'knowledge of God' also has covenantal overtones (cf. Jer. 31: 34).

Since, however, the relation of v. 7 with what precedes has been so much disputed, we must also enquire whether the verse itself offers any clue to the meaning of the prophet's accusation.

The word *kᵉʾādām* is problematic. A recent suggestion is that the half verse to which it belongs should be understood 'they have walked over my covenant like dirt' (*ʾādām* being understood as equivalent to *ʾᵃdāmāh*

---

[2] *Dodekapropheten 1 Hosea*, second edition, BKAT xiv/1, Neukirchen 1965, p. 138; E. trs. *Hosea*, Philadelphia 1974, p. 109.

[3] I owe several observations concerning this passage in Hosea to Dr Graham Davies at Cambridge who is currently preparing a commentary on Hosea.

[4] Davies makes this suggestion.

'earth, soil').[5] Against this, however, it has been correctly pointed out that there is no evidence that *ᵃdāmāh* was regarded as contemptible, and thus provide a simile for disdain, and further that the verb *ʿābar* means 'to cross over, pass by' and not 'to trample upon (with scorn)'.[6] Literally the word means 'like Adam', and a traditional interpretation is that it is a reference to Adam's rebellion against God in the Genesis narrative. But the Old Testament nowhere refers to a covenant between God and Adam, and such an interpretation of Hosea 6: 7 seems therefore improbable.[7] It seems likely that in view of the locative 'there' in the second half of the verse it refers to a place. Most modern commentators accordingly adopt Wellhausen's proposal that the text be slightly emended to *bᵉʾādām* 'at Adam'.[8] Such a reading fits the context well, since specific places are mentioned also in vv. 8 and 9. Adam is probably to be identified with Adam in the Jordan valley (Josh. 3: 16; probably modern Tell ed-Damiye) and in the territory of Gilead, and this provides a further reason for adopting this proposed reading in view of the reference to Gilead in v. 8. The *New English Bible* reading 'at Admah' (cf. Hos. 11: 8; Gen. 14: 2) is to be rejected; it requires yet another textual emendation, and, besides, the people of Admah, wherever it was, were not Israelites.

What of the particular offence 'at Adam' here mentioned? The fact that the second half of the verse states that it was treachery against Yahweh would appear, on the principle of *parallelismus membrorum*, to support the understanding of 'they transgressed the covenant' in the first half of the verse as referring to Yahweh's covenant with Israel, as many commentators have argued. According to Perlitt this does not follow. Rather, he argues, the offence in question was the breaking of a treaty between Israel and some other group or nation.[9] Since, however, treaties were entered into by means of an oath sworn in the name of one's own god, breaking a treaty was *ipso facto* an offence against one's own god, in this instance against Yahweh. The offence is to be understood, therefore, on the analogy of Hosea 10: 4a, 'They utter mere words, with empty oaths

---

[5] See D. J. McCarthy, '*bᵉrît* in Old Testament History and Theology', *Biblica* 53, 1972, p. 113, on the basis of M. J. Dahood, 'Zecharia 9, 1 *ʿēn ʾĀdām*', *CBQ* 25, 1963, pp. 123–4.

[6] See F. I. Anderson and D. N. Freedman, *Hosea*, Garden City, New York, 1980, p. 438.

[7] See Day, op. cit.

[8] *Die kleinen Propheten übersetzt und erklärt*,⁴ in loc.

[9] For Perlitt's discussion of the Hosea texts see *Bundestheologie im Alten Testament*, pp. 139–52.

they make treaties', and thus means 'At Adam they broke the treaty, there they broke faith with me'.[10] Further, the use of the word *bᵉrīt* in 6: 7 without a suffix referring it to Yahweh is in line with Hosea's use of it for 'treaty' in 10: 4 and 12: 2; elsewhere the word, when used with the verb *ᶜābar*, either has such a suffix (Deut. 17: 2; Josh. 7: 11; Jud. 2: 20; 2 Kgs. 18: 12; Jer. 34: 8; Hos. 8: 1—all Deuteronomic/Deuteronomistic including, according to Perlitt, the Hosea text), or is coupled with Yahweh (Josh. 7: 15; 23: 16—also Deuteronomistic). The word *bāgᵉdū* 'they were treacherous' in the second half of the verse is frequently used elsewhere of Israel's treachery against Yahweh, but never within the context specifically of breaking the *bᵉrīt* between him and Israel (cf. for example, Hos. 5: 7; Jer. 3: 8, 11, 20; 5: 11; 9: 1; 12: 1). It cannot be called upon in Hosea 6: 7 as inherent evidence that the *bᵉrīt* here mentioned was between Yahweh and Israel.

Perlitt's view has some support from the record in Ezekiel 17: 11–21 of Zedekiah's breach of his treaty with Nebuchadrezzar where this is described as treachery against Yahweh (v. 20). (A different verb (*māᶜal*) is employed, but clearly it may be taken as an analogy for *bāgᵉdū* in Hosea 6: 7.) Further, the treaty between Nebuchadrezzar and Zedekiah is here referred to as Yahweh's treaty (v. 19), thus underlining that wanton breach of a treaty made with another could at the same time be regarded as treachery against one's own god.

An alternative interpretation of Hosea 6: 7 has been proposed by G. Fohrer.[11] He understands the breach of the *bᵉrīt* here to refer to a covenant between the king and the people in northern Israel, and argues that it was at Adam that the breaking of this covenant, that is, revolution against the king, took place, a revolution which then spread in bloodshed in Gilead and across to Shechem. This may find support, he suggests, from the probability that Shallum (2 Kgs. 15: 10) and Menahem (2 Kgs. 15: 14) were from Gilead, as well as from the fact that Pekah's revolution (2 Kgs. 15: 25) was carried out with the help of men from Gilead.[12]

---

[10] Ibid., p. 143.

[11] 'Der Vertrag zwischen König und Volk in Israel', *ZAW* 71, 1959, pp. 1–22.

[12] pp. 15 ff. Cf. W. Rudolph, *Hosea*, KAT xiii/1, Gütersloh 1966, pp. 145 f.

II

For various reasons, however, I cannot accept Perlitt's understanding of Hosea 6: 7. First, Hosea appears to have vehemently condemned Israel's treaty-making activities (cf. 5: 13; 7: 11; 8: 9; 12: 2); the making of such treaties is regarded as an act of faithlessness against Yahweh. Perhaps, though he opposed the making of a treaty with a foreign nation, he also believed that once made such a treaty should be honoured. Yet it is difficult to accept that he could condemn as treachery against Yahweh the termination of a treaty, the very making of which had been an act of faithlessness against Yahweh in the first instance. In short, it is surely unlikely that he would have regarded such a treaty as 'Yahweh's treaty' (as Ezekiel evidently regarded that between Judah and Babylon).[13] Second, the offences listed in the following verses appear to refer to internal crimes and have no apparent relevance to the breaking of a treaty with an external power. Third, it has also to be asked what conceivable action on the part of the Israelite state at this politically insignificant place on Israel's soil could have constituted the breaking of a treaty with a foreign nation.

The more likely understanding of the verse is that the *bᵉrît* referred to was one between Yahweh and Israel. In this connection the idiom employed (*ʿābar bᵉrît*) is of significance, and, in my opinion, tells strikingly against both Perlitt's and Fohrer's interpretation of the text.

First, in every other occurrence of this idiom it refers to a covenant between Yahweh and Israel (Deut. 17: 2; Josh. 7: 11, 15; 23: 16; Jud. 2: 20; 2 Kgs. 18: 12; Jer. 34: 18; Hos. 8: 1). By contrast, it is never used of the breaking of secular treaties for which the technical term appears to have been *hēpēr bᵉrît* (1 Kgs. 15: 19=2 Chron. 16: 3; Isa. 33: 8; Ezek. 17: 15, 16, 18, 19).[14] If, as Perlitt maintains, Hosea 6: 7 refers to the breaking of a treaty

---

[13] See H. Lubsczyk, 'Der Bund als Gemeinschaft mit Gott. Erwägungen zur Diskussion über den Begriff "berit" im Alten Testament', *Dienst der Vermittlung*, Erfurter Theologische Studien 37, Leipzig 1977, pp. 88 f. My colleague John Day made this observation to me independently of Lubsczyk's article (see his forthcoming article referred to in note 1 above).

[14] See W. Thiel, '*Hēpēr bᵉrît*. Zum Bundbrechen im Alten Testament', *VT* 20, 1970, pp. 214–29. Notwithstanding his conclusion here, Thiel maintains that the *bᵉrît* referred to in Hos. 6: 7, where it is coupled with the verb *ʿābar*, refers to the breaking of a secular treaty; cf. his 'Die Rede vom "Bund" in den Prophetenbüchern', *Theologische Versuche* 9, 1977, p. 12.

between Israel and another nation, it is the only text in which the idiom *hēpēr bᵉrīt* is not employed for breaking a secular treaty, and the only one in which the idiom *ʿābar bᵉrīt* is used in the secular sphere. In short, the onus is on those who argue that the idiom *ʿābār bᵉrīt* in Hosea 6: 7 has a different referent than in the remaining texts which employ it and where it is consistently used for a covenant between Yahweh and Israel.

Second, and yet more significant, there is an important distinction between these two idioms. On the one hand, *hēpēr bᵉrīt* is employed for the nullification of a treaty or covenant; such a treaty or covenant has been terminated and can only be replaced by a new one. One thinks instantly of the 'new covenant' passage in Jeremiah 31: 31–4 which is to replace that made with Israel's ancestors and which has been annulled (*hēpērū*; v. 32) by Israel's apostasy and disobedience. By contrast, it seems that 'to transgress the covenant' (*ʿābar bᵉrīt*) refers to offences which threaten the continuation of the covenant and which, if not purged, will result in its termination—the narrative of the transgression of the covenant by Achan in Joshua 7 provides an example—but not to the nullification of the covenant as such. In other words, the idioms *hēpēr bᵉrīt* and *ʿābar bᵉrīt* are not synonymous and simply interchangeable; a clear distinction must be preserved between them. Thus, for example, whilst it is said of Yahweh that he can annul, terminate (*hēpēr*) his *bᵉrīt* with Israel (cf. Lev. 26: 44; Jud. 2: 1; Jer. 14: 41; Zech. 11: 10 f.), this idiom cannot be replaced by *ʿābar bᵉrīt* in these texts.

In view of this, it seems likely that had Hosea in 6: 7 wished to refer to the annulment of a treaty between Israel and another state, or, as Fohrer argues, between the citizens of northern Israel and their king,[15] he would have used the idiom *hēpēr bᵉrīt*. It is correspondingly likely that by using the different idiom *ʿābar bᵉrīt* he had something different in mind, and the use of this idiom elsewhere in the Old Testament strongly suggests that he was referring to an offence by Israel against Yahweh's covenant. More precisely, it is likely that the idiom refers to a transgression against Yahweh's *tōrāh*, so that in this context the word *bᵉrīt* may be replaced by the word *tōrāh*. This is clearly so in Hosea 8: 1, where the idiom *ʿābᵉrū bᵉrītī* is paralleled by 'they have rebelled against my *tōrāh*'. In several other texts employing the idiom, the *bᵉrīt* is said to have been 'com-

---

[15] Against Fohrer, it should also be noted that in any case we have no evidence that the citizens of northern Israel regularly made a covenant with the ruling dynasty there.

manded' (cf. Josh. 7: 11; 23: 16; Jud. 2: 20; 2 Kgs. 18: 12) and thus in such contexts refers to Yahweh's *tōrāh*. Such an understanding is also supported by the collocation of *ʿābar* with *ḥōq* ('to transgress a statute'; Ps. 148: 6), with *miṣwāh* (Deut. 26: 13; 2 Chron. 24: 20; cf. Esth. 3: 3 where it is used of the command of a king), with *pī* in the sense of Yahweh's command (Num. 4: 41; 1 Sam. 15: 24), and with *tōrāh/tōrōt* (Isa. 24: 5; Dan. 9: 11). On this ground it is probable that as employed in Hosea 6: 7 the word *bᵉrīt* also refers to Yahweh's *tōrāh* —a conclusion which is in keeping with Hosea's concern elsewhere with Yahweh's *tōrāh* (4: 1 f., 6; 8: 12).

To what offence committed by Israel at Adam does the accusation in Hosea 6: 7 refer? J. Lindblom makes the interesting suggestion that since Adam lay close to the place where the Israelites under Joshua crossed the Jordan to take possession of the land (Josh. 3: 16), the prophet is here accusing Israel of having transgressed the covenant from the moment it entered the land long ago.[16] A paraphrase of the verse might be thus 'No sooner were you in the land than you transgressed the covenant'. Such an interpretation should not be ruled out. Against it, however, the offences listed in the following verses seem more likely to refer to more recent events,[17] and it is improbable that the prophet would first have mentioned treachery of the remote past and then moved immediately to actions of the very recent past.

Does the accusation allude to a cultic offence? The word *bāgᵉdū* in the second half of the verse might be taken as some evidence in support of such an interpretation. This word occurs elsewhere in Hosea at 5: 7 where it refers to Israel's 'harlotrous' infidelity to Yahweh. It is a sound exegetical principle to understand its use in 6: 7 on this basis. Thus understood, the word might be taken as characterizing the nature of the offence at Adam as having been an act of Israel's wonted apostasy, a transgression of the law which is so prominent in covenantal texts in the Old Testament: the demand for Israel's exclusive worship of Yahweh. Hence, with Wolff it might be agreed that the verse may refer to some recent cultic action by Israel which demonstrated its unfaithfulness to the covenant.[18] An

---

[16] *Hosea Literarisch Untersucht*, Acta Academiae Aboensis, Humaniora V, Åbo 1927, p. 86. Cf. Noth, 'Die Gesetze im Pentateuch', *Gesammelte Studien zum Alten Testament*,² p. 85, E. trs. 'The Laws in the Pentateuch', *The Laws in the Pentateuch and other Essays*, p. 63.

[17] Lindblom himself suggests that the offences listed in vv. 8 f. refer to events of Hosea's time (p. 86).   [18] *Hosea*, p. 155; E. trs. p. 121.

indictment of Israel's apostasy is a central theme of Hosea's preaching. The only difference is that in 6: 7 he has used the terminology of transgressing a covenant with Yahweh rather than his more familiar 'marriage metaphor' of which, however, it might be argued that the use of the word *bāḡᵉdū* is an echo, an associative signal. But there is no evidence elsewhere in the Old Testament about apostasy at the place Adam. The most plausible interpretation is that this reference to treachery at Adam as well as the references to bloodshed at Gilead and murder at Shechem (or in its vicinity) in the following verses allude to violent acts committed in the course of political upheavals and revolution in the time of Hosea,[19] and which the prophet describes as transgression of Yahweh's covenant.

III

What of Hosea 8: 1? It may be said straight away that if it is the case that 6: 7 does employ the image of a *bᵉrīt* between Yahweh and Israel, the onus of proof upon those who argue that 8: 1b is non-Hoseanic is surely significantly increased. Perlitt (pp. 146 ff.) argues that the terminology finds its closest parallel in the Deuteronomistic literature (cf. especially Jud. 2: 20), and that the line is an interpolation; instead of its generalizing, anticipatory statement of the ground for coming judgement, before any description of Israel's offences has been given, the 'summons to alarm' in v. 1a much more effectively opens the ears for the register of Israel's guilt which follows it.

There is nothing in this line, however, which necessarily points to a Deuteronomistic hand. It employs the same terminology (*ᶜābar bᵉrīt*) as 6: 7; as in the latter, so here also *bᵉrīt* refers to Yahweh's *tōrāh* which Israel has transgressed. The only difference is that in 8: 1b *bᵉrītī* 'my covenant' has a suffix. But this is a slender basis on which to deny it to Hosea; the suffix is surely more plausibly explained as due to a desire to have a strict parallel with *tōrātī* 'my *tōrāh*' in the second half of the verse. Further, the phrase 'they have rebelled against my *tōrāh*' (*uᶜ ᶜal tōrātī pāšāᶜū*) is nowhere attested in the Deuteronomic corpus—even though there are many occasions when it could have been employed—but is peculiar to Hosea 8: 1.

---

[19] See Day in his forthcoming article referred to in note 1 above.

It is the case, as Perlitt points out, that a similar 'summons to alarm'[20] in Hosea 5: 8 (cf. Jer. 4: 5; 6: 1) is not followed by such a line as 8: 1b. But again, this is surely an insufficient ground for arguing that therefore no such line could originally have followed Hosea 8: 1a. The offences in vv. 4–14 can be understood as a spelling out in specific terms of the general indictment announced in v. 1a, as Wolff has suggested.[21] In short, there are good reasons for believing that 8: 1b derives from Hosea himself, and no convincing reasons for regarding it as a Deuteronomistic interpolation.

IV

In view of our conclusions earlier about other 'key texts' relating to the covenant, the evidence of the book of Hosea is crucially significant, for it indicates that the notion of a covenant between God and Israel was known already in the mid-eighth century BC.

The possibility suggests itself that it was Hosea who first coined such a notion and that it was from him that other circles, notably the Deuteronomic movement, derived it and further developed it. Such a possibility should not be ruled out. In favour of it is the remarkable variety of imagery which this prophet employed: 'No other prophet—indeed not one writer in the entire Old Testament—uses so many similes as Hosea does.'[22] His audience 'must have been struck by the great number of metaphors he employed'.[23] To have coined the image of a *berīt* between Yahweh and Israel would certainly have been in keeping with his manifest fondness for a wide variety of imagery. The notion of a *berīt* between Yahweh and Israel may have suggested itself to him as an alternative to his more familiar 'marriage metaphor', so that both metaphors are employed to signal that solemn commitment of Yahweh to Israel and of Israel to Yahweh which Israel's infidelity and treachery betrayed (cf. his use of the same verb (*bāgad*) in 5: 7 and 6: 7, the former employing it for Israel's treachery as an unfaithful 'wife', the latter employing it for Israel's treachery in transgressing the covenant). It is

---

[20] The text of Hosea 8: 1a is unclear, but a 'summons to alarm' appears to be indicated.
[21] *Hosea*, pp. 170–3; E. trs. pp. 133–5.
[22] Ibid., p. xv; E. trs. p. xxiv.
[23] Ibid., p. xvi; E. trs. p. xxiv.

worth recalling in this connection that Wellhausen, though he denied that Hosea used the word *bᵉrīt* for the relationship between Yahweh and Israel, could nevertheless state that in his 'marriage metaphor' the prophet 'certainly presents us as clearly as possible with the thing'.

Against such a suggestion, however, it might be argued that the manner of Hosea's use of the word *bᵉrīt* in the two texts discussed suggests that he was not formulating something new, but was referring rather to something already in circulation. The matter-of-fact, almost incidental nature of his use of the word in 6: 7 and 8: 1 may indicate this: no accompanying explanation for its use is necessary; the references have the character of allusions to something familiar both to Hosea and to his audience.

Even if the latter is the case, however, we have no sound basis for concluding that the covenant concept emerged long before the time of Hosea. He alone among the prophets of the eighth century appears to have known the theological use of the word *bᵉrīt*, and Exodus 24: 3–8 alone among the main convenantal texts can be regarded with any confidence to be of pre-Deuteronomic origin, though it contains nothing which necessitates an origin earlier than the time of Hosea.

All in all, the conclusion is warranted that the concept of a covenant between Yahweh and Israel originated at some point during the second half of the monarchical period. Hosea shows it to have been emerging in his time, and the narrative in Exodus 24: 3–8 is probably a further pre-Deuteronomic anticipation of its use. Its most intensive and expansive usage, however, came with the Deuteronomic movement of the period subsequent to Hosea whose influence on this movement has long been recognized.

To this extent, the thesis that the covenant as a full-blown theological concept was a late arrival in Israel is substantially vindicated, and thus in this respect we seem to have been brought back, like Perlitt and some others recently, to almost the view of Wellhausen a century or so ago. But that the issue cannot be left where these scholars leave it will now be argued in the next, my concluding, chapter.

PART THREE

GOD AND HIS PEOPLE

The Covenant and the Distinctiveness of Israel's Faith

THE notion of a covenant between Yahweh and Israel was not so late a development in Israel as to have been completely unknown in the eighth century BC. On the other hand, it cannot any longer with confidence be traced to an early period in the history of Israel and of its religion. Further, none of the descriptions of the making of a covenant provides evidence that any part of its purpose was to unite diverse tribes into a tribal league, as so often suggested hitherto. That the tribes already belonged together as 'Israel' is the presupposition of each one of these texts; what they concentrate on is Israel's relationship with, and commitment to, Yahweh. We are thus led away from an understanding of the covenant as an ancient 'institution' and pointed towards a consideration of the covenant as a theological innovation of a later time. It seems to have emerged at some point in the late monarchical period, in the time of Hosea or not long before, and subsequently received its most intensive and expansive treatment at the hands of Deuteronomic writers from the late pre-exilic period on into the sixth century. On the whole, therefore, the thesis that the covenant as a full-blown concept of the relation between God and Israel was a late arrival in Israel is vindicated.

A century of scholarly research would thus seem to have brought us back virtually to the view of Wellhausen on the origin of the covenant, and as a result it may be wondered whether the whole debate has run itself into the ground, leaving covenant as a played-out concept for the student of the Old Testament. But there is much more to be said about the covenant, even if on the mere question of its date Perlitt and other recent scholars, like Wellhausen a century ago, have drawn approximately the correct conclusion. For covenant theology proves, on closer examination, to hold the key to a question that has long occupied the attention of Old Testament scholars: the question of the distinctiveness of Israel's religious faith.

My purpose in this concluding chapter is to show why I believe this is so. In part the view to be argued is based upon an insight of Wellhausen which in my opinion scholars since his time have too quickly abandoned, namely, his view that the great prophets of the eighth century effected a decisive change in the understanding of God's relationship with Israel.[1] Briefly stated, the preaching of these prophets, according to Wellhausen, broke the mould of a 'natural bond' between God and the people, and transferred the relationship to the plane of moral response and commitment. I shall argue that this view is correct, and that the notion of a covenant between God and Israel arose as one of the results of the decisive change these prophets brought about.

The ground on which I shall argue differs in two main respects from that of Wellhausen. First, we are today able to draw upon a great deal that has been discovered since his time about Israel and its ancient Near Eastern environment, especially about ancient Near Eastern religion and what Israelite religion owed to it. The brief description which I offer of Israelite religion in the pre-exilic period is therefore necessarily different from his. Second, I shall use some insights which the modern study of the sociology of religion offers. It is well known that there is a variety of theories about the relation between religion and society, some of them sharply conflicting. Further, there are obvious hazards in applying such modern theories to the life and religion of an ancient society such as Israel. The use here made of some insights which this field of study provides does not necessitate wholly accepting any one of these theories. They are insights which, I believe, are generally accepted and which, I shall argue, give a fresh perspective to Wellhausen's understanding of the achievement of the prophets and ultimately to the understanding of the origin and nature of the covenant.

The main insight which I have in mind, and how it may be used in the study of the problem on hand, is as follows. The sociology of religion has been interested not only in the social institutions which religion may generate, but also in the social function of religion and religious ideas in the sense of legitimating the structures and institutions of a society. Writers such as Peter Berger have devoted special attention to an analysis of this role of religion.[2] When such an analysis is applied to the history of Israelite religion, one can trace a highly distinctive development, in which a phase where religion legitimates society is succeeded by one in which a new style of religious thought emerges which challenges and de-legitimates or 'demystifies' the apparently stable and divinely ordained social structures and institutions. The crucial figures in bringing about this transformation were (as Wellhausen correctly maintained) the classical prophets, beginning in the eighth century BC. But if, as concluded above, the notion of a covenant between God and Israel originated in the same period in which these prophets began their preaching, then the conclusion that the covenant concept itself was intimately bound up with the decisive religious change which these prophets initiated lies close to hand. It is this conclusion which will be argued in the following pages.

I

As a general thesis, the history of the development of Israelite religion may be described as having been one of increasingly conflicting world-views, that is, theologically speaking, of increasingly opposed understandings of God and his relation to man and the world. Further, this did not represent primarily a confrontation between Israel as an 'in-group' and a religious cultural 'out-group'; rather, Israel's distinctive world-view as portrayed in the Old Testament was wrought out of a protracted history of controversy within Israel itself which was finally decisively intensified and also resolved by the preaching of the classical prophets. More elaborately, this may be put as follows.

One way of describing religion is that it is part of a society's endeavour to impose meaning upon its experience of the world.[3] Among the nations of Israel's environment religion performed this role in an all-embracing manner. As a microcosm is related to a macrocosm, the humanly perceived 'right order' of the social world was seen as a reflection of the cosmic order created and willed by the gods. This sacred order extended from the world of the gods to the world of men, embracing both in a unity. Society's structures and institutions were in this way believed to be grounded in the sacred order of the cosmos and were accordingly seen

---

[1] For a recent perceptive discussion of this see W. McKane, 'Prophet and Institution', *ZAW* 94, 1982, pp. 251–66.

[2] See especially P. Berger, *The Social Reality of Religion*, London 1969.

[3] See Berger, esp. ch. 1.

as being divinely legitimated.[4] Put differently, the ordering of the human world, including both nature and society, was conceived from the perspective of, and validated by, what we would call a 'theology of creation'.[5]

Creation myths described how this sacred cosmos was created by the gods against the forces of chaos in the *Urzeit*. But though they narrated events of the remote past, to some extent at least these myths reflected society's experience of the continuing threat of chaos, that is, of the continuing confrontation between the 'right order' of the human world and all that threatened it. In other words, creation was not merely an event of the remote past, but also concerned the present: the cosmic order was not merely given; it had to be sustained. It was society's guarantee against the ever present forces of destruction, the forces of chaos, which might manifest themselves in, for example, disruptions of the fertility of nature, attacks by enemies (seen as allies of the cosmic forces of chaos), and the like.

A perception of the 'right order' of the world informed all activities of society's life, the total well-being of which depended upon upholding it.[6] In the cultic sphere the annual New Year festival centred upon a realization in the present, a cultic 'actualization', of the triumph of the creator gods over chaos, and so sought to 'renew' the 'right order' of the world, including the fertility of nature, for the year to come. Or when at any time calamity struck—that is, when the order of things was under assault—the cult and its rituals (lament, sacrifice, magic, etc.) played an important role in restoring the 'right order'. In the political sphere enemies could be viewed as earthly allies of the cosmic forces of chaos, so that defence against them was itself part of the endeavour to maintain the divinely willed order. The sacred order was also reflected in society's laws, understood as having been decreed by the gods at the foundation of the state;[7] in this way the just ordering of society was brought into close relationship with the creation of the world itself. Hence a breach of these laws was *ipso facto* a breach of the order of creation, and could be understood as having

---

[4] Ibid., esp. ch. 2.

[5] See especially H. H. Schmid, *Altorientalische Welt in der alttestamentlichen Theologie*, Zürich 1974, ch. 1.   [6] Ibid., pp. 10 ff.

[7] Ibid., pp. 11 f. Schmid draws attention in this connection to the beginning of the Prologue to the Code of Hammurabi (cf. *AOT*, pp. 380 f.; *ANET*, p. 164).

dire consequences in the sphere of nature or in the sphere of politics, since law, politics, and nature were but different aspects of the one all-embracing ordering of the world.[8]

The perception of the divine ordering of the world likewise informed the ideology of kingship in the ancient Near East. The king—whether as an incarnation of the creator god or as 'son'—was the divinely appointed vicegerent of the creator deity and as such was seen as the earthly guardian of the order of things they willed; he was responsible through his actions and functions for the social and political well-being of the state, including the fertility of the land. The wisdom literature of the ancient Near East provides some further evidence of the belief in the divinely willed ordering of the world: to live wisely was to be in harmony with the cosmic order of which wisdom was fundamentally constitutive[9] (hence, for example, the use in Egyptian wisdom and legal texts of the word *maat* which is also employed to designate the 'right order' of the created world itself).[10]

The sense of the all-pervading order of the world accounts for another familiar feature of ancient Near Eastern thought, namely, the belief in a direct relationship between a misdeed and what must befall as a result of it: a violation of the divinely established order issues in dire consequences for its perpetrator; unless otherwise purged or expiated, the offence rebounds on the malefactor, whether as a necessary result of the inherent nature of things, or as punishment visited directly by the gods, as sustainers of the ordering of the world, upon the offender.

Although allowance has to be made for much variation in detail, it may plausibly be claimed that such in brief was the world-view held in common by Israel's ancient Near Eastern neighbours, including Canaanite society which formed the more immediate background to the development of Israelite religion. The structures and institutions of society were believed to reflect the order willed by the gods, and were thus understood as being divinely legitimated. They were viewed, as we may

---

[8] Ibid., p. 12.

[9] Ibid., p. 12 f., and especially Schmid's two detailed studies *Wesen und Geschichte der Weisheit*, BZAW 101, Berlin 1966, and *Gerechtigkeit als Weltordnung*, Beiträge zur historischen Theologie 40, Tübingen 1968.

[10] Schmid, *Wesen und Geschichte der Weisheit*, pp. 12 f. *Gerechtigkeit als Weltordnung*, pp. 46 ff.

put it, *sub specie aeternitatis.* Put differently, it was a world-view grounded in what we may describe as a 'theology of creation'.

II

There is evidence, as I shall argue below, that this ancient Near Eastern sense of the divine ordering of the world and its reflection in, and legitimation of, society's structures and institutions influenced Israelite religion.[11] Further, it does not seem that this was a secondary influence upon Israelite religion conceived of as having been originally sharply discontinuous with the religious thought-world of its environment, only subsequently to fall into degeneration through contact with Canaanite religion. On the contrary, it may be claimed that whichever of the main views one accepts concerning the origins of Israel, the development of Israelite religion from the earliest stages of its history in Canaan was unavoidably and necessarily shaped in significant respects by the religious thought-world and institutions of its environment.

The most widely accepted view of the emergence of Israel is that the tribes were a consolidation of numerous erstwhile semi-nomadic clans whose original habitat was the desert fringes of Palestine, but who settled permanently in the land itself during the Late Bronze/Early Iron Age. The most widely accepted view of the origin of the worship of Yahweh is that it originated in the territory south of Palestine and that it was associated with a sacred mountain variously named in the Old Testament texts as Sinai, Horeb, or simply 'the mountain of God',[12] whence it was eventually brought into Canaan by the semi-nomadic groups who settled there and gradually constituted the tribes of Israel. If all this was so, however, then the conditions into which the worship of Yahweh was brought in the land will have necessitated considerable development of it if it was to survive, because the life of a settled society such as Israel was now to become will have been much more complex than that of the pastoral clans by whom this God was originally worshipped. In the terminology employed above, the world-view with which Yahweh was originally associated will have

---

[11] See especially Schmid, *Altorientalische Welt in der alttestamentlichen Theologie*, ch. 2.

[12] For a review of the significance of these different descriptions see W. H. Schmidt, *Exodus, Sinai und Mose*, Erträge der Forschung 191, Darmstadt 1983, pp. 122 ff. and the further bibliography cited there.

required extensive elaboration in Canaan. That this elaboration was effected through the appropriation of features and aspects of the cultural and religious tradition of Canaan is strongly suggested by the evidence, as we shall see.

An alternative suggestion is that the name Yahweh was originally a cultic name of the Canaanite high god El, possibly an epithet of this god as patron deity of a Midianite league in the south and associated with Sinai.[13] If such a view could be sustained, it would account for the fact that various features associated with El were also associated with Yahweh.[14] It would also explain how elements of the population of Israel—who, there is reason to believe, had long been resident in Canaan and were not among those enslaved by the Pharaoh in Egypt and who, we may reasonably assume, were already worshippers of El—were able to identify themselves with the worship of Yahweh as the God (El) who had delivered those groups who had been enslaved in Egypt and were now in Canaan. In the present state of our knowledge, however, such a suggestion concerning the origin of the worship of Yahweh is certainly not proven. There is no reference to Yahweh, whether as an epithet of El or as a separate deity, among the gods of the Canaanite pantheon, about which we are relatively well informed, or for that matter among the deities of any other pantheon of the religions of the ancient Near East. But even if such a hypothesis could be proved, it would still point, even more so indeed than the alternative view outlined above, to an involvement of Canaanite religion in the emerging religion of Israel, since, *ex hypothesi*, Israel's own God was originally a manifestation of the Canaanite high god El. That is, if such was the origin of the worship of Yahweh, it is inherently unlikely that the 'radical differentiation'[15] of Yahweh from Canaanite religion would have been accomplished all at once and without some permanent debt to that religion.

According to an alternative understanding of Israelite origins currently favoured by some scholars, the tribes of Israel were not constituted by

---

[13] F. M. Cross, *Canaanite Myth and Hebrew Epic*, Cambridge Mass., and London 1973, ch. 3 (esp. pp. 60–75).

[14] Ibid., esp. pp. 40–60, and his article on *ʾēl* in *Theologisches Wörterbuch zum Alten Testament*, vol. I, ed. G. J. Botterweck and H. Ringgren, Stuttgart, Berlin, Cologne, Mainz 1973, cols. 259–79; E. trs. *Theological Dictionary of the Old Testament*, vol. I, Grand Rapids 1977, pp. 242–61. See also the well-known article by O. Eissfeldt, 'El and Yahweh', *JSS* 1, 1956, pp. 25–37. [15] Cross's phrase, *Canaanite Myth and Hebrew Epic*, p. 71.

movements of peoples into the land from outside but were in fact the rural population of the land itself in which it had long been resident alongside the city-state citizenry.[16] With the decline of the city-state system in the Late Bronze Age, it is argued, the tribes gained the upper hand in what had hitherto been a delicate balance between them and the monarchically governed city-states. If such was the origin of Israel as a society, the implications it would have had for the development of the worship of Yahweh are self-evident: brought into the land by numerically small groups from the desert fringes, it would have had to establish itself among these tribes of the Canaanite countryside who, it may plausibly be inferred, would have been worshippers of indigenous Canaanite gods. Once again, on such a view it is inherently probable that the cult of Yahweh would have had to accommodate itself in significant ways to a long established Canaanite world-view.[17]

III

Whichever of these theories one decides upon, there is no shortage of evidence that Israel became significantly indebted to the religious thought-world of its environment. For example, it is probable that in Israel too there was an annual New Year festival which centred upon Yahweh's triumph over chaos in creation, and thus proclaimed his divine kingship as creator and sustainer of the world (e.g. Pss. 47; 93; 95–99). The motif of the battle against chaos, which belonged to the creation typology of Canaanite and Mesopotamian religions, appears also to have been associated with Yahweh (e.g. Isa. 27: 1; 51: 9; Pss. 74: 13 f.; 89: 10 f.; 104: 6–9; Job 9: 13; 26: 12; 38: 8–11); further, this motif is found not only in cosmological contexts but also in political contexts, thus indicating that in

[16] See especially G. E. Mendenhall, 'The Hebrew Conquest of Palestine', *BA* 25, 1962, pp. 66–87, and *The Tenth Generation*, Baltimore 1973; C. H. J. de Geus, *The Tribes of Israel*, Assen and Amsterdam 1976; N. K. Gottwald, *The Tribes of Yahweh*, London 1979; D. N. Freedman and D. F. Graf (eds.), *Palestine in Transition: The Emergence of Ancient Israel*, Sheffield 1983.

[17] It will be seen from what follows that I do not accept the view of Mendenhall, Gottwald, and others that Israel came into existence through a religiously inspired 'peasant revolution' against the city-state rulers of the Late Bronze Age. For some observations, especially on Gottwald's work, see my 'Israelite Religion in the Pre-Exilic Period: A Debate Renewed', to be published in a *Festschrift* for William McKane, 1986.

Israel too enemies could be regarded as none other than a manifestation of chaos.[18] In Israel too, at least in the case of the Davidic dynasty, there emerged an ideology of kingship which bears close resemblances to that of the surrounding nations: the king is Yahweh's 'son' on whose behalf Yahweh defeats the enemies (e.g. Pss. 2; 89; 110); he exercises the role of Yahweh's vicegerent as the guardian and maintainer of Yahweh's righteousness among the people, and associated with the role of the king in this respect is the very fertility of the land (e.g. Ps. 72). Likewise in Israel wisdom was believed to be grounded in, and a reflection of, the divinely created 'right order' of things; wisdom and righteousness were closely related to one another.[19] In the ethical sphere there is evidence that Israel shared with its neighbours a belief in the 'deed-and-its-effect' syndrome, that is, an order built into the structure of things.[20]

There are further strong indications of what may be termed the 'Canaanization' of Yahweh. There is evidence, especially in traditions deriving from Jerusalem, that Yahweh was identified with El, the highest god of the Canaanite pantheon, a number of whose epithets and descriptions have been associated with Yahweh.[21] In this way Yahweh would have assumed the role of El as creator, sustainer, and guardian of the divinely willed order of the world. Further, there is some evidence that, in typical Canaanite fashion, a number of subordinate deities were worshipped alongside the national God Yahweh (e.g. Shalim, Shamash, Astarte),[22] and there is of course abundant evidence that Baal, the most active god of the Canaanite pantheon, was widely worshipped in Israel, in some circles probably identified with Yahweh.[23] It seems also likely that the cult of the Canaanite goddess and Baal's consort Anath among the fifth-century Jews at Elephantine was inherited by them from much earlier Israelite times. To this must be added now the evidence of recently

[18] See F. Stolz, *Strukturen und Figuren im Kult von Jerusalem*, BZAW 118, Berlin 1970, pp. 12-101. Cf. J. Day, *God's Conflict with the Dragon and the Sea*, Cambridge 1985, ch. 3.

[19] Cf. Schmid, *Altorientalische Welt in der alttestamentlichen Theologie*, p. 16; *Gerechtigkeit als Weltordnung*, esp. pp. 96 ff.

[20] Cf. K. Koch, 'Gibt es ein Vergeltungsdogma im Alten Testament?', *ZTK* 52, 1955, pp. 1-42; Schmid, *Altorientalische Welt in der alttestamentlichen Theologie*, pp. 14 f., 49 f.; J. Barton, 'Natural Law and Poetic Justice in the Old Testament', *JTS*, NS 30, 1979, pp. 1-14.

[21] See, for example, Schmid, *Altorientalische Welt in der alttestamentlichen Theologie*, pp. 38 ff.; Stolz, esp. ch. 4. Cf. the articles by Cross and Eissfeldt cited in footnote 14 above.

[22] See Schmid, *Altorientalische Welt in der alttestamentlichen Theologie*, pp. 42 f.; Stolz, ch. 5. [23] See H. W. Wolff, *Hosea*, p. 60; E. trs. pp. 49f.

discovered inscriptions dating from the mid-monarchical period which lends support to the view that the goddess Asherah, the worship of whom is attested in the Old Testament as having been at least at times part of Israel's national cult, was associated with Yahweh as his consort, just as she was a consort of El in Canaanite religion.[24]

It seems, therefore, on this evidence that Israel adopted a world-view which in significant respects resembled that typical of its ancient Near Eastern neighbours. Israel too understood itself, its structures and institutions *sub specie aeternitatis*, as we may put it; religion in Israel performed a legitimating role no less than the religions of other nations of the time. Religion, that is, contained a crucially important 'state-ideology' component.[25]

Over against all this, however, there are other aspects and features which can be gathered from the Old Testament and which radically differentiate Old Testament religion from the religious thought-world of its environment. Instead of the many there is but one God to whom alone Israel's allegiance is commanded; against polytheism, which was of the essence of the religions of the ancient Near East, came a zealously exclusive monolatry and eventually monotheism. Further, the creation-theology which predominates in the Old Testament and which is represented most notably by the opening chapters of Genesis is far removed from the cosmogonic mythology of the ancient Near East with which, as noted above, Yahweh may at one time have been associated. In the Old Testament Yahweh is creator but radically transcends his creation. The distance between him and the human world is polarized, and in between is a universe emptied of gods. He bestows the gifts of the earth upon the people, but is sharply dissociated from the fertility gods who were so common a feature of the religions of antiquity. He chooses his people, delivers them from bondage in Egypt, and brings them into possession of the land he had sworn to give them; he further delivers them from their enemies. Yet his purposes are not fulfilled simply in the establishment of this people among the nations; his purposes are not 'to the greater glory of

---

[24] For a recent discussion see J. A. Emerton, 'New Light on Israelite Religion: The Implications of the Inscriptions from Kuntillet ʿAjrud', *ZAW* 94, 1982, pp. 2–20. On the goddess Asherah see the excellent survey by J. Day, 'Asherah in the Hebrew Bible and Northwest Semitic Literature', forthcoming in *JBL*.

[25] Cf. Schmid, *Altorientalische Welt in der alttestamentlichen Theologie*, pp. 53, 60.

Israel'; rather, Israel's life in every aspect is to be 'to the greater glory of God'. Over against the common world-view of the nations of its time which centred upon the well-being of the state, and was thus, as suggested above, a sort of 'state-ideology', over against Israel's own apparent belief that its well-being was permanently secured by Yahweh, is a world-view in which the fulfilment of God's righteousness is the goal, the very *raison d'être*, of the nation. Hence Yahweh's will confronts Israel and in its name a faithless Israel can be and is rejected, the goal of its promised reconstitution being again the service of Yahweh and the uncompromising demands of his will.

Here then we have evidence that Israel adopted significant aspects and features of the characteristic religious thought-world of its environment, with strong indications that the innate polytheism of that thought-world made deep inroads into Israelite life, but at the same time evidence also that in the most decisive and far-reaching manner Israelite religion as it finally found expression in the Old Testament rejected such a world-view and arrived at a radically different understanding of God and his relation to man and the world. Such is the gulf which separates them that we must think of it as the rejection of one world-view, initially significantly influential upon Israel, and the working out of a radically different one.

It is this latter world-view which we identify as the distinctive religion of the Old Testament. It has been variously described: by Wellhausen, for example, as 'the denaturalization of ancient religion', by Weber as 'the disenchantment of the world', by others as 'the desacralization of the world', or as a 'demythologized world-view', and the like. But in whatever way it is described, the point to be made is that its character was not given in one creative, founding period at the beginning; rather, as the evidence outlined above already suggests, it was wrought out of controversy within Israel, a controversy which centred upon the nature of God and his relation to the world and to Israel, upon the nature of his will for Israel and what this demanded of Israel in response, and so consequently upon what Israel itself was to be in the world.

IV

The decisive stage in the history of this inner-Israelite controversy began in the eighth century with the preaching of the great prophets, and it was from this period onwards that a radically new and distinctive Israelite world-view emerged. The resultant transformation of Israel's understanding of God and his relation to Israel provided the basis for, and found expression in, the concept of a covenant between Yahweh and Israel, as I shall argue below. But the controversy which the eighth-century prophets sharply intensified had antecedents which go further back.

Evidence for this can be found, for example, in connection with the demand for Israel's exclusive allegiance to Yahweh which is so central a feature of the covenant theology where it has the status of nothing less than a principle upon which the religious community stood or fell. It is similarly conceived of in the preaching of Hosea, most notably among the eighth-century prophets.

Controversy on this issue did not first emerge in the time of this prophet. The traditions about Elijah a century or so before Hosea bear witness to an earlier history of controversy concerning it. Indeed, it is not unlikely that it had still earlier origins. In the indisputably ancient traditions of Yahweh's deliverance of Israel's ancestors from bondage in Egypt and of his victories on behalf of the tribes of Israel against their enemies during the early generations of Israel's emergence in Canaan, Yahweh was acknowledged to be the God who alone stood at the foundation and beginnings of Israel.[26] Traditions such as these provide the evidence for how Yahweh became the God of Israel, and it is likely that some circles in Israel from the earliest period maintained an exclusive relationship with Yahweh. But the evidence strongly suggests that for Israelites in general—not only at the level of a popular 'folk religion' but also in official religion in the pre-exilic period—the worship of the national God Yahweh was not believed to be incompatible with the worship of other gods as well, and it seems highly unlikely that exclusive worship of Yahweh was regarded as of the very essence of the national religion, much less that it was the principle upon which the community stood or fell.

[26] On this period see R. Smend, *Jahwekrieg und Stämmebund: Erwägungen zur ältesten Geschichte Israels*, FRLANT 84, Göttingen 1963; E. trs. *Yahweh War and Tribal Confederation: Reflections upon Israel's Earliest History*, Nashville and New York 1970. Cf. H.-P. Müller, 'Gott und die Götter in den Anfängen der biblischen Religion. Zur Vorgeschichte des Monotheismus', in *Monotheismus im Alten Israel und seiner Umwelt*, ed. O. Keel, Biblische Beiträge 14, Fribourg 1980, pp. 99–142.

However, though controversy on this issue may have had early beginnings, in particularly heightened form and with violent consequences it erupted in the ninth century at the hands of Elijah and the circles associated with him. Such is the development which the traditions about Elijah have undergone, and such the Deuteronomistic re-working to which they have been subjected in being placed in their present context, that particular caution is required in attempting to reconstruct the events of the period and to discern the religious motivations behind Elijah's activity.

His name itself has the appearance of a sort of confessional assertion which on the basis of the declaration of the people at Carmel 'Yahweh, he is God' (1 Kgs. 18: 39) may be rendered 'Yahweh is God'.[27] It may have been acquired by him as a nickname, and suggests that he belonged to conservative Yahwistic circles in Israel and now entered the scene as the leader of a movement of militantly self-conscious Yahwism. That he came from Gilead in Transjordan, and thus well away from the centre of the kingdom, has frequently been seen as also suggestive of his conservative background. The policies and behaviour of the dynasty of Omri, and most notably the role of the evidently formidable Tyrian princess and fervent patroness of Baal, Jezebel, occasioned his activity; indeed it was partly as a result of this that the dynasty met its violent end—he himself is described as having announced its rejection by Yahweh and as having inaugurated the dynasty which was to succeed it (1 Kgs. 19: 15-18; 21: 17-24)—and that Jezebel met her bloody death.

It has been suggested that his stand for Yahweh was nationalistically inspired and motivated: Yahweh is Israel's God, and not a foreign deity. In the name of Yahweh, Israel's national God, it is suggested, he waged rebellion against this dynasty's recognition and patronage of foreign cults—the installation of the cult of the Tyrian Baal, Jezebel's own ancestral state god, in Samaria (1 Kgs. 16: 31 f.), and Ahaziah's quest for a cure for his sickness not from Yahweh but from Baalzebub ('Is it because there is no God in Israel that you are going to enquire of Baalzebub, the god of Ekron?' (2 Kgs. 1: 3)).

Though there is some justification for such a view, it may be questioned whether the royal patronage of foreign cults was the sole

[27] For this see R. Smend, 'Der biblische und der historische Elia', *SVT* 28, 1975, pp. 176–80.

motivation of Elijah's 'jealousy' for Yahweh, and whether what he represented is adequately described as a nationalistically inspired Yahwism. He is described as the 'troubler of Israel' and not just of the house of Omri (1 Kgs. 18: 7), and it was Israelites at Mount Carmel whom he confronted with the uncompromising choice 'Yahweh or Baal?'. In my opinion, these elements in the traditions about him, as well as his name and background, suggest a controversy not merely between him and the ruling dynasty, but the sort of inner-Israelite controversy referred to above, a controversy between, on the one hand, a tradition that Yahweh alone stood at the foundation and beginnings of Israel's life and that to him alone Israel's allegiance was due, and, on the other, the polytheistic religion and *praxis* which not merely rivalled but, on the evidence of the Old Testament, prevailed against it throughout the pre-exilic period with at best only sporadic reversals.

Conflict within Israel concerning the nature of Yahweh and his relation to, and claims upon, Israel was not, however, confined to this issue of the worship of the one as against that of the many. In addition, though in important respects related to it, was a further issue of which the Elijah narratives again provide some evidence. It may be described as follows.

As I have suggested, Israelite religion, no less than the religions of its environment, contained a 'state-ideological' component; Israel believed its social order and institutions to have been established by God and thus to be legitimated by him as permanent. The order which Yahweh willed and his actions on Israel's behalf were seen as a manifestation of the righteousness which Yahweh both possessed and safeguarded. It was not considered that the demands of Yahweh's righteousness posed any ultimate threat to Israel. When offences were committed or when there was any other sign that Yahweh's favour had been lost, the organs of the cult (lament, sacrifice, etc.) were there to restore it. Thus Israel's well-being (*šālōm*) was believed to be permanently guaranteed by Yahweh; fundamentally Yahweh's will and Israel's well-being were identified: 'Is not Yahweh in the midst of us? No evil shall befall us' (Mic. 3: 11).

In acute form controversy within Israel on this issue did not come until the prophets of the eighth century who turned Yahweh's righteousness against Israel, placing it at the centre and vehemently denying the belief that his will and Israel's well-being were simply identical. No one before that period had polarized Yahweh's righteousness and Israel's offences against it to such an extent as to announce that Yahweh had rejected Israel (see further below).

Nevertheless, there is evidence that tension arose at an earlier time between, on the one hand, the 'state-ideology' component of Israel's understanding of Yahweh's ordering of the world, and, on the other, the demands of Yahweh's righteousness. Thus, for example, the demands of Yahweh's righteousness were the basis of the prophetic condemnation of Ahab's violent appropriation, at the instigation of Jezebel and with her energetic help, of Naboth's land, understood as his inalienable patrimony from Yahweh. In the prophetic denunciation and condemnation of the king 'Have you murdered and also taken in possession?' (2 Kgs. 21: 19) is already indicated the claims of Yahweh's righteousness, if not at the cost of Israel as such, then certainly at the cost of the state's dynasty. Similarly, at a still earlier time David's adultery with Bathsheba and his ensuing treacherous murder of Uriah were confronted by the divine righteousness at the hands of Nathan, and although the Davidic dynasty remained intact, lasting punishment was announced against it (2 Sam. 12: 10).

Just as religion in Israel was a legitimating agency, these two instances are testimony to its significant role as a 'de-mystifying' agent. That is, the very institutions, in this instance kingship, which religion legitimated *sub specie aeternitatis*, religion could also relativize, 'de-mystify', *sub specie aeternitatis* by declaring them in the face of God's righteousness to be devoid of inherent sanctity or divinely willed permanence.[28]

The fervent exclusivism of Elijah and the circles associated with him in the face of traditional polytheism, and the 'de-mystifying' role of religion in the face of its traditional role of legitimating the social order and its institutions, bear witness to a history of controversy within Israel concerning the nature of Yahweh and his claims upon Israel. But as suggested above, there are good reasons for believing that the most decisive stage in the history of this controversy, and that which gave a qualitatively new dimension to Israel's understanding of God, man and the world, began in the eighth century with the preaching of the great prophets. The notion of a covenant between Yahweh and Israel was conceived of at this time, both contributing to, and reflecting leading aspects of, the radically transformed world-view which now began finally to emerge in Israel.

[28] Cf. Berger, esp. ch. 4.

V

Elijah announced Yahweh's rejection of the dynasty of Omri and arranged for Jehu to be anointed to rule over Israel. He did not announce the rejection of Israel, but saw its continuation under a new dynasty. In this respect he stood in the tradition of, for example, Ahijah at an earlier time. But the prophets of the eighth century, beginning with Amos *c*.760 BC, announced Yahweh's rejection of Israel.

Israel believed its well-being to be permanently guaranteed by Yahweh. But if tradition declared 'You only have I known of all the nations of the world', Amos added in Yahweh's name 'therefore I will punish you for all your iniquities' (3: 2), 'The end has come upon my people Israel' (8: 2; cf. 5: 2). If from ancient times Israel believed itself to be Yahweh's people, Hosea now announced 'You are not my people and I am not your God' (1: 9). When Judaeans and citizens of Jerusalem confidently boasted that since Yahweh was in their midst 'No evil shall befall us', Micah prophesied 'Zion shall be ploughed like a field; Jerusalem shall become a heap of ruins' (3: 11 f.).[29] The Zion tradition declared that Yahweh would devastate any enemies who dared assault it (e.g. Pss. 2; 46: 6 f.; 48: 5–7), but Isaiah announced that Yahweh was about to summon enemies to execute his wrath upon its inhabitants for their sins (7: 18).

The grounds of their indictment of Israel were not simply uniform. But consistently present in the preaching of all four prophets of this period is their condemnation of Israel in the ethical sphere, in the sphere of Yahweh's righteousness, that is, on the basis of Yahweh's divine 'order' in the sphere of interpersonal relationships.[30] In unprecedented manner they intensively focused upon Yahweh's righteousness against which, again in unprecedented manner, they rigorously measured Israel's life and pronounced it as standing condemned by God (cf. Isa. 1: 16 f., 21–3; 3: 13–15; 5: 7, 8, 23; 10: 1–4; Hos. 4: 1; 6: 6–9; 7: 1–7; 8: 3; Amos 2: 6–8; 3: 10; 4: 1; 5: 7, 10–15, 24; 8: 4–6; Mic. 2: 1 f.; 3: 1–4, 9–12);[31] no amount of cultic religiosity (sacrifice, lament, etc.) could uphold a relationship between this

---

[29] For evidence of a possible background in controversy for some of the material in Micah see A. S. van der Woude, 'Micah in Dispute with the Pseudo-prophets', *VT* 19, 1969, 244–60.

[30] Cf. Schmid, *Altorientalische Welt in der alttestamentlichen Theologie*, pp. 14 f., 49 ff.

[31] Ibid.

righteous God and this unrighteous people (cf. Isa. 1: 10–17; Hos. 6: 6; Amos 5: 21–4; Mic. 3: 4). That is, these prophets sharply augmented the clash, of which there were already some signs at an earlier time, between the demands of Yahweh's righteousness and the 'state-ideological' component in Israel's understanding of Yahweh's ordering of the world; not the *šālōm* ('well-being') of Israel, but Yahweh's righteousness now occupies the centre, if needs be at the cost of Israel.[32]

Put differently, in the preaching of these prophets the role of religion as a de-legitimating agent entered its most vigorous period in the history of Israel, and with far-reaching consequences. No longer merely the king-ship or any other individual institution, but the social order as a whole was relativized in the face of a radicalized perception of Yahweh's righteousness.

The presupposition of such a relativizing of the social order was a radical differentiation between the divine and the human world, between God and his creation, so that the human world is not viewed as simply continuous with the divine: the divine-human continuum is split apart, so that the human world even can be viewed as being at loggerheads with its creator. In short, the transcendence of God over the human world is emphasized.[33]

Such a relativizing of the human world in the face of a transcendent God and his will for righteousness is one of the hallmarks of Old Testament religion, and the view is warranted that it was fundamentally this that effected the decisive departure of this religion from the religious thought-world of its environment, including what appears to have been the predominantly polytheistic religion of Israel in the pre-exilic period. Herein lies the justification for the description of Old Testament religion as the rationalization of life on the basis of the 'disenchantment of the world', to employ the phrase made popular by Weber.[34] Such 'dis-enchantment of the world' is represented by, for example, the decisive break with the typical creation-theology of the ancient Near East: God is not continuous with his creation, does not permeate it, is not to be identified with, or represented by, anything within it, but stands outside

---

[32] Ibid., p. 53.   [33] See Berger, pp. 115 ff.

[34] Cf. Berger, pp. 111 f. The description 'Entzauberung der Welt' was evidently first coined by Schiller. For a brief description of Weber's use of this phrase see H. H. Gerth and C. Wright Mills, *From Max Weber: Essays in Sociology*, London 1948, pp. 51 ff.

his creation confronting it with his righteous will. More than anything else, more than any traditional monolatry which may have existed among some circles in Israel from early times, this emphasis upon the transcendence of God polarized the difference between Yahweh and other gods and eventually led from monolatry to monotheism proper. Further, because of this 'disenchantment of the world', the world, seen as inimical to God's righteousness, becomes a world not merely to be sustained, as in the cosmogonic religions of antiquity, but a world to be transformed. Hence Israel is more and more viewed as having been called by God as a manifestation of his will for righteousness in the world, and is eventually conceived of as the divine means of bringing blessing, salvation, Yahweh's righteousness, to the world. That is, the emphasis upon the transcendence of God and the relativizing of the human world in the face of God's righteousness necessarily involved the development of soteriology.

The understanding of the role of Israel among the nations was itself a new understanding of Israel's existence: from being a state among other states, Israel was conceived of as 'the people of God', performing a role for God in history among the nations. The break with traditionalism represented by the 'disenchantment of the world' yielded a rationalization of life within the world. For example, all magic and ritual conceived of as a means of sustaining the world from within, of maintaining the immanent order of the cosmos, were eliminated—a more literal translation of Weber's description *Entzauberung der Welt* is 'demagicalization of the world'—and life was rationalized in terms of service to a transcendent and righteous God whose will was declared and known. This insistence upon the totality of life in the service of God imposed a 'cohesive and, *ipso facto*, rational structure upon the whole spectrum of everyday life'.[35]

'The prophet is significant as the initiator of a great process of rationalization in the interpretation of the "meaning" of the world and the attitudes men should take toward it.'[36] It was pre-eminently the prophets of the eighth century in Israel who broke with traditionalism by denying that Israel's life was divinely guaranteed as permanent. Such an

---

[35] Cf. Berger, p. 120.

[36] Talcott Parsons, *The Structure of Social Action*, vol. II, New York and London 1968 (originally published 1937), p. 567. (Parsons at this point is discussing Weber's notion of rationalization and of prophets as initiators of the process of rationalization.)

unprecedented relativizing of Israel's life in the face of God's righteousness was in itself a decisive advance in the perception of the nature of
Yahweh as transcendent. To claim that the 'disenchantment of the world'
which is such a characteristic of Old Testament religion had its sole
source in, or received its sole impulse from, the preaching of these
prophets would be an oversimplification. But the view is justified that
what they preached was crucial for its development and that without
their preaching such potential as Israelite religion may already have had
for such a 'disenchantment of the world' would not have been fully
realized. At their hands the inner-Israelite controversy to which attention
has been drawn above (concerning the nature of Yahweh and his claims
upon Israel) entered its decisive stage; to the extent that the history of the
development of Israelite religion was a history of two increasingly conflicting world-views, the preaching of these prophets may be said to have
marked the beginning of the triumph of the one over the other.

In their condemnation of Israel and in the prophecies which some of
them announced of a transformed Israel beyond judgement, they gave a
qualitatively new dimension not only to the perception of the nature of
Yahweh as transcendent, but also to the concept of Israel as 'the people of
Yahweh'. Theirs was a radically theocentric understanding of Israel's
existence; whether explicitly or implicitly their vision of Israel was of a
people summoned to live in single-minded obedience to the claims of
God: herein lay Israel's very *raison d'être*, and short of this it had none. To
the extent that tension had earlier emerged in Israel between the 'state-
ideological' component in Israel's religion and the claims of Yahweh's
righteousness, they roundly broke it in favour of Yahweh's claims, which
they viewed as being uncompromisingly totalistic.

They themselves did not engage in any systematic rationalization of
Israel's life on this basis. But what came to the fore in their preaching and
the desacralized understanding of Israel which it embodied initiated, at
the hands of others, just such a rationalization. And it was this that found
expression in the notion that Israel's relationship with Yahweh was a
covenant relationship.

Covenant-theology is through and through a theology of 'the people of
Yahweh'. Appropriated by Yahweh as his own, Israel is commanded to
live in exclusive allegiance and total commitment to him. As in the
preaching of the prophets of the eighth century and their successors, here

too this is Israel's *raison d'être*. By its very nature the notion of a covenant between God and his people disposed of any belief that Israel's election was simply Israel's destiny in the sense that Yahweh automatically guaranteed Israel's existence. No less than in the preaching of the prophets of the eighth century, the covenant-theology opposed a false traditionalism which believed this to be so. Rather, Israel's election is understood as Israel's vocation, that is, something which had to be realized in Israel's life as a society. The making of a covenant thus involved choice and decision on Israel's part no less than on God's. The requirement of a covenant is itself the clearest evidence of this, for it may justifiably be claimed that it was addressed to an Israel which was not wont to serve Yahweh in the exclusive manner for which it calls. That is, its very formulation, the fervent imperative which it placed upon Israel's allegiance to Yahweh alone and to his will, could not simply be assumed or taken for granted: from such a people the most solemn pledge of loyalty to Yahweh alone, the solemnly binding pledge of a covenant, was evidently necessary. Further choice and decision confronted each generation of Israel, for again by its very nature the making of a covenant carried with it the possibility that the relationship between Yahweh and Israel could be terminated, something which is made explicit in, for example, the 'new covenant' passage in Jeremiah 31: 31-4 (see below). The very fact that the making of a covenant confronted Israel with such a choice is itself an indication of the goal of the covenant-theology: the transformation of Israel from what it historically had been into what it had been summoned to be: the people of Yahweh. Put differently, the covenant-theology represented at once an indicative and an imperative: the indicative, Israel's constitution as the people of Yahweh; the imperative, Israel's vocation to be the people of Yahweh.

VI

In various formulations in the Old Testament the description of the making of a covenant between God and Israel is characterized by two foci: on the one hand, Yahweh's appropriation of, and commitment to, Israel; on the other, the solemn binding of Israel to the service of Yahweh alone and obedience to his commandments. Against Kutsch, therefore, it is to be insisted that God's covenant with Israel was conceived of as bilateral in nature.

This is already indicated in what is probably the earliest description of the making of such a covenant, Exodus 24: 3–8. Whilst emphasizing Israel's pledge of obedience to the commandments, this pledge is related to a ceremony which effected the solemn consecration of Israel as Yahweh's people: those over whom the blood of Yahweh's sacrifices was cast now belonged peculiarly to him as his holy people. And this consecration of Israel as Yahweh's holy people is immediately underlined by the apt attachment to this narrative of the tradition of the *visio dei* vouched to the representatives of Israel upon the mountain of God (vv. 9–11).

The essence of the making of the covenant described in Exodus 34: 10–28 is the same. It is not here a case of the making of one *bᵉrīt* followed by the making of another separate *bᵉrīt*, as Kutsch's understanding of the meaning of the word would appear to imply for its usage here in vv. 10 and 27, the first an obligation which Yahweh takes upon himself (v. 10; *eine Selbstverpflichtung*),[37] the other an obligation which he imposes upon Israel (v. 27; *eine Verpflichtung des Volkes*).[38] Rather, one covenant is here announced, encompassing both Yahweh's commitment to Israel as his people, and the commitment this requires of, and lays upon, Israel precisely as his people.

The matter is again the same in the case of the formulation which immediately follows the giving of the law in Deuteronomy 26: 17–19 and which (again contrary to Kutsch's view) should certainly be understood as a covenantal formulation. Israel's solemn declaration 'this day' that Yahweh is its God is accompanied by Yahweh's declaration that Israel 'this day' has become 'a people for his own possession' in fulfilment of his promise (vv. 17–18). In the keeping of Yahweh's commandments Israel on its part will fulfil its vocation which has now been made manifest in the making of the covenant: to be 'a people holy to Yahweh your God', set high as such by Yahweh 'above all nations that he had made in praise and fame and glory' (v. 19).

Whatever precisely the theological content of the 'new covenant' passage in Jeremiah 31: 31–4 may be, it offers confirmation of the bilateral nature of Yahweh's covenant with Israel. As it is in the nature of the

---

[37] *Verheissung und Gesetz*, pp. 18, 72 f., 132.
[38] pp. 89, 92.

covenant that it could be annulled, so it has been annulled by Israel (v. 32). The terminology employed is significant (*hēpērū*). It is not merely that Israel has committed transgressions for which it has been punished, and that this is now to be followed by a return to the situation prior to transgression and judgement. The matter is not such as is described in, for example, the book of Judges with its well-known pattern: apostasy, punishment, forgiveness, a return to the situation before apostasy and judgement. Rather, Israel's transgressions have been such that the covenant has been brought to nought, and with this Israel's standing as Yahweh's people. What has now come about—the devastation of the land, exile from the land once given to Israel as Yahweh's people—has signalled Yahweh's rejection of Israel. The presupposition of the declaration which stands at the centre of the 'new covenant'—'I will be their God, and they shall be my people' (v. 33)—is 'I am not your God, and you are not my people' (cf. Hos. 1: 9).

What is announced here is a new beginning; and, just as elsewhere Israel is once again to experience a new exodus from bondage, a new journey through the wilderness, a new entry into the land, so the making of a new covenant is promised to a new Israel newly appropriated by Yahweh as his own. Further, just as in the making of the former covenant Yahweh's law was addressed to Israel, so in the new dispensation Israel is to live as Yahweh's people obedient to his will. In short, formally the 'new covenant' follows the same pattern of, and has the same goal as, the covenant which Israel's infidelity has annulled. What is different is that in a new act of grace Yahweh is so to transform the will of Israel that it will henceforth spontaneously live as his people: 'I will put my law within them, and I will write it upon their hearts' (v. 33); all, 'from the least of them to the greatest', will 'know' Yahweh (v. 34). The same thought is expressed in Jeremiah 32: 36–41 which speaks of the making of an 'everlasting covenant, that I will not turn away from doing good to them; and I will put the fear of me in their hearts, that they may not turn from me' (v. 40; cf. Jer. 52: 4 f.; Ezek. 37: 15–28).

That the covenant entailed the solemn submission of Israel to Yahweh's will expressed in his commandments, with which the making of the covenant is invariably associated, is abundantly clear. The emphasis and scope of the commandments are grounded in, and directed to, the understanding of Israel as 'the people of Yahweh'.

First, a consistent viewpoint permeates them: 'they are provisions which seek to ensure the exclusive nature of the relationship between God and people, between Yahweh and the Israelite tribes, or (in other words) which guard against a defection in any form from the sole God, who is thought of as the partner to the covenant'.[39] A glance at the main covenant texts is sufficient to show how justified this conclusion is, and warrants the view expressed above that the covenant-theology was addressed to an Israel which was not wont to serve Yahweh in the exclusive manner for which it calls. That Israel's allegiance is to be to Yahweh alone and that therefore Israel is to guard against all things which may lead to a defection from Yahweh is the hallmark of all these texts. Thus in various ways, as has often been noted, they seek to mark off Israel's life from the religious, cultic and other aspects of its Canaanite environment. In the form of a commandment that Israel is to worship no god but Yahweh, it is found in the Book of the Covenant (Exod. 22: 19); it heads the commandments of the decalogue, and no less 'the words of the covenant' in Exodus 34: 11–26; it is the focal issue in Joshua 24; it is the basis of Deuteronomy.[40] Similarly, the 'breaking', 'transgressing', 'not keeping', 'forsaking', and 'forgetting of' the covenant are most frequently described precisely in terms of 'going after other gods', 'going whoring after other gods', 'serving other gods' (cf. Deut. 17: 2 f.; 29: 24 f.; 31: 16, 20; Josh. 23: 16; Jud. 2: 19 f.; 1 Kgs. 11: 10 f.; 2 Kgs. 17: 38; Jer. 11: 10; 22: 9).

Second, allegiance to Yahweh alone as 'the people of Yahweh' informs not only the emphasis of the commandments but also their scope. All areas of Israel's life come within their ambit. An endeavour to be all-embracing in this respect is apparent in the wide spectrum of life's activities and duties dealt with in the Book of the Covenant and, most notably, in Deuteronomy. It is also apparent in the endeavour to summarize in easily remembered manner the content of God's will in the decalogue, which in both Exodus and Deuteronomy is presented as the foundation of the covenant law and as having been addressed directly by Yahweh to Israel at Sinai/Horeb. Those responsible sought to place all

---

[39] M. Noth, 'Die Gesetze im Pentateuch', *Gesammelte Studien zum Alten Testament*, p. 70; E. trs. 'The Laws in the Pentateuch', *The Laws in the Pentateuch and Other Essays*, p. 51.

[40] On the translation of the opening clause of the *Shema* in Deuteronomy 6: 4, with which the original book of Deuteronomy may have begun, 'Hear O Israel, Yahweh is our God, *Yahweh alone*', see A. D. H. Mayes, *Deuteronomy*, p. 176.

aspects of Israel's life, both sacral and secular, under the all-ruling will of Yahweh. The presupposition of this is that it is Yahweh alone who watches over all aspects of life in the world. No other divine powers enter the picture in the way that polytheistic religion allocated different areas and aspects of life to different deities (with a resultant frequent clash of wills).[41] Nor do any magical forces have to be reckoned with. In short, life in the world is rationalized on the basis that it is Yahweh's will alone which counts and is effective.

In both emphasis and scope, then, the covenant commandments represent the ordering of Israel's life in all its aspects as 'the people of Yahweh'. Third, however, this is underlined by a further significant feature of the commandments.[42] This is that none of the law-codes in the Pentateuch can be regarded as state laws promulgated, as in other ancient Near Eastern nations, by its kings, but are governed by, and oriented to, the concept of Israel not as a state among other states but as a holy people whose king—dealt with only circumspectly in one of these law-codes (Deut. 17: 14-20)—is himself to live under Yahweh's instruction for all his people. It is not that Israel's nationhood has become of no account (cf. for example Deut. 26: 19), but rather that in being 'the people of Yahweh' Israel's nationhood is to find its divinely willed character and destiny. This is underlined by the way in which the covenant contexts are the locus for the declaration of great promises concerning Israel's destiny and role among the nations if it remained faithful to its vocation: thus, as 'the people of Yahweh' consecrated to his service, Israel will be Yahweh's 'peculiar possession' among the nations (Exod. 19: 5; Deut. 7: 6; 14: 2; 26: 18), will be set high 'above all nations which he has made, in praise and fame and glory' (Deut. 26: 19), and will be his 'kingdom of priests, and a holy nation' (Exod. 19: 6).

Yet these promises are conditional upon Israel's response to Yahweh; they reaffirm that the making and keeping of the covenant involved a choosing and deciding on Israel's part throughout its generations. Thus at Sinai Israel chose to enter the covenant, twice over giving its pledge in response to Moses's reporting and subsequent reading of the commandments (Exod. 24: 3-8). On the plains of Moab a subsequent generation

---

[41] Cf. W. G. Lambert, 'Destiny and Divine Intervention in Babylon and Israel', *OTS* 17, 1972, p. 66.

[42] For this see especially Noth, 'Die Gesetze im Pentateuch', pp. 23 ff.; E. trs. pp. 12 ff.

chose and declared 'this day' that Yahweh had become its God (Deut. 26:
19). At Shechem Israel was again called upon to choose (Josh. 24). It was a
choice between life and death which each generation was called upon to
make (cf. Deut. 30: 15–20; Josh. 24: 19 f.).

That Israel was conceived of as having such a choice indicates that it
was not understood as being endowed with an inherent sanctity which
permanently guaranteed its existence; in this respect the covenant-
theology, no less than the prophets of the eighth century, rejected the false
traditionalism in Israel which believed this to be so. Here Israel is revealed
for what it was: a human society which can exercise choice for good or ill,
for blessing or curse, for the way of life or the way of death. No powers or
mysterious forces exist within the world which can impede Israel's choice
against Israel's own will. Israel is denied appeal to any supposed circumstances on the basis of which its allegiance to Yahweh and to the fulfilment of his will might be qualified or limited. A world 'disenchanted' is
'humanized' in the sense that it becomes the arena for human resolve and
purposefulness informed by God's will and in the service of God alone.

If in the covenant-theology religious action was given a different focus
in that it called for the worship of one God as against the worship of
many, it also represented a qualitatively different understanding of the
nature of religious action stemming from a distinctive understanding of
the nature of Yahweh. The making of the covenant was not only upon
Yahweh's initiative; more than that, he himself was a partner to it. In no
sense, therefore, did the covenant-theology conceive of life as mere
observance, upon penalty of disaster, of divinely decreed laws. Rather, life
for Israel was understood as fellowship with Yahweh who had entered a
covenant with this people, and the fulfilment of Yahweh's commandments was to be an expression of this fellowship. Hence keeping the commandments can be described as loving Yahweh (cf. Exod. 20: 6 = Deut. 5:
10; Deut. 7: 9; 10: 12; 11: 1, 13, 22; 13: 3; 19: 9; 30: 16, 20; Josh. 22: 5).

VII

The conclusion to which this book has led is that covenant-language
served as the focal point for that desacralization of a religious society of
which the prophets were the chief agents. The concept of a covenant
between Yahweh and Israel is, in terms of 'cash value', the concept that

religion is based, not on a natural or ontological equivalence between the divine realm and the human, but on *choice*: God's choice of his people and their 'choice' of him, that is, their free decision to be obedient and faithful to him. Thus understood, 'covenant' is the central expression of the distinctive faith of Israel as 'the people of Yahweh', the children of God by adoption and free decision rather than by nature or necessity. This has been obscured somewhat by too narrow a concentration on questions of terminology, and lost sight of altogether in the (fruitless) quest to find ancient parallels in the sphere of social institutions. So far from being a social institution, the covenant represents the refusal of prophets and their disciples to encapsulate Yahweh's relationship with his people in institutions, and to insist that it depends on a moral commitment on both sides which needs to be continually reaffirmed in faithful conduct, not taken for granted (as were institutions such as the monarchy in the ancient world) as though it were part of the order of nature.

Just how dominant was this element of response and freely-given commitment in the covenant concept may be seen from the 'new covenant' prophecy in Jeremiah 31: 31–4, where an insistence on the non-automatic character of the covenant is maintained even in a passage which is precisely concerned to say that God's grace is in the future to be bestowed without the requirement of any human response, and that it is, indeed, guaranteed: so imbued is the author with the idea that the covenant was a two-sided affair with no built-in guarantees that he is constrained to produce a paradoxical theory according to which God himself promises to make possible the very response which he inexorably demands.

In one sense this does, indeed, take us back to Wellhausen: the distinctiveness of Israel's faith lies in the way it breaks the mould of a 'natural bond' between God and the people, and transfers the relationship on to the plane of moral response and commitment; and it was the prophets and their disciples in the Deuteronomic tradition who were the architects of this new vision. But the intervening years of debate have given the issue a far sharper focus. Sociological analysis has thrown the freshness of this point of view into even sharper relief by showing how far religion was (and is) normally the legitimation of an existing social order, in which such a relativizing and conditionalizing of the divine-human nexus is customarily unthinkable: covenant-theology is thus much more radical than even Wellhausen could have imagined. And the evolution of the covenant-model has implications not just for the relation between God and Israel, but for that between God and the world, for we can now see that Israel's God was, even in the early years, no mere tribal god, but the Creator; and by producing the covenant theory Israel's thinkers introduced a note of choice and of the need for freely-given faith even into the cosmic aspects of their religion. None of this could have been seen a hundred years ago. Properly understood, then, the study of covenant leads into a rich vein of enquiry which has implications not only for the history of Israelite religion but for the theology of the Old Testament. My hope is that this book may help to generate further research into it.

Bibliography

Alt, A., *Der Gott der Väter*, BWANT III: 12, Stuttgart 1929, reprinted in *KS* I, Munich 1953, pp. 1–79, E. trs. 'The God of the Fathers', *Essays on Old Testament History and Religion*, Oxford 1966, pp. 1–77.

— *Die Staatenbildung der Israeliten in Palästina*, Reformationsprogramm der Universität Leipzig, 1930, reprinted in *KS* II, Munich 1953, pp. 1–65, E. trs. 'The Formation of the Israelite State in Palestine', *Essays on Old Testament History and Religion* ,pp. 171–237.

— *Die Ursprünge der israelitischen Rechts*, Leipzig 1934, reprinted in *KS* I, pp. 278–332, E. trs. 'The Origins of Israelite Law', *Essays on Old Testament History and Religion*, pp. 79–132.

— 'Das Königtum in den Reichen Israel und Juda', *VT* 1, 1951, pp. 2–22, reprinted in *KS* II, pp. 116–34, E. trs. 'The Monarchy in Israel and Judah', *Essays on Old Testament History and Religion*, pp. 239–59.

Anderson, F. I. and Freedman, D. N., *Hosea*, The Anchor Bible, Garden City, New York 1980.

Anderson, G. W., 'Israel: Amphictyony: ʿAM; ḲĀHĀL; ʿĒDÂH', *Translating and Understanding the Old Testament, Essays in Honor of H. G. May*, ed. H. T. Frank and W. L. Reed, Nashville and New York 1970, pp. 135–51.

Andrew, M. E. and Stamm, J. J., *Der Dekalog im Lichte der neueren Forschung*, second revised and enlarged edition, Bern and Stuttgart 1962, E. trs. *The Ten Commandments in Recent Research*, London 1967.

Auer, F., 'Das Alte Testament in der Sicht des Bundesgedankens', *Lex tua veritas, Festschrift für H. J. Junker*, ed. H. Gross and F. Mussner, Trier 1961, pp. 1–15.

Baentsch, B., *Exodus–Leviticus–Numeri*, Göttingen 1903.

Baltzer, K., *Das Bundesformular*, WMANT 4, Neukirchen-Vluyn 1964, E. trs. *The Covenant Formulary*, Oxford 1971.

Barr, J., 'Some Semantic Notes on the Covenant', *Beiträge zur Alttestamentlichen Theologie, Festschrift für Walther Zimmerli zum 70. Geburtstag*, ed. H. Donner, R. Hanhart, R. Smend, Göttingen 1977, pp. 23–38.

— 'The Typology of Literalism in Ancient Biblical Translations', *Nachrichten der Akademie der Wissenschaften in Göttingen. I. Philogisch-Historische Klasse*, Nr. 11, 1979, pp. 279–325.

Barton, J., 'Natural Law and Poetic Justice in the Old Testament', *JTS* NS 30, 1979, pp. 1–14.

Baumann, E., '*Yāda*ᶜ und seine Derivate. Ein sprachlich-exegetische Studie', *ZAW* 28, 1908, pp. 22–41 and 110–41.

Beer, G., *Mose und sein Werk. Ein Vortrag*, Giessen 1912.

—— *Exodus*, Tübingen 1939.

Begrich, J., 'Berit. Ein Beitrag zur Erfassung einer alttestamentlichen Denkform', *ZAW* 60, 1944, pp. 1–11.

Bendix, R., *Max Weber: An Intellectual Portrait*, London 1966.

Berger, P., *The Social Reality of Religion*, London 1969.

Beyerlin, W., *Herkunft und Geschichte der ältesten Sinaitraditionen*, Tübingen 1961, E. trs. *Origins and History of the Oldest Sinaitic Traditions*, Oxford 1965.

Bickerman, E., 'Couper une alliance', *Archives d'Histoire du Droit Oriental*, 5, 1950–1, pp. 133–56.

Borger, R., 'Zu den Asarhaddon-Verträgen aus Nimrud', *ZA* 54 (NF 20), 1961, pp. 173–96.

Boston, J. R., 'The Wisdom Influence upon the Song of Moses', *JBL* 87, 1968, pp. 198–202.

Botterweck, G. J., 'Form- und überlieferungsgeschichtliche Studie zum Dekalog', *Concilium* 1, 1965, pp. 392–401.

Bredencamp, C. J., *Gesetz und Propheten. Ein Beitrag zur alttestamentlichen Kritik*, Erlangen 1881.

Brekelmans, G. H. W., 'Exodus xviii and the origins of Yahwism in Israel', *OTS* 10, 1954, pp. 315–24.

—— 'Éléments Deutéronomiques dans le Pentateuque', *Recherches Bibliques*, 8, Bruges 1967, pp. 77–91.

Bright, J., *A History of Israel*, London 1960.

—— *Covenant and Promise: The Future in the Preaching of the Pre-exilic Prophets*, London 1977.

Budde, K., *The Religion of Israel to the Exile*, New York and London 1899.

—— *Die Religion des Volkes Israel bis zur Verbannung*, Giessen 1900.

Caspari, W., *Die Gottesgemeinde am Sinai und das nachmalige Volk Israel*, BFChrTh 27, Gütersloh 1922.

Cassuto, U., *A Commentary on the Book of Exodus*, Jerusalem 1967.

Childs, B. S., *Biblical Theology in Crisis*, Philadelphia 1970.

—— *Exodus*, London 1974.

Clements, R. E., *Prophecy and Covenant*, London 1965.

—— *Abraham and David: Genesis 15 and its Meaning for Israelite Tradition*, London 1967.

—— 'Baal-Berith of Shechem', *JSS* 13, 1968, pp. 21–32.

—— *Prophecy and Tradition*, Oxford 1975.

Cogan, M., *Imperialism and Religion: Assyria, Judah and Israel in the Eighth and Seventh Centuries B.C.E.*, Missoula 1974.

Cross, F. M., *Canaanite Myth and Hebrew Epic*, Cambridge Mass. and London 1973.

—— ''el', *Theologisches Wörterbuch zum Alten Testament*, I, ed. G. J. Botterweck and H. Ringgren, Stuttgart, Berlin, Cologne, Mainz 1973, cols. 259–79, E. trs. *Theological Dictionary of the Old Testament*, I, Grand Rapids 1977, pp. 242–61.

Dahood, M., 'Zecharia 9, 1 ᶜên 'Ādām', *CBQ* 25, 1963, pp. 123–4.

Davidson, A. B., 'Covenant', *HDB*, Edinburgh 1898, vol. I, pp. 509–15.

Davies, G. H., *Exodus*, London 1967.

Day, J., *God's Conflict with the Dragon and the Sea. Echoes of a Canaanite Myth in the Old Testament*, University of Cambridge Oriental Publications 35, Cambridge 1985.

—— 'Pre-Deuteronomic Allusions to the Covenant in Hosea and Psalm lxxviii' (forthcoming in *VT*).

—— 'Asherah in the Hebrew Bible and Northwest Semitic Literature' (forthcoming in *JBL*).

Dillmann, A., *Die Bücher Exodus und Numeri*, third edition by V. Ryssel, Leipzig 1897.

Driver, G. R., 'Studies in the Vocabulary of the Old Testament. VI', *JTS* 34, 1933, pp. 375–85.

—— 'Linguistic and Textual Problems: Isaiah i–xxxix', *JTS* 38, 1937, pp. 36–50.

—— 'Problems in Job and Psalms Reconsidered', *JTS* 40, 1939, pp. 391–4.

—— 'Problems and Solutions', *VT* 4, 1954, pp. 225–45.

—— 'Abbreviations in the Massoretic Text', *Textus*, 1, 1960, pp.112–31.

—— '"Another Little Drink"—Isaiah 28: 1–22', *Words and Meanings. Essays Presented to David Winton Thomas*, ed. P. R. Ackroyd and B. Lindars, Cambridge 1968, pp. 47–67.

Driver, S. R., *The Book of Exodus*, Cambridge 1911.

Eerdmans, B. D., 'Oorsprung en beteekenis van de "Tien Woorden" ', *Theologisch Tijdschrift* 37, 1903, pp. 19–35.

Eichrodt, W., *Theologie des Alten Testaments*, I, Leipzig 1933, II, 1935, III, 1939, E. trs. *Theology of the Old Testament*, I, London 1961 (from the sixth German edition of vol. I, Stuttgart 1959), II, London 1967 (from the fifth German edition of vols. II and III, Stuttgart 1964).

—— 'Darf man heute noch von einem Gottesbund mit Israel reden', *TZ* 30, 1974, pp. 193–206.

Eissfeldt, O., *Hexateuch-Synopse*, Leipzig 1922, reprinted Darmstadt 1962.

—— 'El and Yahweh', *JSS* 1, 1956, pp. 25–37.

Emerton, J. A., 'New Light on Israelite Religion: The Implications of the Inscriptions from Kuntillet ᶜAjrud', *ZAW* 92, 1982, pp. 2–20.

Fensham, F. C., 'Malediction and Benediction in Ancient Near Eastern Vassal-Treaties and the Old Testament', *ZAW* 74, 1962, pp. 1–9.

—— 'Common Trends in Curses of the Near Eastern Treaties and *Kudurru*-Inscriptions Compared with Maledictions of Amos and Isaiah', *ZAW* 75, 1963, pp. 15–75.

—— 'Clauses of Protection in Hittite Vassal-Treaties and the Old Testament', *VT* 13, 1963, pp. 133–43.

—— 'Did a Treaty between the Israelites and the Midianites Exist?', *BASOR* 175, 1964, pp. 51–4.

—— 'Father and Son as Terminology for Treaty and Covenant', *Near Eastern Studies in Honor of William Foxwell Albright*, ed. H. Goedicke, Baltimore and London 1971, pp. 121–35.

Field, F., *Origenis Hexaplorum Quae Supersunt; sive Veterum Interpretum Graecorum in Totum Vetus Testamentum Fragmenta*, I, Oxford 1875.

Fitzmyer, J. A., *The Aramaic Inscriptions of Sefire, Biblica et Orientalia* 19, Rome 1967.

Fohrer, G., 'Der Vertrag zwischen König und Volk in Israel', *ZAW* 71, 1959, pp. 1–22.

—— ' "Priesterliches Königtum", Ex. 19, 6', *TZ* 19, 1963, pp. 359–62.

—— 'Altes Testament—"Amphiktyonie" und "Bund"?' *TLZ* 91, 1966, cols. 801–16 and 894–904.

—— *Geschichte der israelitischen Religion*, Berlin 1969, E. trs. *History of Israelite Religion*, London 1973.

Fox, M., 'ṬÔḆ as Covenant Terminology', *BASOR* 209, 1973, pp. 41–2.

Frankena, R., 'The Vassal-Treaties of Esarhaddon and the Dating of Deuteronomy', *OTS* 14, 1965, pp. 123–54.

Freedman, D. N. and Graf, D. F. (eds.), *Palestine in Transition: The Emergence of Ancient Israel*, The Social World of Biblical Antiquity Series, 2, Sheffield 1983.

—— See also under Anderson, F. I.

Gall, A. F. von, *Der hebräische Pentateuch der Samaritaner*, Giessen 1918.

Galling, K., *Die Erwählungstraditionen Israels*, BZAW 48, Giessen 1928.

Gerleman, G., 'Die "Besonderheit". Untersuchung zu bᵉrît im Alten Testament', *Studien zur alttestamentlichen Theologie*, Heidelberg 1980, pp. 24–37.

Gerth, H. H. and Mills, C. Wright, *From Max Weber: Essays in Sociology*, London 1948.

Geus, C. H. J. de, *The Tribes of Israel*, Assen–Amsterdam 1976.

Giesebrecht, F., *Die Geschichtlichkeit des Sinaibundes*, Königsberg 1900.

Ginsberg, H. L., *The Israelian Heritage of Judaism*, New York 1982.

Görg, M., 'Etymologisch-semantische Perspektiven zu bᵉrît, *Bausteine biblischer Theologie, Festgabe für G. J. Botterweck*, BBB 50, ed. H.-J. Fabry, Cologne–Bonn 1977, pp. 25–36.

Gottwald, N. K., *The Tribes of Yahweh*, London 1979.

Graf, D. F., see under Freedman, D. N.

Gressmann, H., *Die älteste Geschichtsschreibung und Prophetie Israels (von Samuel bis Amos und Hosea)*, Göttingen 1910.

— *Mose und seine Zeit. Ein Kommentar zu den Mose-Sagen*, FRLANT, NF 1, Göttingen 1913.

— 'Die Aufgaben der alttestamentlichen Forschung', *ZAW* 42, 1924, pp. 1–33.

Grønbech, V., *Vor Folkeaet in Oldtiden*, Copenhagen 1909-12, E. trs. *The Culture of the Teutons*, London and Copenhagen 1931.

Gunkel, H., *Schöpfung und Chaos in Urzeit und Endzeit. Eine religionsgeschichtliche Untersuchung über Gen I und Ap Joh 12*, Göttingen 1895.

— *Genesis, übersetzt und erklärt*, Göttingen 1901.

— 'Mose', *RGG*¹, vol. IV, 1913, cols. 516–24.

— 'Mose', *RGG*², vol. IV, 1930, cols. 230–7.

— 'Sagen und Legenden Israels', *RGG*¹, vol. V, 1913, cols. 179–98.

— 'Sagen und Legenden: II. Zu Israel', *RGG*², vol. V, 1931, cols. 49–60.

Hahn, H. F., *The Old Testament in Modern Research*, London 1956.

Halbe, J., *Das Privilegrecht Jahwes. Ex. 34, 10-26: Gestalt und Wesen, Herkunft und Wirken in vordeuteronomischer Zeit*, FRLANT 114, Göttingen 1975.

Harvey, J., *Le Plaidoyer prophétique contre Israël après la rupture de l'alliance. Étude d'une formule littéraire de l'Ancien Testament*, Studia 22, Paris and Montreal 1967.

Hempel, J., *Gott und Mensch im Alten Testament. Studie zur Geschichte der Frömmigkeit*, BWANT III: 2, Stuttgart 1926.

Hillers, D. R., *Treaty Curses and the Old Testament Prophets*, Biblica et Orientalia 16, Rome 1964.

— 'A Note on Some Treaty Terminology in the Old Testament', *BASOR* 176, 1964, pp. 46–7.

— *Covenant: The History of a Biblical Idea*, Baltimore 1969.

Hoftijzer, J., *Die Verheissung an die drei Erzväter*, Leiden 1956.

— 'Enige Opmerkingen rond het israëlitischen 12-Stammensysteem', *Nederlands Theologisch Tijdschrift* 14, 1959-60, pp. 241–63.

Holzinger, H., *Exodus*, Tübingen 1900.

Huffmon, H. B., 'The Covenant Lawsuit in the Prophets', *JBL* 78, 1959, pp. 285–95.

— 'The Treaty Background of Hebrew YĀDAʿ', *BASOR* 181, 1966, pp. 31–7.

— 'A further Note on the Treaty background of Hebrew YĀDAʿ' (with S. B. Parker), *BASOR* 184, 1966, pp. 36–8.

Humbert, P., 'Étendre la main', *VT* 12, 1962, pp. 383–95.

Hyatt, J. P., *Exodus*, New Century Bible, London 1971.

Jepsen, A., 'Berith. Ein Beitrag zur Theologie der Exilszeit', *Verbannung und*

Heimkehr. Beiträge zur Geschichte und Theologie Israels im 6. und 5. Jahrhundert v. Chr., *Wilhelm Rudolph zum 70. Geburtstag*, ed. A. Kuschke, Tübingen 1961, pp. 161-79.

Johag, I., '*Tōb*. Terminus technicus in Vertrags- und Bundnisformularen des Alten Orients und des Alten Testaments', *Bausteine biblischer Theologie, Festgabe für G. J. Botterweck*, BBB 50, ed. H.-J. Fabry, Cologne-Bonn 1977, pp. 3-23.

Johnson, A. R., 'The Rôle of the King in the Jerusalem Cultus', *The Labyrinth*, ed. S. H. Hooke, London 1935, pp. 71-111.

— *Sacral Kingship in Ancient Israel*, Cardiff 1955, second edition 1967.

Kaiser, O., 'Traditionsgeschichtliche Untersuchung von Genesis 15', *ZAW* 70, 1958, pp. 107-26.

Kalluveettil, P., *Declaration and Covenant*, Analecta Biblica 88, Rome 1982.

Karge, P., *Geschichte des Bundesgedankens im Alten Testament*, Alttestamentliche Abhandlungen, II: 1-4, ed. J. Nikel, Münster 1910.

Kautzsch, E., 'Religion of Israel', *HDB*, extra volume, Edinburgh 1904, pp. 612-734.

— *Biblische Theologie des Alten Testaments*, Tübingen 1911.

Kimbrough, S. T., *Israelite Religion in Sociological Perspective: The Work of Antonin Causse*, Studies in Oriental Religions, vol. 4, Wiesbaden 1978.

Kittel, R., *Geschichte der Hebräer*, vol. I, Gotha 1888, E. trs. *A History of the Hebrews*, vol. I, London and Edinburgh 1895.

— 'Die Zukunft der alttestamentliche Wissenschaft', *ZAW* 39, 1921, pp. 84-99.

Knight, D. A., *Rediscovering the Traditions of Israel*, SBL Dissertation Series 9, Missoula 1975.

Koch, K., 'Gibt es ein Vergeltungsdogma im Alten Testament?', *ZTK* 52, 1955, pp. 1-42.

Köhler, L., 'Problems in the Study of the Language of the Old Testament', *JSS* 1, 1956, pp. 3-24.

Köhler, L. and Baumgartner, W., *Hebräisches und aramäisches Lexikon zum Alten Testament*, third edition, Leiden 1967-.

Kraeling, E. G., *The Brooklyn Museum Aramaic Papyri: New Documents of the Fifth Century B.C. from the Jewish Colony at Elephantine*, New Haven and London 1953.

Kraetzschmar, R., *Die Bundesvorstellung im Alten Testament in ihrer geschichtlichen Entwickelung*, Marburg 1896.

Kraus, H.-J., *Die prophetische Verkündingung des Rechts in Israel*, Theologische Studien 51, Zollikon 1957.

— *Gottisdienst in Israel*, Munich 1962, E. trs. *Worship in Israel*, Oxford 1966.

— *Geschichte der historisch-kritischen Erforschung des Alten Testaments*, second edition, Neukirchen 1969.

Kutsch, E., '*bᵉrīt* Verpflichtung', *Theologisches Handwörterbuch zum Alten Testament*, I, ed. E. Jenni and C. Westermann, Munich and Zürich 1971, pp. 339–52.

— *Verheissung und Gesetz. Untersuchungen zum sogenannten "Bund" im Alten Testament*, BZAW 131, Berlin and New York 1973.

— 'Gottes Zuspruch und Anspruch. bᶜrît in der alttestamentlichen Theologie', *Questions disputées d'Ancien Testament. Méthode et théologie*, Bibliotheca Ephemeridum Theologicarum Lovaniensium 33, Leuven-Gembloux 1974, pp. 71–90.

— *Neues Testament—Neuer Bund? Eine Fehlübersetzung wird korrigiert*, Neukirchen 1978.

— 'Bund', *Realenzyklopädie*, vol. 8, New York and Berlin 1980, pp. 397–410.

Lambert, W. G., 'Destiny and Divine Intervention in Babylon and Israel', *The Witness of Tradition, OTS* 17, 1972, pp. 65–72.

Lindblom, J., *Hosea Literarisch Untersucht*, Acta Academiae Aboensis, Humaniora V, Åbo 1927.

Lohfink, N., *Das Hauptgebot: Eine Untersuchung literarischer Einleitungsfragen zu Dtn 5–11*, Analecta Biblica 20, Rome 1963.

— *Die Landverheissung als Eid. Eine Studie zu Genesis 15*, Stuttgarter Bibel Studien 28, Stuttgart 1967.

Loretz, O., '*bᶜrīt* "Band-Bund" ', *VT* 16, 1966, pp. 239–41.

Lotz, W., 'Der Bund vom Sinai', *NKZ* 12, 1901, pp. 561–80, 631–55, 859–75; *NKZ* 13, 1902, pp. 181–204; *NKZ* 14, 1903, pp. 128–53; *NKZ* 15, 1904, pp. 281–304, 532–59.

Lubsczyk, H., 'Der Bund als Gemeinschaft mit Gott. Erwägungen zur Diskussion über den Begriff "bᶜrit" im Alten Testament', *Dienst der Vermittlung*, Erfurter Theologisches Studien 37, Leipzig 1977, pp. 61–96.

Luther, B. and Meyer, E., *Die Israeliten und ihre Nachbarstämme. Alttestamentliche Untersuchungen*, Halle 1906.

McCarthy, D. J., *Treaty and Covenant*, Analecta Biblica 21, Rome 1963, second revised and enlarged edition, Analecta Biblica 21A, Rome 1978.

— 'Notes on the Love of God in Deuteronomy and the Father–Son Relationship between Yahweh and Israel', *CBQ* 27, 1965, pp. 144–7.

— '*bᶜrît* in Old Testament History and Theology', *Biblica* 53, 1972, pp. 110–21.

— *Old Testament Covenant: A Survey of Current Opinions*, Oxford 1972.

McKane, W., 'Prophet and Institution', *ZAW* 94, 1982, pp. 251–66.

McKay, J. W., *Religion in Judah under the Assyrians*, London 1973.

Malamat, A., 'Organs of Statecraft in the Israelite Monarchy', *BA* 28, 1965, pp. 34–65.

Mayes, A. D. H., *Israel in the Period of the Judges*, London 1974.

— *Deuteronomy*, New Century Bible, London 1979.

—— *The Story of Israel Between Settlement and Exile: A Redactional Study of the Deutero-nomistic History*, London 1983.

Meek, T. J., *Hebrew Origins*, New York 1936.

Mendenhall, G. E., 'Covenant Forms in Israelite Tradition', *BA* 17, 1954, pp. 50-76.

—— 'The Hebrew Conquest of Palestine', *BA* 25, 1962, pp. 66-87.

—— *The Tenth Generation*, Baltimore 1973.

Mettinger, T. N. D., *King and Messiah: The Civil and Sacral Legitimation of the Israelite Kings*, Coniectanea Biblica, Old Testament Series 8, Lund 1976.

Meyer, E., see under Luther, B.

Mills, C. Wright, see under Gerth, H. H.

Moberly, R. W. L., *At the Mountain of God*, *JSOT* Supplement Series 22, Sheffield 1983.

Moran, W. L., 'A Kingdom of Priests', *The Bible in Current Catholic Thought*, ed. J. L. McKenzie, New York 1962, pp. 7-20.

—— 'The Ancient Near Eastern Background of the Love of God in Deutero-nomy', *CBQ* 24, 1963, pp. 77-87.

—— 'A Note on the Treaty Terminology of the Sefire Stelas', *JNES* 22, 1963, pp. 173-6.

Mowinckel, S., *Psalmenstudien II. Das Thronbesteigungsfest Jahwäs und der Ursprung der Eschatologie*, Kristiania 1922.

—— *Le Décalogue*, Paris 1927.

—— *Offersang og Sangoffer*, Oslo 1951, E. trs. *The Psalms in Israel's Worship*, I and II, Oxford 1962.

—— *Erwägungen zur Pentateuch Quellenfrage*, Oslo 1964.

Muilenburg, J., 'The Form and Structure of the Convenantal Formulations', *VT* 9, 1959, pp. 345-65.

Müller, H.-P., 'Gott und die Götter in den Anfängen der biblischen Religion. Zur Vorgeschichte des Monotheismus', *Monotheismus im Alten Israel und seiner Umwelt*, ed. O. Keel, Biblische Beiträge 14, Fribourg 1980, pp. 99-142.

Nestle, E., 'Ein Vorgänger Goethe's über den zweiten Dekalog', *ZAW* 24, 1904, pp. 134-5.

Nicholson, E. W., *Exodus and Sinai in History and Tradition*, Oxford 1973.

—— 'The Interpretation of Exodus XXIV 9-11', *VT* 24, 1974, pp. 77-97.

—— 'The Antiquity of the Tradition in Exodus XXIV 9-11', *VT* 25, 1975, pp. 69-79.

—— 'The Origin of the tradition in Exodus XXIV 9-11', *VT* 26, 1976, pp. 148-60.

—— 'The Decalogue as the Direct Address of God', *VT* 27, 1977, pp. 422-33.

—— 'The Covenant Ritual in Exodus XXIV 3-8', *VT* 32, 1982, pp. 74-86.

—— 'Israelite Religion in the Pre-Exilic Period: A Debate Renewed' (forthcoming in a *Festschrift* for W. McKane 1986).

Nielsen, E., *Shechem: A Traditio-Historical Investigation*, second edition, Copenhagen 1959.

Noth, M., *Die israelitischen Personennamen im Rahmen der gemeinsemitischen Namengebung*, BWANT III: 10, Stuttgart 1928.

—— *Das System der zwölf Stämme Israels*, BWANT IV: 1, Stuttgart 1930.

—— *Die Gesetze im Pentateuch*, Halle 1940, reprinted in *Gesammelte Studien zum Alten Testament*, second edition Munich 1960, pp. 9–141, E. trs. 'The Laws in the Pentateuch', *The Laws in the Pentateuch and Other Essays*, Edinburgh and London 1966, pp. 1–107.

—— *Überlieferungsgeschichtliche Studien*, Tübingen 1943, E. trs. *The Deuteronomistic History, JSOT* Supplement Series 15, Sheffield 1981.

—— *Überlieferungsgeschichte des Pentateuch*, Stuttgart 1948, E. trs. *A History of Pentateuchal Traditions*, Englewood Cliffs, 1972.

—— 'Das Amt des Richters Israels', *Festschrift für A. Bertholet*, ed. W. Baumgartner, O. Eissfeldt, K. Elliger, and L. Rost, Tübingen 1950, pp. 404–17.

—— 'Das alttestamentliche Bundschliessen im Licht eines Mari-textes', *Annuaire de l'Institut de Philologie et d'Histoire Orientales et Slaves* 13, 1953, pp. 433–44, reprinted in *Gesammelte Studien zum Alten Testament*,[2] pp. 142–54, E. trs. 'Old Testament Covenant-making in the Light of a Text from Mari', *The Laws in the Pentateuch and Other Essays*, Edinburgh and London 1966, pp. 108–17.

—— *Geschichte Israels*, Göttingen 1950, E. trs. *The History of Israel*, second edition, London 1960.

—— *Das zweite Buch Mose, Exodus*, ATD 5, Göttingen 1959, E. trs. *Exodus*, London 1962.

Parker, S. B., see under Huffmon, H. B.

Parsons, Talcott, *The Structure of Social Action*, II, New York and London 1968 (originally published 1937).

Patrick, D., 'The Covenant Code Source', *VT* 27, 1977, pp. 145–57.

Pedersen, J., *Der Eid bei den Semiten*, Strasburg 1914.

Perlitt, L., *Bundestheologie im Alten Testament*, WMANT 36, Neukirchen–Vluyn 1969.

Pfeiffer, R. H., 'Facts and Faith in Biblical History', *JBL* 70, 1951, pp. 1–14.

—— *Religion in the Old Testament*, London 1961.

Phillips, A., *Ancient Israel's Criminal Code. A New Approach to the Decalogue*, Oxford 1970.

—— 'Prophecy and Law', *Israel's Prophetic Tradition. Essays in Honour of Peter Ackroyd*, ed. R. Coggins, A. Phillips, M. Knibb, Cambridge 1982, pp. 217–32.

—— 'A Fresh Look at the Sinai Pericope. Part I', *VT* 34, 1984, pp. 39–52.

Plöger, J. G., *Literarkritische, formgeschichtliche und stilkritische Untersuchungen zum Deuteronomium*, BBB 26, Bonn 1967.

Porteous, N. W., 'Volk und Gottesvolk im Alten Testament', *Theologische Aufsätze: Karl Barth zum 50. Geburtstag*, ed. E. Wolf, Munich 1936, pp. 146–63.

Preuss, H. D., *Deuteronomium*, Erträge der Forschung 164, Darmstadt 1982.

Procksch, O., *Das nordhebräische Sagenbuch. Die Elohimquelle*, Leipzig 1906.

— 'Die letzten Worte Davids. 2 Sam. 23: 1–7', *Alttestamentliche Studien: Rudolph Kittel zum 60. Geburtstag dargebracht*, BWAT 13, Leipzig 1913, pp. 112–25.

Rad, G. von, *Das formgeschichtliche Problem des Hexateuch*, BWANT IV: 26, Stuttgart 1938, reprinted in *Gesammelte Studien zum Alten Testament*, Munich 1958, pp. 9–81, E. trs. 'The Form-Critical Problem of the Hexateuch', *The Problem of the Hexateuch and Other Essays*, Edinburgh and London 1966, pp. 1–78.

— *Deuteronomium-Studien*, FRLANT 58, second edition, Göttingen 1948, E. trs. *Studies in Deuteronomy*, London 1953.

— *Das erste Buch Mose, Genesis*, ATD 2–4, fifth edition, Göttingen 1958, E. trs. *Genesis*, London 1961.

— *Der heilige Krieg im alten Israel*, Göttingen 1958.

Roberts, J. J. M., 'The Hand of Yahweh', *VT* 21, 1971, pp. 244–51.

Robinson, H. Wheeler, *Inspiration and Revelation in the Old Testament*, Oxford 1946.

Rodd, C. S., 'Max Weber and Ancient Judaism', *SJT* 32, 1979, pp. 457–69.

Rost, L., *Die Überlieferung von der Thronnachfolge Davids*, BWANT III: 6, Stuttgart 1926, reprinted in *Das kleine Credo und andere Studien zum Alten Testament*, Heidelberg 1965, pp. 119–253, E. trs. *The Succession to the Throne of David*, Historic Texts and Interpreters in Biblical Scholarship, 1, Sheffield 1982.

— 'Sinaibund und Davidsbund', *TLZ* 72, 1947, cols. 129–34.

Rowley, H. H., *The Biblical Doctrine of Election*, London 1950.

— *From Joseph to Joshua: Biblical Traditions in the Light of Archaeology*, London 1950.

Rudolph, W., *Der 'Elohist' von Exodus bis Josua*, BZAW 68, Berlin 1938.

— *Hosea*, KAT xiii/1, Gütersloh 1966.

Ruprecht, E., 'Exodus 24, 9–11 als Beispiel lebendiger Erzähltradition aus der Zeit des babylonischen Exils', *Werden und Wirken des Alten Testaments. Festschrift für Claus Westermann zum 70. Geburstag*, ed. R. Albertz, H.-P. Müller, H. W. Wolff, and W. Zimmerli, Göttingen 1980, pp. 138–73.

Schäfer-Lichtenberger, C., *Staat und Eidgenossenschaft im Alten Testament. Eine Auseinandersetzung mit Max Webers Studie 'Das antike Judentum'*, BZAW 156, Berlin and New York 1983.

Scharbert, J., ' "B^crit" im Pentateuch', *De la Tôrah au Messie*, (Studies in honour of H. Cazelles), ed. M. Carrez, J. Doré, and P. Grelot, Paris 1981, pp. 163–70.

Schluchter, W., *Max Webers Studie über das antike Judentum. Interpretation und Kritik*, Frankfurt 1981.

Schmid, H. H., *Wesen und Geschichte der Weisheit*, BZAW 101, Berlin 1966.

— *Gerechtigkeit als Weltordnung*, Beiträge zur historischen Theologie 40, Tübingen 1968.

— *Altorientalische Welt in der alttestamentlichen Theologie*, Zürich 1974.

Schmidt, W. H., *Exodus, Sinai und Mose*, Erträge der Forschung 191, Darmstadt 1983.

Schwally, F., *Semitische Kriegsaltertümer, I (Der Heilige Krieg im alten Israel)*, Leipzig 1901.

Seitz, G., *Redaktionsgeschichtliche Studien zum Deuteronomium*, BWANT 93, Stuttgart, Berlin, Cologne, Mainz 1971.

Sellin, E., *Geschichte des israelitisch-jüdischen Volkes*, I, Leipzig 1924.

— 'Seit welcher Zeit verehrten die nordisraelitischen Stämme Jahwe?', *Oriental Studies dedicated to Paul Haupt*, Baltimore and Leipzig 1926, pp. 124–34.

Simon, M., *Babli Berakoth*, London 1948 (in *The Babylonian Talmud*, translated and edited under the editorship of I. Epstein).

Simpson, C. A., *The Early Traditions of Israel*, Oxford 1948.

Slotki, J. J., *Numbers* (in *Midrash Rabbah*, translated under the editorship of H. Freedman and M. Simon), vol. I, London 1939.

Smend, R., *Lehrbuch der alttestamentlichen Religionsgeschichte*, Freiburg-im-Breisgau and Leipzig 1893.

Smend, R., *Die Bundesformel*, Theologische Studien 68, Zürich 1963.

— *Jahwekrieg und Stämmebund: Erwägungen zur ältesten Geschichte Israels*, FRLANT 84, Göttingen 1963, E. trs. *Yahweh War and Tribal Confederation: Reflections upon Israel's Earliest History*, Nashville and New York 1970.

— 'Der biblische und der historische Elia', *SVT* 28, 1975, pp. 167–84.

— *Die Entstehung des Alten Testaments*, Stuttgart, Berlin, Cologne, Mainz 1978.

Smith, W. Robertson, *Kinship and Marriage in Early Arabia*, Cambridge 1885.

— *The Religion of the Semites*, London 1889, second edition 1894, third edition by S. A. Cook 1927.

Smyth, H. W., *Aeschylus*, The Loeb Classical Library, London 1922.

Snaith, N. H., *The Distinctive Ideas of the Old Testament*, London 1944.

Spieckermann, H., *Juda unter Assur in der Sargonidenzeit*, FRLANT 129, Göttingen 1982.

Stade, B., Review of C. J. Bredencamp, *Gesetz und Propheten, TLZ* 7, 1882, cols. 241–8.

— *Geschichte des Volkes Israel*, I, Berlin 1887.

— 'Die Entstehung des Volkes Israel', *Ausgewählte akademische Reden und Abhandlungen*, Giessen 1899, pp. 99–121.

—— *Biblische Theologie des Alten Testaments*, Tübingen 1905.

Stamm, J. J., see under Andrew, M. E.

Steuernagel, C., 'Der jehovistische Bericht über den Bundesschluss am Sinai', *ThStK* 72, 1899, pp. 319–50.

—— 'Alttestamentliche Theologie und alttestamentliche Religionsgeschichte', *Vom Alten Testament. Festschrift für K. Marti*, ed. K. Budde, BZAW 41, Giessen 1925, pp. 266–73.

Stolz, F., *Strukturen und Figuren im Kult von Jerusalem*, BZAW 118, Berlin 1970.

Thiel, W., 'Hēfēr bᵉrīt. Zum Bundbrechen im Alten Testament', *VT* 20, 1970, pp. 214–29.

—— 'Die Rede vom "Bund" in den Prophetenbüchern', *Theologische Versuche* 9, 1977, pp. 11–36.

Trumbull, H. C., *The Blood Covenant*, New York 1885.

Valeton, J. J. B., 'Bedeutung und Stellung des Wortes bᵉrīt im Priestercodex', *ZAW* 12, 1892, pp. 1–22.

—— 'Das Wort bᵉrīt in den jehovistischen und deuteronomischen Stücken des Hexateuchs, sowie in den verwandten historischen Bücher', *ZAW* 12, 1892, pp. 224–60.

—— 'Das Word bᵉrīt bei den Propheten und in den Ketubim. Resultat', *ZAW* 13, 1893, pp. 245–79.

Van Seters, J., 'Joshua 24 and the Problem of Tradition in the Old Testament', *In the Shelter of Elyon. Essays on Ancient Palestinian Life and Literature in Honor of G. W. Ahlström*, ed. W. Boyd Barrick and J. R. Spencer, *JSOT* Supplement Series 31, Sheffield 1984, pp. 139–58.

Vaux, R. de, *Les Institutions de l'Ancien Testament*, II, Paris 1960, E. trs. *Ancient Israel: Its Life and Institutions*, London 1961.

—— *Histoire ancienne d'Israël: la periode des Juges*, Paris 1973, E. trs. *The Early History of Israel: From the Entry into Canaan to the Period of the Judges*, London 1978.

Vriezen, T. C., 'The Exegesis of Exodus xxiv 9–11', *The Witnes of Tradition, OTS* 17, 1972, pp. 100–33.

Wächter, L., 'Die Übertragung der Beritvorstellung auf Jahwe', *TLZ* 99, 1974, cols. 801–16.

Weber, M., *Die protestantische Ethik und der Geist des Kapitalismus, Gesammelte Aufsätze zur Religionssoziologie*, I, Tübingen 1920, pp. 17–206, E. trs. *The Protestant Ethic and the Spirit of Capitalism*, London 1930.

—— *Das antike Judentum, Gesammelte Aufsätze zur Religionssoziologie*, III, Tübingen 1921, E. trs. *Ancient Judaism*, London 1952.

Weinfeld, M., 'Traces of Treaty Formulae in Deuteronomy', *Biblica* 41, 1965, pp. 417–27.

—— 'Covenant', *Encyclopaedia Judaica*, vol. 5, Jerusalem 1971, cols. 1012–22.

— *Deuteronomy and the Deuteronomic School*, Oxford 1972.

— 'bᵉrîth', *Theologisches Wörterbuch zum Alten Testament*, I, ed. G. J. Botterweck and H. Ringgren, Stuttgart, Berlin, Cologne, Mainz 1973, cols. 781–808, E. trs. *Theological Dictionary of the Old Testament*, II, Grand Rapids 1977, pp. 253–79.

— 'Bᵉrît—Covenant vs. Obligation' (a review of E. Kutsch, *Verheissung und Gesetz*), *Biblica* 56, 1975, pp. 120–8.

Weiser, A., *Die Bedeutung des Alten Testaments für den Religionsunterricht*, Giessen 1925, reprinted in *Glaube und Geschichte im Alten Testament und andere ausgewählte Schriften*, Göttingen 1961, pp. 19–50.

— Review of S. Mowinckel, *Le Décalogue* in *TLZ* 53, 1928, cols. 553–7.

— *Glaube und Geschichte im Alten Testament*, BWANT IV: 4, Stuttgart 1931, reprinted in *Glaube und Geschichte im Alten Testament und andere ausgewählte Schriften*, pp. 99–182.

— *Einleitung in das Alte Testament*, Göttingen 1948, second edition 1949, E. trs. (from the fourth German edition) *Introduction to the Old Testament*, London 1961.

— *Die Psalmen*, fifth edition, Göttingen 1959, E. trs. *The Psalms*, London 1962.

Wellhausen, J., *Geschichte Israels I*, Berlin 1878.

— *Prolegomena zur Geschichte Israels*, Berlin 1883, E. trs. *Prolegomena to the History of Israel*, Edinburgh 1885.

— 'Israel', *Encyclopaedia Britannica*, vol. XIII, 1881, reprinted as an Appendix to *Prolegomena to the History of Israel*, pp. 429–548.

— *Reste arabischen Heidentums*, Berlin 1887.

— *Die kleinen Propheten übersetzt und erklärt*, Berlin 1892, fourth edition 1963.

— *Die Composition des Hexateuchs und der historischen Bücher des Alten Testaments*, third edition, Berlin 1899.

— *Israelitisch-jüdische Religion, Die Kultur der Gegenwart*, ed. P. Hinneberg, I: 4, Berlin and Leipzig 1905, pp. 1–38, reprinted in J. Wellhausen, *Grundrisse zum Alten Testament*, ed. R. Smend, Munich 1965, pp. 65–109.

Westermann, C., *Genesis (12–36)*, BKAT 1, Neukirchen 1981.

Whitley, C. F., 'Covenant and Commandment in Israel', *JNES* 22, 1963, pp. 37–48.

Wildberger, H., *Jahwes Eigentumsvolk*, ATANT 37, Zürich and Stuttgart 1960.

Wiseman, D. J., *The Vassal Treaties of Esarhaddon*, London 1958.

Wolff, H. W., *Dodekapropheten I, Hosea*, BKAT xiv/1, second edition, Neukirchen 1965, E. trs. *Hosea*, Philadelphia 1974.

— *Dodekapropheten, II, Joel und Amos*, BKAT xiv/2, second edition, Neukirchen 1975, E. trs. *Joel and Amos*, Philadelphia 1977.

Woude, A. S. van der, 'Micah in dispute with the Pseudo-prophets', *VT* 19, 1969, pp. 244–60.

Wright, G. E., 'How did Early Israel differ from her Neighbours?', *BA* 6, 1943, pp. 1–20.

—— *The Challenge of Israel's Faith*, Chicago 1944, London 1946.

—— *The Old Testament Against Its Environment*, London 1950.

—— *God Who Acts*, London 1952.

—— 'The Lawsuit of God. A Form-Critical Study of Deuteronomy 32', *Israel's Prophetic Heritage*, (*Festschrift* for J. Muilenburg), ed. B. W. Anderson and W. Harrelson, London 1962, pp. 26–67.

Würthwein, E., 'Amos-Studien', *ZAW* 62, 1949–50, pp. 10–52, reprinted in *Wort und Existenz*, Göttingen 1970, pp. 68–110.

Zenger, E., *Die Sinaitheophanie: Untersuchungen zum jahwistischen und elohistischen Geschichtswerk*, Forschung zur Bibel 2, Würzburg 1971.

Zimmerli, W., *The Law and the Prophets*, London 1965.

—— *Ezechiel I*, BKAT xiii/1, Neukirchen 1969, E. trs. *Ezekiel I*, Philadelphia 1979.

Author Index

Index of Scripture References